The Concise Guide to

SOUNDING

SMART

at PARTIES

The Concise Guide to

SOUNDING

SMART

at PARTIES

An Irreverent Compendium of
Must-Know Info from
Sputnik to Smallpox
and Mao to Marie Curie

David Matalon & Chris Woolsey

BROADWAY

PUBLISHED BY BROADWAY BOOKS

Published in the United States by Broadway Books, an
imprint of The Doubleday Broadway Publishing Group,
a division of Random House, Inc., New York.
www.broadwaybooks.com

BROADWAY BOOKS and its logo, a letter B bisected on the
diagonal, are trademarks of Random House, Inc.

Book design by Donna Sinisgalli
Chapter opening illustration by Adam McCauley

Library of Congress Cataloging-in-Publication Data

Matalon, David.
    The concise guide to sounding smart at parties : an
irreverent compendium of must-know info from *Sputnik* to
smallpox and Mao to Marie Curie / David Matalon and
Chris Woolsey.— 1st ed.
        p. cm
    1. Curiosities and wonders. 2. Interpersonal
communication—Miscellanea. I. Woolsey, Chris. II. Title.

    AG243.M354 2006
    031.02—dc22

ISBN-13: 978-0-7679-2299-9
ISBN-10: 0-7679-2299-9

PRINTED IN THE UNITED STATES OF AMERICA

10 9 8 7 6 5 4 3 2 1

First Edition

David Matalon

For my parents, Ahron and Leah, for showing me that sounding smart is only the beginning.
For my brother, Marc, for being there when I needed him, and to Lisa, Jessica and Gabrielle.

Chris Woolsey

For Nicole, my wife, for not letting me get a real job and without whom none of this would be possible, and for my mom and dad, Gary and Judy, and sisters, Kelly and Leslie, for filling the house with laughter in my formative years.

The Conversations

Foreword

"*E*ducation is not the filling of a pail, but the lighting of a fire." So said William Butler Yeats, one of the preeminent, um . . . preeminent . . . guys, I guess, of the last—oh, I don't know—four . . . *thousand* years? Does that sound right?

The fact is, I don't know. And under what circumstances might it be the most helpful to know exactly who this Yeats character is and what it is he wants from us? Would it be in school, when the teacher calls on us and asks us (rather brusquely, I think) who he is (assuming William isn't a woman)? Not hardly. Ignorance is clearly one of the most regarded commodities in the whole of the education system, coming in right behind "tenure" and "a concealed weapon."

Would it be at work? I think not. Rare is the time when Jim from Marketing, that weird guy with the crew cut who smells like imitation bacon bits, approaches an underling's desk and demands, "I need the data on that ConTriTech account. And give me all you've got on William Butler Yeats, or I'm giving your promotion, *and* the smoked turkey you won in that sales contest, to Pam. Got it, Cap'n? Or do I have to put it in a memo and CC all relevant parties?" Jim would never do that, if I know Jim even half as well as I think I do.

No, the most valuable place to be in possession of information on Bill Yeats, and a whole bunch of these other eggheads, is of course at a party. Think about it: You are lingering near the bean dip, which you despise, hoping to get a word in with the cute girl who looks a little like Reese Witherspoon, or maybe like that lady who was in that one black-and-white film directed by that fat guy who did a lot of movies starring that one actor. Unexpectedly, given that you are licking sour cream off your forearm, she approaches and says, "Great party. But it's hotter than Dante's *Inferno* in here, don't you think?"

Dante? you think. Dante Culpepper? The quarterback of the Minnesota Vikings? He has an inferno? Why? And what exactly is an inferno?

"Yeah," you finally manage. "And his inferno sure is hot compared to, say, Trent Dilfer's." You have blown it. After faking a kidney stone, she's off and is soon seen chatting warmly with Chuck, your rival, and a man who still believes in applying great lashings of Polo cologne to his large rubbery cheeks.

This could have been avoided. Chuck could have come up empty, which is more than he deserves, and you could have been sharing deep and meaningful conversations with the woman of your dreams. You should have read Chris and David's book, *The Concise Guide to Sounding Smart at Parties*.

With erudition and humor they would have coached you through that utterly humiliating moment (what were you thinking?) with their wonderful book. Read it. Study it. Follow their advice and soon you too can be as smart as, um, that one guy, with the weird hair, who did that math thing.

Enjoy.

—Michael J. Nelson, former host and head
writer of *Mystery Science Theater 3000*
and author of *Love Sick*

Introduction

*S*o, you're invited to a party. Maybe it's the company picnic, a wine tasting, the hottest night at the hottest club in town, your friend's ex's cousin's July Fourth barbecue, or just your next-door neighbor having a few folks over for Flag Day. Whatever the occasion, the art of conversation requires far more knowledge than most people's immediate frame of reference, which includes the score of last night's big game and the name of the starlet who dry-gulched a paparazzo outside an awards show. While ideally anybody with a mouth and a caucus of brain cells can carry on a basic conversation, what we're talking about here is the ability to converse intelligently and humorously on a variety of subjects.

Now you might at this point be asking, "Why should I care about sounding smart? I've got Netflix." Yet this same question is asked by painfully lonely people across the planet as they crack open another bag of Funyuns and prepare for the *Sex and the City* marathon. Well, a whole bunch of studies done by a whole bunch of experts with university funding and far too much time on their hands indicate the top two character traits that cause attraction between people are intelligence and humor (although a yacht-load of cash or being smoking hot surely runs a close second). Since the majority of us don't have shares in an IPO or a top-of-the-line Beverly Hills plastic surgeon, the smart, funny members of the herd have a considerable advantage in the realms of dating, career, and life in general (and yes, a cute pair of heels doesn't hurt either). When you consider that more than half the adult population of this country will not read a book this year (Oprah fans excluded), the gap widens even further between those in the know and the know-nothing-at-alls.

No doubt, you've experienced that mystifying moment when people you've judged as social write-offs (you know the ones, with the sweaters over the shoulders, penny loafers, and collars flipped up Scott Baio style) are suddenly holding court, dazzling the crowd, charming the opposite sex, winning hearts and minds, and turning us green with envy (and really, who looks good in green?). So what's their secret? The answer lies in the palm of your hands . . . no, we're not talking love lines and life lines; we're talking about this book.

How many of us have negative impressions of people who are smart (brainiacs, nerds, geeks)? How many times have we heard the terms "smarty-pants" or "know-it-all" or been ridiculed into believing we should be less smart than we are ("What are you? Some kind of genius?"). Believe it or not, you've been brainwashed to think being smart isn't cool. When it comes to intelligence, there is an evil voice inside our heads (that might sound like Pat Robertson) that labels smart people as stuck-up, boring, and unsexy. Even our political leaders try to subvert their intellects (which, admittedly, these days doesn't seem to take much effort) in order to appeal to the "common person" (. . . and that'd be you).

Meanwhile, a not-so-secret society of success-driven citizens have been training their brains to get ahead in this marathon we call life. And so where does that leave you? Eating their dust, my friends. Eating their dust. The good news is it's never too late. You can still break through the glass ceiling of success and get back in the running. Fear not humiliation, ridicule, or the cruel barbs of flying spitwads. The only things people shoot at smart people these days are envious glances. Don't believe us? Just ask Mssrs. Gates, Jobs, and Trump. Okay? Moving on . . .

Beauty fades, fortunes are lost, but intelligence remains to serve you steadfastly through thick and thin. So if life hasn't turned out to be the fairy tale you had hoped for, don't despair, *The Concise Guide to Sounding Smart at Parties* is like that winged godmother and her magic wand, ready to transform you into the prince or princess of your social scene . . . Pumpkin sold separately.

The Concise Guide to

SOUNDING

SMART

at **PARTIES**

The War Conversation

*T*he sadly useful thing about the war conversation is that there's always some kind of bloodshed going on somewhere in the world, and so it's easy to bring up. Though military history has been traditionally a guy topic, these days it's quite likely that in a room full of people of either sex someone will have served or at least had a sibling, significant other, or "ex" who did. Certainly, if you're attending any armed forces related affair, familiarizing yourself with a few topics in the war conversation will help you win friends and get people talking. However, be mindful that you are likely to find a handful of Experts (see the Appendix, Who's Who at the Party) in the crowd who will give you a run for your military money. So once things are rolling, consider where to take the talk next. Generally, military buffs tend to like video games, sports, action flicks (war movies), and politics. It's worth noting, if you're dealing with people in the actual military, it's a good rule of thumb to stay clear of criticizing the government, unless you get the sense that the people you're dealing with have liberal, or at the very least, tolerant views.

Hannibal Was Republic Enemy Number One

When Are We Talking About: 247 BC–183 BC

Why Are We Even Talking About This: Hannibal was one of the most famous military commanders in history, who impossibly led his army (including cavalry and elephants), across the Swiss Alps into the heart of the Roman Empire, not only surprising the Roman legions but nearly destroying them.

What You Need to Know to Sound Smart: Hannibal Barca was born in Carthage (near modern-day Tunis), North Africa, in 247 BC, the son of Hamilcar (boy, they sure had great names in Carthage, didn't they?), the general who defended Sicily against the Romans in the First Punic War (nothing like the Pubic War waged by penis enlargement companies on the Internet). While most dads teach their boys to play baseball and fish, Hamilcar despised the Roman Empire and kindled the same hatred in Hannibal. With training-spear in hand, ten-year-old Hannibal traveled with his father to war in Spain, and by age twenty-six was a general, replacing his dead brother-in-law, Hasdrubal (a name ripe for telemarketer screwups: "Is Mr. Haysdrooble in? Well, is Mrs. Haysdrooble there?") In 223 BC, Hannibal attacked and conquered Saguntum, modern-day Sagunto (wherever the hell *that* is . . . just kidding, it's in Spain), and won the support of his native city, thus laying the foundation for what would become the Second Punic War (218–201 BC).

Fed up with Roman imperialism (he preferred his own), Hannibal decided to surprise the Roman army by taking the fight to them. In a daring and nearly suicidal move, Hannibal led his Carthaginian army, including baggage train (that is, food supplies, not that blind date you had who unloaded all of his problems on you the first time you got together for tuna rolls), on foot across the Alps, a total of 1,500 miles with not a freeway or HoJo's in sight. Hannibal appeared unexpectedly in Northern Italy and fell upon the undefended Po Valley (218–217 BC), catching the Roman soldiers with their togas down around their ankles.

As word of Hannibal's victories spread, new recruits from Rome's other enemies (like everyone in civilization) flocked to his banner, following Hannibal as he defeated several Roman armies (mind you, the mightiest military force in the world at that time), sometimes while outnumbered four to one. At the famed Battle of Cannae, Hannibal brilliantly used his cavalry to outflank the Romans, who had twice as many soldiers, and destroyed their army to a man. (His name was Frederico and he was a snappy dresser.) Between 25,000 and 50,000 Romans were slain and 10,000 captured, compared to Hannibal's 5,700, of which the vast majority were Celts and Iberians (Spanish).

With this great victory, Southern Italy rose up against the empire, joining Hannibal, as he threatened to end the power of Rome a few centuries earlier than scheduled. However, internal squabbles from the nimrods back in Carthage resulted in the loss of financial support, and Hannibal was left to survive on traveler's checks. ("Hey, guys, just like twenty more bucks and I could finish this.") Hannibal refused to go home, and instead hung out in Italy, touring the cities with his army, sacking wherever he went if his rigatoni wasn't al dente and crushing any who dared to face him, until Roman generals were too afraid to take the field (imagine if Mexicans invaded Texas and took over the entire southern half of the state and the U.S. government was helpless to stop them . . . well, just imagine Texas). Hannibal was at last recalled to defend his home city against a young Roman commander, Scipio Africanus, who at the Battle of Zama (Africa), finally conquered the Carthaginian commander.

Hannibal retired from military life in 200 BC, but four

years later, began to publicly lash out at his city's corrupt aristocracy. The powers that be, fearing Hannibal's influence, sold him out to the Romans (who still had a Punic bone to pick with him for rubbing their noses in the elephant poo he left all over their country) by falsely accusing him of plotting another attack on Rome. In an incredible strategic blunder, Hannibal launched a surprise assault against the Empire ("They think I'm gonna attack, but what they don't know is . . . I'm gonna attack!"). But as we said, the Romans *did* know and had a massive welcome back party waiting. Consequently, Hannibal was forced to retreat to Asia Minor in 183 BC, where the Romans pressured the local ruler, Prusias I, for his surrender ("If you give us Hannibal, we'll give you working toilets. Whaddya say?"). Trapped and out of options, rather than give in to his lifelong enemy, Hannibal poisoned himself in Libyssa, Turkey. Death by street kebab, what a way to go.

Interesting Tidbit: When his son was just nine years old, before departing on the Spanish campaign, Hamilcar took Hannibal to the altar and made him repeat this oath, "I swear that so soon as age will permit, I will use fire and steel to arrest the destiny of Rome." Hatred truly does begin in the home.

Ways to Bring Up Hannibal in Conversation

- ☀ There's more foreigners here than in Hannibal's army.
- ☀ That guy is the Hannibal of my existence, always popping up unexpectedly and making my life miserable.
- ☀ I'm having a Hannibal day. I feel like I'm winning the battle, but losing the war.

Saladin Won the Noble Prize During the Crusades

When Are We Talking About: 1138–1193

Why Are We Even Talking About This: Saladin was the

notoriously fair and chivalrous sultan of Egypt and the greatest general to face the European crusaders. He conquered Jerusalem and restored Sunnism to Egypt and Syria.

What You Need to Know to Sound Smart: Salah ad-Din Yusuf Ibn Ayyub (or Saladin, to anyone living west of the Nile) was born in Tikrit, Mesopotamia, around 1138, to a wealthy Kurdish family in northern Iraq (you know, the people from the old "no fly zone"), but grew up in the court of Nur ad-Din, the ruler of Syria, the caliph of Damascus, kind of like a state governor but with camels. In the court, he studied the Koran, philosophy, the Koran, military history, the Koran, the Koran, poetry and followed that up with a little bedtime Koran. At age fourteen, when most young boys are mastering Halo2, Saladin (meaning Righteous of the Faith) joined his uncle Shirkuh's military staff on a campaign into Egypt.

When the Egyptian sultan died, a three-way landgrab ensued between Sharwah, the shifty vizier of the Egyptian Fatimid caliph (a ruler who was an incompetent boob), the European crusaders of the kingdom of Jerusalem, and Saladin's guys. From 1164 to 1168, Saladin jockeyed for control of these rulerless lands, eventually luring Sharwah into an ambush and killing him. When his uncle died shortly thereafter in March of 1169, the thirty-two-year-old Saladin, a reputedly short and frail man, was given the title al-Malik al-Nasir (the prince defender). Uncle Shirkuh would be the first of several people who would conveniently expire just in time for the charismatic commander to rise to power, the second being the Al-Adid, last of the Fatimid caliphs (Shi'a nobles believed to descend from Mohammed's youngest daughter, Fatima, who reigned from 969 to 1171), whose passing gave our Islamic idol command of all Egypt.

Leading a Seljuk army made up mostly of former slaves, Saladin marched to Kahira, where the royal compound was located, and kicked out the caliph's 18,000 lazy relatives who were crashing there, opening the city to the people. Saladin was a humble man who did not hoard money or live in palaces, and under his fair rule slaves who earned their freedom (known as Mamluks) could gain rank in his army and royal court. People flocked to this new and noble ruler and the population of Kahira swelled. Today it is known as Cairo, which means "the subduer."

Luckily, before Nur ad-Din could become jealous of his nephew, he died right on cue in May 1174, making Saladin sultan of all Egypt and Syria and the first supreme ruler of the new Ayyubid caliphate. In May 1176, while attacking the town of Aleppo, the Assassins Cult of Rashideddin made their first attempt on Saladin's life, but failed because they didn't count on his judo chop. Saladin responded by besieging the fortress of Masyaf, the Assassin stronghold, in 1176, but withdrew only a few weeks later, some say as a result of threats to his family. ("Ooops sorry, wrong stronghold. We wanted the one two mountains down. Our bad.")

Around the same time, Saladin began improvements on Cairo, constructing mosques, hospitals (which he even equipped with mental asylums and separate quarters for women), and colleges of Islamic study. He also swept away the governmental corruption that had plagued the Fatimid rule. In a time of physical and spiritual war, Saladin wanted Cairo to be a bastion of Islamic faith, military strength, and a source of income to fund his campaign against the double-crossing crusaders and their infidel-ity. Domestically, Saladin revitalized the Egyptian economy, reorganized the military, and restored Islamism in Egypt, but preferring the Sunni side of the street, he replaced the prevalent Shi'a Islamic doctrines with those of his own faith.

In 1182, Saladin left Egypt in the hands of his brother and marched off to attack the crusaders' kingdom of Jerusalem, commanding a vast army of Muslims that the crusaders dubbed the Saracens, from the Greek word *sarakenoi* meaning "easterner," or "Hey, watch where you're waving that scimitar." At the Battle of Hattin in 1187, provoked by the underhanded French crusader Raynald de Chatillon and his threats to sack the Islamic holy centers of Medina and Mecca ("Oh, no he di'nt!"), Saladin met and crushed the Christian forces. This battle would ultimately lead to the crusaders' fall from grace (and power) in the Middle East. Although his army captured several European nobles, Saladin forbade his men from murdering them. He also prohibited raping and pillaging the holy city (but then, where's the fun?), granting the Christians safe passage home, as opposed to the crusaders who, when sacking Jerusalem back in 1099, butchered everybody in sight.

In 1189, the king of England, Richard I, Coeur de Lion (the Lionhearted guy everyone's waiting for to come back in *Robin Hood*), led the Third Crusade to recover the holy city (because the abysmal failure of the first two had been so inspirational), beginning a military rivalry with Saladin that became the stuff of legend. Because of his chivalry, Saladin has been called the "noble Arab" (though despite his fancy galabia he was never called the "chic sheik"), once even sending his enemies fruit and water when Richard fell ill, hoping it would help his upset tummy. Richard's Crusade, also known as the King's Crusade, ultimately failed.

In 1192 Saladin reached an agreement with the Western warriors called the Peace of Ramla, allowing them to peacefully withdraw from the region, while still generously permitting Christian pilgrims to trek to Jerusalem unmolested, unless they brought one of those naughty priests, in which case it was out of his hands. In the meantime, Saladin smashed nearly all other Christian cities except Tyre and Jaffa, reducing the once great crusaders' kingdom to ruin. At its height, Saladin's empire spanned the Middle East and

North Africa for hundreds of miles, but when he died in Damascus in 1193 at the age of fifty-five, he'd given away all his money to the needy and was buried penniless.

Interesting Tidbit: While he had the city under siege, Saladin once gave a crusader permission to retrieve his family from Jerusalem and leave unscathed. His only condition was that the soldier swore not to stay and fight. When the crusader reached the holy city, the outnumbered defenders persuaded him to take charge of their defenses and he sought release from his oath to Saladin. The noble Arab understood his plight and gave the man's family safe passage out of the area anyway.

Ways to Bring Up Saladin in Conversation

- ☼ Larry really pulled a total Saladin by forgiving Laura for cheating.
- ☼ Look out. The way Amy is rising through the ranks, before you know it, we'll be calling her Saladin.
- ☼ I want my Middle Eastern chicken salad Saladin style . . . with chopped white meat.

Manfred von Richthofen's Life Was a Flying Circus

When Are We Talking About: 1892–1918

Why Are We Even Talking About This: More commonly known as the Red Baron, Manfred von Richthofen is arguably the most famous name in the history of aerial combat and a modern-day legend.

What You Need to Know to Sound Smart: Manfred Albrecht Freiherr von Richthofen was born on May 2, 1892, in Breslau, Germany, now located in Poland. He was the son of a Prussian nobleman, Maj. Albrecht Richthofen, and his wife, Kunigunde (oh, those erotic Prussian names, "Give it to me, Kunigunde"). An excellent athlete and an even better equestrian, Richthofen was an arrogant, charismatic, and cocky young man, who spent his life in military school, punishment for being unable to pronounce his mother's name. After graduating from the Royal Military Academy at Lichterfelde, Richthofen became a cavalry officer (like his daddy) in the kaiser's army and got to wear a cool pointy helmet. When his unit was obliterated in a bloody skirmish, Manfred realized that in modern war the horseman would be put out to pasture and so traded in his saddle for a flight stick.

Inspired by the exploits of German flying ace Oswald Boelcke (who would become both a mentor and a friend), Richthofen began studying piloting and proved himself an apt aerial pupil. His aviation career first took flight in 1915 when he soloed after only twenty-four hours of training. Richthofen quickly soared to fame as a deadly dogfighter but didn't gain his legendary nom de guerre (French for "my real name sucks monkey butt") until his fellow Germans, never renowned for their good judgment, mistook his plane for an enemy aircraft and opened fire as he flew overhead. Cursing, Richthofen limped from his newly air-conditioned craft to the supply shed and covered the entire plane in a coat of red paint to ensure that troops in the future could tell Manfred from foe. Thus, the Red Baron was born.

In 1917, Richthofen formed and commanded the Flying Circus, a squadron of Germany's top aces, though they were never known to cram thirty pilots into a single plane. This "brat-wurst pack" instantly became the terror of the skies during World War I, causing their British enemies to spontaneously "drop fuel" as Richthofen led them screaming out of the clouds. During his career, Manfred and his Fokker DR-1 triplane were credited with eighty kills, giving him the high score for WWI. However, by the end of the war, Richthofen, disenchanted and disillusioned, suffered from headaches, combat wounds, and terrible bouts of depression having watched all his friends die in battle. On April 21, 1918, near Sailly-le-Sac, France, the Red Baron was finally killed by a single bullet through his chest while, contrary to his own tactical teachings, he flew deep over enemy lines at low altitude in pursuit of a novice British pilot. He was only twenty-five.

Controversy persists to this day as to whether Manfred was shot down by the pilot he was chasing or the Australian infantry gunners he was soaring over. Richthofen was such a respected adversary that the British buried him with full military honors in France, but his body was eventually moved to his family's cemetery in Wiesbaden in 1976.

Interesting Tidbit: Richthofen was the most famous man in Germany during WWI and, like a modern-day sports star, he even had his own trading cards as well as other types of "merch," which kids collected throughout the country.

Ways to Bring Up von Richthofen in Conversation
- I don't trust that airline. They've had more confirmed kills than Richthofen.
- That guy's a killer. He's the Red Baron of dating.
- Amanda lives like Richthofen flew, fast and furious.

No One Outfoxed Erwin Rommel
When Are We Talking About: 1891–1944
Why Are We Even Talking About This: Better known as the Desert Fox this Nazi field marshal was in charge of troops in the Third Reich's North African Campaign during World War II and is considered one of the finest tacticians in the history of warfare.
What You Need to Know to Sound Smart: Rommel's first major victory occurred when he was born on November 15, 1891, in Heidenheim, Germany. The battle map of Rommel's childhood campaign was relatively free of minefields until

age fourteen, when, like any good middle-class boy, lil' Erwin decided he wanted to be an engineer. Erwin Sr., a class-conscious schoolmaster, forbade such an ordinary pursuit ("Zer vill be *no* engineering in zis 'ouse!"), demanding his boy join the military for the glory of the new German Empire established about thirty years earlier. At nineteen, the dutiful son enlisted in the 124th Württemberg Infantry and began studying in Danzig (the Germany city, *not* the frightening speed-metal band), at the nation's leading war academy.

A hot dog young officer, Rommel mustered out a second lieutenant, and like any graduate, decided to take a year and tour Europe, or in his case, the Western Front. Rommel and his camouflaged Kampfgruppe backpacked across France, Italy, and Romania, staying in the most hostile hostels, where he encountered fascinating foreigners and shot them. For his bravery and cunning, Rommel was awarded the Iron Cross (first and second class) and promoted to captain. However, despite his MVP status, war is a team sport, and his fellow German players repeatedly fumbled the ball, resulting in their surrender in 1918, where the Treaty of Versailles reduced the country's army strength to that of an angry Baptist Women's League.

In 1929, Rommel found work teaching at the Dresden Infantry School (where he hated subbing for the arts and crafts teacher on clay day), honing his tactical brilliance. By 1935, Rommel had shot up the ranks to lieutenant colonel and begun teaching in Potsdam, where he published his WWI diaries, *Infanterie Greift an* (*Infantry Attacks,* 1937). This detailed account of his experiences and strategies is considered a classic of modern military technique and was a best seller among peace-loving Aryans such as Adolf Hitler. In September 1939 Rommel was promoted to major general just in time for the next German Invasion Festival, sponsored by the unwitting people of Poland. As former commander of Hitler's personal bodyguard, Rommel had his choice of command.

He was fascinated by the destructive power of the panzer tanks during the blitzkrieg across Poland, and even though he couldn't drive stick, he requested a division to take out for a spin. Leading what at the time was the most sophisticated motorized force on the planet, Rommel's panzers decimated the French "military" in May 1940, catching the enemy with their pants down while in bed with their neighbor's wives. Unlike the Great War where armies struggled over six feet of mud for months on end, Rommel's blitzers plowed through the French defense, sacking the entire country in an unheard of six weeks, or about the time it takes your average Parisian to shower twice. Rommel's Seventh became known as the Ghost Division, traveling swiftly and with next to no communication, so that his own Nazi superiors often had no idea of his location.

In January 1941, Rommel, now a lieutenant general in charge of the Fifteenth Panzer Division, was sent to support the German Africa Corps, assisting the nearly exhausted Italian Army in Libya, who were losing primarily because they were Italian. Rommel had a secret recipe for victory. Transforming his limp noodle Italian units into an al dente fighting force, he served up double helpings of punishment, spilling plenty of red sauce while gobbling up territory lost to the British. Rommel, who inspired his men by leading from the front, blazed through all opposition reaching the Egyptian border by April 1941, and proved such hot stuff that he earned the name Desert Fox. One of his most famous tactics was dragging piles of wood behind ordinary trucks in the desert, creating huge dust clouds, and the appearance of a tank division to his enemies while his actual armor attacked elsewhere.

At age fifty, Rommel became German field marshal, making him the youngest man to ever achieve the rank. He was also a hero among Arabs who saw him as their liberator from oppressive British rule, causing them to leap into the welcoming arms of the freedom-fostering Third Reich with its love for dark-skinned, dark-eyed people. In August 1942, Rommel took command of all "battle-ready" Axis troops in North Africa, both German and Italian, so in other words, just the Germans. Though winning terrific victories at Benghazi and Tobruk, by the end of 1942 the combination of American troop presence, the Allied use of their German code cracker, the Ultra, to decipher Axis battle communiques, and an inability of the German high command to keep him supplied took its toll, culminating in a crushing defeat at the Kasserine Pass.

Despite this failure, Hitler appointed Rommel commander of the reorganized Army Group Africa, a job which, though he respectfully declined, he was forced to accept. In March, the Desert Fox tried to convince the führer that Africa was a dog that wouldn't hunt, but instead was awarded the Knight's Cross with Oakleaves, Swords and Diamonds, a broach that made him the envy of cross dressers everywhere. Two months later, fighting on fumes (from gas siphoned from disabled Allied tanks), the African Corps surrendered, raising money for their trip home with an Italian rifle sale: "Never fired, only dropped once."

By mid-1943, Rommel was back in Europe commanding Army Group B and constructing barriers to defend the Atlantic wall, which he named "Rommel's Asparagus" and which we hope sounds a lot more impressive in German. Rommel recommended his tanks be placed right on the beachhead to protect them from Allied aircraft and to assist in repelling the coming D-day invasion. His direct superior, Field Marshal Gerd von Rundstedt, disagreed, advising Hitler to leave the armor in Paris for mop-up. Hitler, a painter renowned for his military genius, split the difference and put them in the middle, where they were absolutely useless.

On July 20, 1944, Rommel was implicated in a failed bomb assassination attempt on the führer and, in return for his years of service, was given the choice of suicide or state execution. Wow, talk about a horserace. On October 14 the Desert Fox, still recovering from injuries inflicted by a strafing enemy aircraft months before, swallowed cyanide in a hospital in Ulm, though it was publicly announced that he had died from his wounds. Four days later, he was buried with full honors, and Hitler himself declared a national day of mourning for this fallen hero.

Interesting Tidbit: Other than the fact that he was a Nazi stooge with a silly name, Erwin was an okay guy. Unlike his Third Reich kameraden, Rommel felt anti-Semitism weakened his country, was never connected to any war crimes, and even cut his own troops' water supply to make sure POWs under his care didn't die of thirst in the desert.

Ways to Bring Up Erwin Rommel in Conversation

☸ Watch Tom and that girl. He's got better moves than Erwin Rommel.

☸ They pulled a Rommel on Sue. She worked like a dog, and they fired her.

☸ I heard that guy's got a bigger turret than Erwin Rommel.

Relaying the Bataan Death March

When Are We Talking About: 1942–1945

Why Are We Even Talking About This: The Bataan Death March was one of the most vicious examples of POW abuse in the history of warfare.

What You Need to Know to Sound Smart: Just over eight hours after Pearl Harbor was bombed on December 7, 1941, the Japanese attacked the Philippines, a commonwealth of the United States (think international protection racket—

where America annexed this sovereign, self-governing nation, for their own safety) and the location of several American military bases. Allied troops in the region, mostly untested Filipinos armed with rifles made when Woodrow Wilson was in office, although aware Japan was on the move, failed to prepare for the attack and were decimated. Gen. Douglas MacArthur retreated to the Bataan Peninsula establishing a defensive line to await reinforcements. Meanwhile the Pentagon had decided resupplying Bataan was not worth the cost and resources and abandoned the province . . . along with the GIs stationed there. ("We just can't afford shipping bullets all the way to the Philippines. I'm sorry waiter, *I* had the filet, *he* had the lobster.")

That was January. Meanwhile the Allied soldiers struggled to hold out against overwhelming assaults by well-stocked Japanese troops. When defeat seemed inevitable, MacArthur made his famous "I will return" speech and then evacuated to Australia on March 11 (but it wasn't until he had a Vegemite sandwich that he really began to regret his decision), making the new commander, Maj. Gen. Edward P. King, a sitting duck. The Japanese dropped surrender pamphlets, promising special preferential treatment to demoralized Allied troops ("If you give up now we've got two words for you: Pizza Party!").

A month later, on April 9, 1942, known as Black Saturday, without rations, medical supplies, or even ammunition, King surrendered his emaciated 10,000 American and 65,000 Filipino troops. The Japanese commander, Gen. Masaharu Homma, decided to march the tens of thousands of POWs to the prison dubbed Camp O'Donnell in Nueva Ecija, more than fifty-five miles away. King informed Homma that nearly all the men under his care were wounded, sick, or malnourished. (Come on, how much *sinigang*—sour boiled fish—can a fella eat?) While a fit, well-fed soldier might make this march in a few days, for the POWs it was a death sentence. Still possessing numerous Allied vehicles, King even offered to drive his wounded to the POW camp, but Homma insisted they walk. Things went bad before they even started out, as the guards executed on the spot any enemy soldiers in possession of Japanese souvenirs (those little snow globes of Mount Fuji just pissed them off).

In temperatures exceeding 100 degrees, the Allied POWs set out from Mariveles on April 10, 1942. Given no water or protective headgear by their Japanese escorts, prisoners collapsed left and right, often brutally beaten to death where they lay or crushed under the treads of rolling tanks (if this was the advertised "preferential treatment," we'd hate to see the other guys). Those who asked for water or tried to take a sip from the dysentery-ridden puddles lining the trail were bayoneted, shot, or beheaded. At night, the prisoners were packed into tiny containment shacks, unable to move, dying on top of one another. After reaching San Fernando, Pampamga, they were loaded onto trains, one hundred men per car (perhaps normal to the Japanese considering how they pack 'em in on their rush-hour subways) in the sweltering heat. By the time they'd walked another seven miles to Camp O'Donnell, a week had passed and only 54,000 POWs remained. Nearly 20,000 unarmed men had been killed or left for dead while those who'd survived would soon wish they had not.

O'Donnell was a disease-ridden, unsanitized pit equipped to house about one-third the number of prisoners now arriving through its gates. The POWs remained malnourished and were subjected to routine beatings and forced labor, including burial detail for those well enough to dig. Red Cross supplies were confiscated by the guards and given to Japanese troops—after all, killing and maiming is *hungry* work. By June, another 25,000 helpless Filipino and 1,500 American POWs had died or been killed—the Japanese were particularly hard on the natives, whom they viewed as traitors. ("You're Asian but your last name is Hernandez! What's wrong with you?!") American prisoners were soon packed into the cargo holds of modified oil rigs called "hell ships" (actually, a far too flattering term) without food, water, or toilet. They were transported to slave labor camps in Japan, China, and Korea where they remained (if they lived) until the end of the war, working for companies such as Mitsubishi and Kawasaki.

Some claim General Homma, a liberal and cultured man fluent in English, would never have approved, let alone ordered, the mistreatment of his prisoners, and instead place blame on his subordinate, Col. Masanobu Tsuji. After all, Homma was a world traveler, Oxford educated, and called the Poet General, while Tsuji was a notorious Jabroni, a rumored pedophile, and a cannibal (allegedly once feasting on the liver of a downed American pilot in a ritual meal). There are those who blame the atrocities of Bataan on Homma's need to stand by the actions of his officers, while others claim he was ignorant of the extent of the suffering since Japanese brass never toured the camps. However, in either case, a man in Homma's position was all the more guilty for failing to control the activities of the men under his command. (Can you say Abu Ghraib?) Another argument posits that the "honor-based" Japanese disapproved of the American surrender, feeling that because they did not fight to the death, they were unworthy of respect and so treated them like dogs. Still another theory suggests the Japanese fancied themselves the master race, superior to all others, and therefore justified in their treatment of the POWs. Finally, some point the blame to Prime Minister Hideki Tojo, who instructed his military commanders not to let their feelings sway them when dealing with prisoners. Interestingly, the Japanese never signed the Geneva Convention, which might explain why they felt so okay with violating it. Conditions eventually became so bad at O'Donnell that the prisoners were dying faster than their captors could kill them. On June 6, 1942, the Japanese moved what was left of the camp's populace north to a camp at Cabanatuan, where they could execute them at their leisure.

All the POW camps were eventually liberated after MacArthur returned (you gotta give it up for the guy, he kept his promise), beginning the Second Battle of the Philippines, which ended in April 1945 with an Allied victory. Homma was found guilty of war crimes for his action (or inaction) in Bataan and killed by a firing squad on April 3, 1946. Hideki Tojo survived a failed suicide attempt and lived to be hung on December 23, 1948. Tsuji escaped prosecution after the war, wrote several best-selling autobiographies (which doubled as cookbooks), and lived in luxury until 1961 when he disappeared during a trip to Laos where it is theorized he was eaten by a tiger. While over 300,000 Japanese soldiers were charged with war crimes, only 6,000 were put on trial with 920 receiving the death sentence and another 3,000 sent to prison. The 1,500-some-odd allied survivors still alive today call themselves the Battlin' Bastards of Bataan.

Interesting Tidbit: A less well-known fact about Bataan is that a group of American troops stationed at nearby Corregidor Island suffered an equally evil and inhumane march through downtown Manila to Fort Santiago, where they were imprisoned.

Ways to Bring Up the Bataan Death March in Conversation

☀ That's as feeble an excuse as Japan had for the Bataan Death March.

☀ It's not that long a walk. Hey, just be thankful you weren't on the Bataan Death March.

☀ I'll wait, but don't leave me waiting the way MacArthur did General King at the Bataan Death March.

The Science Conversation

*T*hough the science conversation can admittedly be a bit of a snoozer, the attraction is that people love to learn how and why things do what they do. If you can present scientific information in a palatable (tasty) and easy to understand way, people will be excited to hear what you have to say. Lucky for you, we do just that in the pages that follow. If, by some cosmic equation, you find yourself at a science party, don't even try to b.s. a scientist when talking on their field of expertise. Generally speaking, it is going to be hard to sound smarter than a scientist (unless you are one), since they do one hundred brain push-ups per day (compared to our usual ten). However, your advantage is that most scientists are socially awkward. While their brains may be in gold medal shape, their people skills are a fat guy in biker shorts. Sorry guys, despite modern Hollywood casting, 99.99 percent of the microbiologists in the world don't look and party like Miss

December, and ladies, let's face it, men who look like George Clooney are too busy dating to study nuclear fission. Most laypeople (that's what scientists call folks like you and me . . . but don't get too excited, it has nothing to do with sex) don't know a beaker from a Bunsen burner, so if you have even a rudimentary knowledge of a scientist's field, they will be unable to contain their excitement or resist sharing and debating their latest theories. Don't be afraid to ask questions here. Those in the science fields understand that their ideas are confusing, and in fact they sometimes have difficulty understanding one another. The edge you have over your average scientist is your ability to bridge their world with the Beavis and Butthead mentality of the average Joe.

Galileo Didn't Think the World Revolved Around Him

When Are We Talking About: 1564–1642

Why Are We Even Talking About This: Galileo transformed the world of science from a speculative practice to one based on the sound principle of testing hypotheses through repeated experimentation.

What You Need to Know to Sound Smart: Not just a poor boy from a poor family, Galileo Galilei was born near Pisa (as in, Leaning Tower of) on February 15, 1564. His father, Vincenzo, was a wool merchant who had forgone his true love, composing music, in order to provide the world with itchy clothing. Despite his pedestrian occupation, Vinny was an iconoclast, a trait inherited by his little silhouetto, much to the chagrin of Galileo's mother, who felt her artistic husband was more like an autistic idiot, and well below her station. The family moved to Florence, where Galileo was tutored by monks at Vallombrosa though his papa soon yanked him out to spare him a life of too much "brotherly love." Later, studying at the University of Pisa in 1581, Galileo turned from medical studies to pursue mathematics and philosophy. Unfortunately, his "out of the box" thinking left him "out of the cash" since his scholarship was revoked in 1585, before he could earn a degree. Ironically, working as a private tutor to make ends meet earned Galileo such renown as a teacher that his "almost mater" offered him a position as a professor in the mathematics department, but due to budget cuts he was also forced to coach the girl's bocce team.

Senior professors were outraged by Galileo's gall when at age twenty-five he challenged Aristotle's theory that objects fall at speeds directly proportionate to their weight. ("You're a teacher! It's not your job to question things!") According to history, after climbing to the top of the Leaning Tower, Galileo defied his detractors with brass balls by tossing two lead balls of differing weights over the side (in one of the most famous experiments of all time) proving once and for all what a big dummy Aristotle was and sending tourists scrambling for cover. The fact that this theory had actually *already* been proven by a number of other scientists didn't prevent Galileo from making a huge name for himself. Though university officials, apparently distant relatives of Aristotle, decided in 1592 not to invite Galileo back, the Italian math stallion already had been offered a bigger piece of the "pi" at the University of Padua, where he taught the powers of force to eager young Paduans until 1610. But supporting his lazy relatives and three illegitimate children from his relationship with Marina Gamba quickly drained his income, so Galileo moonlighted as a tutor to Prince Cosimo, the son of Tuscany's grand duchess (who, it's said, had a grand tuchus), a relationship that would serve him well later in life.

While teaching at Padua, Galileo turned from speculative physics (guessing at stuff) to this crazy new idea of taking careful measurements when conducting experiments (an innovation that would one day lead to the establishment of the scientific method). He also spent time studying pendulums (note to reader: they go back and forth), observing the parabolic path of projectiles, creating the Law of Falling Bodies, and developing the first calculator, called a calculating compass (which was probably more powerful and slightly smaller than the first TRS-80s sold by Radio Shack).

While many people believe Galileo invented the telescope, they also believe that Freddy Prinze Jr. is a good actor. They are wrong on both counts, since that distinction goes to Dutch researcher Hans Lippershey and *She's All That* was unwatchable. But Galilei *did* make significant improvements to the Lippershey model and presented one of his new and improved telescopes to the Venetian Senate, whose members were so thrilled they could spy into their neighbor's windows that they doubled his salary. Galileo soon improved on his own design and created a 400-power telescope (he just didn't want to give the senate the good one!), which he used to prove that the moon was covered in craters and mountain ranges, an amazing new discovery that had, once again, already been proven months before by someone else; Thomas Harriot in 1609. However, in all fairness to the pasta-stronomer, Galileo did make several important original discoveries (finally), including the moon's light is reflected off the sun, the universe is made up of an uncountable number of stars (the exact number, if you must know, is two bajillion), and that Jupiter has four moons, which he named the Medician stars for his patrons, the Medici family. And to think movie stars only get a filthy square on Hollywood Boulevard. This final discovery led Galileo to fully embrace Copernicus's heliocentric universe model (which sounds like a beauty contest with hot Italian women, but isn't) that stated that the sun was the center of the universe, as opposed to the Earth, or New York.

In March of 1610, Galileo published his findings as *Sidereus Nuncius* ("Starry Messenger") and dedicated it to his old pupil, Cosimo, who now happened to be the doge of Venice. Hey, he knew who buttered his *pané*. His theories shook the European world, calling into question long-held beliefs from both Aristotle and biblical misinterpretation about the structure and age of the universe. Cosimo rewarded Galileo with a title (Court Philosopher and Mathematician) as well as cash. This scaramouch then did a fandango, abandoning his wife and family to join the doge under the Tuscan sun. In his new locale, Galileo enjoyed incredible celebrity ("Come on, do long division for us!") while studying the movement of the planets and the relationship to their moons. In 1613, Galileo published *Letters on the Solar Spots*, again demanding an end to the Church's stratos fear and the rejection of the dominant theories previously established by Aristotle and Ptolemy.

Galileo's chief rival, a narrow-minded, inferior mathematician named Ludovico de Colombe, pressured the Church to prosecute the starstruck math-debater on charges of heresy, claiming all his heliocentric hogwash was basically a rejection of God. Galileo, never missing an opportunity to thumb his nose (or being Italian, more likely his chin) at the Church allowed the publication of a letter to a friend where he scathingly expressed his opinion that the Bible was no more a science textbook than *The Da Vinci Code*. As a result, in February 1616, Galileo was forced to travel to Rome to explain himself to the Church ("Wrong? I said the Bible was 'long.'") where he was harshly scolded by Cardinal Robert Bellarmine and told to drop the Copernican crap if he knew what was good for him. The Vatican also officially declared the heliocentric model "wrong" in 1616 and that anyone daring to believe otherwise would face the business end of a burning stake.

Apparently no one explained the severity of the situation to G.G. because he continued with his writing and research. *The Assayer* (1623), a book on comets and their usefulness in detecting longitude in naval navigation (on the off chance you're ever on a boat and lost when you see a comet), was Galileo's next published work, and shortly thereafter, unwilling to let sleeping dogmas lie, he tried to convince the new, and supposedly more hip, Pope Urban VIII, that his new book, *The Dialogue Concerning the Chief Two World Systems* was cool for Christmas, though in it he unabashedly bashed the whole Earth-is-the-center-of-the-universe thing again. But Urban didn't have a modern point of view, and in 1632, Galileo went before God's own *Crossfire,* better known as the Inquisition. Found guilty of heresy in 1633 and already ill, Galileo knew he could not endure their questionable "questioning," and so on May 10, he foreswore his beliefs and life's work, admitting he had supported heretical views, because everyone knows torturing someone into changing their mind makes it true. On June 22, after signing his confession, and allegedly telling the Inquisitors, "And yet, it turns," Galileo was punished with life in prison, but, mama-mia, mama-mia, the pope let him go and mercifully commuted his sentence to house arrest, like Martha Stewart except without the anger and bitterness.

Galileo was mocked by his peers yet managed to get his proscribed book published by the Dutch, because the Dutch are *so* progressive; hashish cafés, public brothels, and more bicycles per square yard than any country in the world. In 1638, half-blind and with one foot in the grave, Galileo published *Discourses Concerning Two New Sciences*, exploring his theories of mechanics and motion. Several years later, now seventy-eight, with a raging fever and crippling arthritis, Galilei's star finally fell from the sky in Arcetri, near Florence, on January 8, 1642.

Interesting Tidbit: An investigation into the astronomer's condemnation was opened in 1979 by Pope John Paul II. In October 1992 a papal commission acknowledged the Vatican's error. So 350 years after the fact, the Vatican officially pardoned Galileo and admitted that he had been right about that sun thing all along. No kidding.

Ways to Bring Up Galileo in Conversation

☀ I admire your conviction. But make sure you don't end up like Galileo.

☀ Ooh, look at the stars. Let's pretend I'm Galileo and pick one to name after you.

☀ I've been trapped in my house like Galileo Galilei, only at least I've got a TV.

An Ounce of Prevention Is Worth a Pound of Curie

When Are We Talking About? 1867–1934

Why Are We Even Talking About This? This two-time Nobel Prize–winning scientist, Marie Curie, was the leading female researcher of her day and her work has been a major influence on modern medicine.

What You Need to Know to Sound Smart: Maria Sklodowska began her half-life in Warsaw on November 7, 1867, which was no Polish joke under the oppressive Russian occupation (as opposed to any other kind of Russian occupation?) that had stripped her nation of its identity. The Russians had denied the Poles the right to speak their own language, and those who broke the law received an all-expense-paid trip to the Siberian gulags, a fate that befell many of Curie's relatives. Maria's parents had descended from nobility, but her mother and father were now humble schoolteachers. Both of her folks were fiercely patriotic, even running an underground school with other Polish intellectuals to keep the lifeblood of their culture circulating.

Marie, or Manya, as she was nicknamed, attended a local school while Dad laid down some science at home (no really, he taught her science). As a young girl, Marie possessed a Curie-ous mind and a nearly photographic memory. By sixteen, she had completed her Russian secondary school with gold medal honors, which in those days actually meant something, as opposed to now, where, for the sake of kids' *feeeeelings*, everyone gets a medal as long as they don't eat paste or touch their wieners. When the family fell into dire financial straits, it was decided that older sister Bronya would go to medical school and that Maria would get a job to pitch in. Now eighteen, serious and unassuming, Curie became a governess (just who you want taking care of your kids), spending what spare time she had from her "home work" to pursue chemistry and physics homework. When her mother passed away, Maria's father nobly insisted she join Bronya, who was now married to a doctor (boy, med school *really* paid off) and in a position to help. ("Don't worry about your ol' Dad. I'll just sit here in the dark . . . and eat the cat food.")

In Paris in 1891, the twenty-four-year-old Curie studied at the Sorbonne while living in an attic and subsisting on scraps. Despite not speaking French, Curie was one of only two women to receive a degree in physics in 1893. Graduating at the head of her class, she also received a second degree in mathematical sciences in 1894. (Sure, we could have two degrees if we took all the easy classes too.)

That same year while studying magnetism at the lab of her mentor, Gabriel Lippmann (a genius who would later win the Nobel Prize for pioneering color photography), she met another brilliant scientist who was experimenting with crystals and electricity named Pierre Curie. Pierre, thirty-five, was an idealist liberal, somewhat shy yet full of lighthearted exuberance. Working in close quarters ("Is that an Erlenmeyer flask in your pocket or are you just happy to see my pipette titrations?"), these two science-minded humanitarians fell in love and married in a town hall civil ceremony at Sceaux on July 25, 1895. They spent their wedding money on bicycles, taking long relaxing rides together, discussing their work, while Marie shocked Parisian pedestrians in her men's pants. ("François, zat young woman was wearing trousers! *And* she actually appears to be in love wiz her *husband*. I am outraged!!!")

In 1896, Henri Becquerel discovered uranium salts caused exposures on photographic plates, though the discovery received little attention (wow, go figure). But the curious Curies suspected there was something more to be mined, and they decided to direct their energies toward "radioactivity," the term Curie coined for the phenomenon, having rejected the phrase "cancercausingactivity." Utterly unaware of the carcinogenic side-effects of radiation, the Curies began experimenting with an ore containing small quantities of uranium called pitchblende (mixed with a hint of delicious paprika) and discovered that though cheaper than the *pure* stuff, it was far more radioactive, which just proves the old saying that you don't have to spend a lot of money to get high-quality nuclear materials. After exhaustive experimentation, Marie discovered two new elements within her spicy mixture: polonium, named after her native Poland, and radium, from the Latin, "this crap is killing me."

The Curies spent their next few years in a glass-roof "lab" donated by Pierre's school, which later a visiting German chemist would describe as "a cross between a stable and a potato shed." Marie spent endless days sifting through literally tons of pitchblende (and you *know* it smells good too!), stirring huge boiling pots of the stuff with an iron rod the size of her body, trying to isolate the radioactive substance. Even the birth of Curie's first daughter, Irène, in 1897 (miraculously arriving with only one head), didn't keep her from her work. In 1890, Curie became the first female professor at École Normale Supérieure for girls in Sévres, where she campaigned for better education for young women and was the first to teach through experimental demonstration. ("Now watch carefully as I handle this uranium. See how my arm swells and turns red? Very good, now you try.")

Marie hit "pitch-dirt" by isolating a decagram (nerdspeak for ten grams) of chloride with an atomic weight of 225. Glowing with excitement (actually, by this point, she was probably pretty much glowing in general), she presented her findings in 1903 and became the first woman to receive her doctorate of science and the Royal Society's Davy Medal for her "outstandingly important" discovery. She was also hailed by members of her examination committee for making the greatest discovery *ever* in a doctoral thesis.

Utterly oblivious to the dangers, Pierre kept a radium sample in his coat to show folks around town, gleefully explaining how it was a million times more radioactive than uranium. ("This stuff can kill a full-grown rhino in about fourteen seconds and it's right here in my pocket.") The researcher even mailed samples of the fun glowing powder to friends ("Happy Birthday! We hope you don't already *have* cancer!") and went so far as to wrap a radium salt bandage around his arm for ten hours until it burned his skin, the results of which he then studied (and this guy's a genius?), while Marie used it as a nightlight for little Irene. ("Don't be scared of the dark, honey. This lump of toxic material next to your bed will keep you safe.") Not surprisingly, Pierre soon grew ill, and Marie's skin suffered scars and cracks (making her look like Jan-Michael Vincent in drag), and both of them were often tired and pale.

In 1903, the cauterized couple would share the Nobel Prize for Physics (making Marie the first woman to receive the honor) with Becquerel, having to split the cash three ways, which was a bummer. Marie became a hero of the science world (though sadly, never had her own action figure) and one of the first champions of women's rights. Over the next few years Marie did a whole lot of other major stuff including earning her doctor of science degree (the first woman in Europe to do so) and giving birth to her second daughter, Eve. On April 19, 1906, Pierre was killed in a freak wagon accident in Paris where his head was isolated from the rest of his body. Marie, devastated, plunged herself into her work, taking over Pierre's post and becoming the first female professor of general physics in the faculty of sciences.

In November of 1911, Curie now in her forties met Paul Langevin, a scientist five years her junior, who set her Bunsen burner on high, and despite his being married, the two began a torrid affair. When Langevin's wife exposed their twisted tryst to the local papers, scandal rocked Curie's world like a nuclear explosion, and she was depicted as a foreign home-wrecker, taking jobs away from the myriad local French home-wreckers. She was forced to go into seclusion to avoid the crowds that surrounded her home hurling insults and nonglowing stones through her windows. The affair divided friends and families, as some rallied around the assailed scientist, while others abandoned her to *les lupins*.

As a result, a letter arrived from the Nobel committee requesting Curie not accept her second Nobel Prize, this time for chemistry, making her the first person to win two of them and only one of two people to win in two different categories (the other would be biochemist Linus Pauling). Curie fired back with a letter of her own, effectively telling the ignoble Nobel committee that her private life was her business and no reflection on her scientific work. In December of 1911, in a testament to her personal strength, Curie journeyed to Stockholm and claimed her prize, making it the only nonradioactive metal she had in the house.

However, Marie soon became depressed, staying with a friend in England and out of the public eye. Three years later, the French forgave all and founded the Radium Institute of the University of Paris with Curie as director.

During World War I, Marie designed and helped build 150 X-ray vans, some of which she drove to the battlefront herself, and trained nurses to use the machinery to locate bullets in wounded soldiers, saving their lives by blasting them with radioactivity. Curie journeyed to America in 1921 where she was greeted like a superstar. The decade only got better for Marie, as President Warren G. Harding, on behalf of the women of America (who had only earned the right to vote in 1920), presented her with one gram of radium in recognition of her service to science. ("And as a sign of our thanks for proving women are our equals, here's a box of death. Choke on it.") In 1932, Marie founded the Curie Foundation and the Radium Institute of Warsaw (later renamed the Curie Institute), appointing her sister Bronya the director (why does Bronya always get to do everything?).

At the age of sixty-seven, Curie died in Savoy, France, on July 4, 1934, of leukemia, probably from radiation exposure during her long years of research. In 1995, she was honored by having her remains moved to the dome of the Pantheon in Paris, making her *again* the first woman to be so honored solely on her own merits. Curie's discoveries paved the way for radiation research that would become the core of the atomic age, opening up the fields of physics, quantum mechanics, nuclear energy, and medicine.

Interesting Tidbit: Since the Curie lab was so soaked with radium, anyone wishing to view their papers today must sign a waiver saying they are doing so at their own risk.

Ways to Bring Up Madame Curie in Conversation

☼ You're positively glowing my dear. Madame Curie would have been jealous.

☀ That girl's like Madame Curie. Smart, ambitious, and she radiates heat.

☀ Baby, if you're the radioactive thing that's melting my heart, then I'm your Madame Curie.

J. Robert Oppenheimer Was Da Bomb

When Are We Talking About: 1904–1967

Why Are We Even Talking About This: Oppenheimer was the Father of the Atomic Bomb who led the design team that created the nukes dropped on Hiroshima and Nagasaki.

What You Need to Know to Sound Smart: Julius Robert Oppenheimer was born in New York City, April 22, 1904, the son of wealthy German immigrants. Brilliant, awkward, and bullied, Oppenheimer spent a year bedridden with dysentery before growing up to build his doomsday bomb (when will we learn?). Oppenheimer graduated Harvard in three years and received his doctorate from the University of Cottingen in Germany (literally making him the "Dr. J" of science). He worked as a professor at both Berkeley and Cal Tech, educating an entire generation of *Star Trek* fans while conducting groundbreaking research on atomic structure, theoretical physics, and black holes. In the second half of the 1930s, Oppenheimer dabbled in leftist political organizations, though he probably just thought he looked cool in black turtlenecks. In 1940, Oppy married Katherine Harrison, a biologist and card-carrying member of the Communist Party. Not long after, when applying for a job with Uncle Sam, Oppenheimer thought it best to blow off his pinko friends and was soon appointed to lead the Manhattan Project—the government team responsible for creating the first nuclear bomb, not to be confused with the Alan Parson's Project, the rock band responsible for creating explosive pop music.

Oppenheimer and his posse assembled at the sandbox of

Los Alamos, New Mexico, to play with their radioactive toys, and on July 16, 1945, the first plutonium bomb (which they called "the gadget") was exploded . . . and there was much rejoicing. Oppenheimer became deeply troubled upon seeing the destructive power he had unleashed on the world and quoted the Bhagavad Gita (a Hindu holy book): "I have become Death, destroyer of worlds," which must have really brought everyone down. Less than a month later, Oppenheimer's research was incarnated as a uranium bomb nicknamed "Little Boy," originally named "Thin Man" after Roosevelt, which would be dropped from the aircraft *Enola Gay* to atomize the Japanese city of Hiroshima, killing somewhere between 66,000 (American figures) and 200,000 people (Japanese figures—we can assume they had a slightly better view). Three days later a plutonium bomb, called "Fat Man" after Winston Churchill, was dropped over Nagasaki (killing between 39,000 and 79,000), causing the Japanese to surrender before all those dangerous children and elderly women could join the war effort. This effectively ended WWII.

Racked with guilt over the deaths of hundreds of thousands, Oppenheimer joined a group of scientists that lobbied to ban the newly developed hydrogen bombs, ten times more powerful than his temperamental baby. As a result, he was declared persona non grata by the U.S. government, fired, stripped of security clearance, and had his phone tapped. Oppenheimer died in Princeton, New Jersey, on February 18, 1967, of all things, from cancer.

Interesting Tidbit: Before becoming the leading name in global annihilation, Oppenheimer wrote an article on geology for the New York Mineralogy Club. The piece won high praise from the society, which was later shocked to learn the author had just celebrated his twelfth birthday.

Ways to Bring Up Oppenheimer in Conversation
☼ Girl, you bombed like Oppenheimer!

☀ Don't feel guilty, at least you're not Oppenheimer.

☀ Sorry, didn't mean to go Oppenheimer on you.

We *Sputnik* in Your Face, America

When Are We Talking About: October 4, 1957

Why Are We Even Talking About This: The launch of the first *Sputnik* satellite showed the world that the United States was indeed trailing the Russians in the space race and shot terror into the hearts of Cold War Americans.

What You Need to Know to Sound Smart: Our story actually begins in 1687, with Sir Isaac Newton's landmark opus, *Philosophiae Naturalis Principia Mathematica*, in which he wrote that a cannonball with enough power could potentially be shot into space.

Cut to: Russia, 1903, where scientist Konstantin Tsiolkovsky mathematically demonstrated that an object attaining a minimum velocity of 8,000 miles per second (the average speed at which folks leaving a Weight Watchers support group head for a Krispy Kreme) could actually break free of the atmosphere and enter the Earth's orbit. Tsiolkovsky, who oddly believed that intergalactic exploration would lead to human immortality, gave the Soviets invaluable research on the nature of orbiting bodies, multistage booster rockets, orbital stations, and space suit design, making him the Gucci of the galaxy. However, these innovations were largely ignored at the time, and space flight was left to the fancies of science fiction writers.

Cut to: 1950. Elvis does something.

Now Cut to: 1952, when the International Council of Scientific Unions decided that 1954 would be the best year to get a satellite in space because there was some cosmic mumbo-jumbo going on they called the International Geophysical Year (IGY). The IGY was a two-year period (1957–1958) when solar activity would be at its height, making it possible to map the planet, and to read at night without ruining your eyes. This race to space commenced in September 1953, at NII-4, a Soviet military research group led by top aircraft engineer, M. K. Tikhonravov, famed for designing the first liquid-propellant engine rocket. M. K. passed his findings on a satellite launch to Chief Designer S. P. Korolev, a master of aeronautical engineering (who would die during a botched surgery on his hemorrhoids, which must have been a real pain in the ass).

Korolev suggested that the satellite should be assisted by a booster rocket traditionally used to carry a five-ton hydrogen warhead with enough radiation to keep New York traffic-free for nine million years. Ironically, in the 1930s, Korolev had been imprisoned in a Siberian gulag for experimenting with *liquid* fuels instead of *solid* fuels. Fact: Joseph Stalin *hated* liquid fuels! Korolev labored in the accursed Kolyma gold mine until Big Joe realized a rocket designer might come in handy for his army, especially since his infantry couldn't hit the broad side of the Kremlin. Initially, the Soviet government was loath to spend money (since, being communists, they had none) on such a risky endeavor, but all that changed in the summer of 1955, when the Americans announced *their* satellite program as well as their intention to be number one in the space race.

In the States, companies and government-sponsored research groups petitioned for the opportunity to utterly waste tax dollars, but it was Dr. John P. Hagen's Project Vanguard working with the Naval Research Laboratory that won the contract in September of that same year. (Hagen would later be a leading force with NASA.)

By the New Year, the Soviets had approved the NII-4 proposal, renaming it Project D (for "*D*is better work or your family is *D*os Vedanya"). The plan was to launch a 1200 kg capsule (So? What's so dang hard about that?), but it was hampered by problems with the booster rocket that was supposed to carry the satellite out of orbit. In September 1956 word reached Korolev and Tikhonravov that the Americans' Jupiter C missile had flown more than 53,000 km, demonstrating they *could have* put a dummy satellite into space. If only those dummies *had* put a satellite in space the whole thing would have been over.

The Soviets panicked, and fearing that the United States would beat them to the punch (or more likely, that Stalin would beat them to a pulp), immediately decided to design and put two smaller 100 kg satellites up instead (*"Go! Go! Go! Put anything up there! I don't care what it is! Use my toaster oven!"*), called PS-1 and PS-2, though you couldn't play decent video games on either one. On Monday, September 30, at a six-day conference at the National Academy of Sciences in Washington, D.C., where Comité Speciale de L'année Geophysique International (CSAGI, aka Committee with the very long, annoying name), a community of international scientists, were discussing the future of rocketry, the Soviets hinted that a launch was perhaps just days away. ("No, we can't make the Tuesday meeting, because we're having launch with some coworkers. Did I say 'launch'? Oops, how silly of me.")

With the U.S. Vanguard project behind on its timetable and overbudget (so *right* on schedule for government contractors), the Americans were praying the Russians were bluffing. They were not. On Friday, October 4, 1957, at the Soviet Union's embassy in Washington, American scientists gathered with their Russian rivals for a friendly bragfest to show off who had the bigger warhead. Suddenly, news spread like wildfire that the Soviets had successfully launched *Sputnik I* (from the phrase "Sputnik Zemli," meaning "traveling companion of the world") from a desert facility near Tyuratam in the Kazakh Republic, making it the world's first space satellite. Over the next ninety-eight minutes, the 183-pound, watermelon-sized hunk of metal made its first orbit of the earth at 28,003 km per hour

(17,400 mph), officially announcing that the space race was on. *Sputnik*'s orbit was actually low enough that it could be observed with the naked trembling eye as a tiny ball of light traveling across the nighttime sky.

Space superiority was believed to be the key to tactical dominance, and in the eyes of America's warhawks, the launch put the Soviets out in front, striking doubt deep into the heart of a country that believed itself the *most* advanced civilization on the planet, after all we invented the hula hoop. Humankind wondered if Premier Nikita Khrushchev was right as he banged his shoe on the desk of the UN, telling the world, "We will bury you!" even though since no one else there spoke Russian most of the diplomats had assumed he was just killing a spider. In a time when democracy and communism were battling for supremacy, this glaring evidence of technological dominance was a devastating blow to the United States. *Sputnik* was not only the first, but was also a far larger satellite than the ones the Americans had been planning to launch. But remember, it's not the size of your missile, it's the motion in the space ocean that truly counts.

American panic turned to terror on November 3, when the Soviets launched a *second* satellite (two times!), *Sputnik II*, honoring the fortieth anniversary of the Great October Revolution, great if you weren't a Romanov, that is. It weighed a whopping 1,120 pounds and carried with it the first space traveler, a dog named Layka, causing American pooches to tell Eisenhower to forget about a second term. Unlike *Sputnik I*, which fell from orbit after only a few months, *Sputnik II* remained aloft for almost two hundred days, although Layka (which means "Barker") wouldn't enjoy the view for long, since on the sixth day all life-support systems crapped out and the pup's road trip became a journey to that big dog park in the sky (Awwww!). The Reds had actually never intended to fetch Layka back alive (THE BASTARDS!), a fact that sparked animal rights debates across the planet. The silver lining was that upon recovery, the Russians discovered that the reentry heat had baked Layka to a deliciously toasty golden brown.

But why had America been beaten to the punch? As early as the mid-1940s there'd been talk of a space program among the nation's higher-ups, and in fact, more than $1 million had been spent researching a satellite launch (which maybe covered the cost of a government hammer and a box of nails), but for some reason the idea was abandoned. Under attack from Democrats led by LBJ, the Ike administration started throwing buckets of money at the space program in a desperate attempt to catch up. The first Vanguard launch fizzled miserably on December 6, 1957, and a second attempt exploded just four miles above the launchpad in front of news cameras. America was humiliated. Not "having to watch our president discuss oral sex on C-SPAN" humiliated, but close.

In July 1958, Congress passed the National Aeronautics and Space Act, leading to the formation of the National Aeronautics and Space Administration (NASA), which pursued alternative programs with the mandate to be the first to create dehydrated ice cream. Oh, and also put a human in space. NASA was actually an expansion of a civilian group called NACA (National Advisory Committee for Aeronautics), which was formed in 1915 . . . so now you know that too.

Among the new hires was an American army scientist, Wernher von Braun, formerly a Nazi Army scientist, who with his team had designed the V-2 ballistic missile before defecting. This group was based out of the Redstone Arsenal in Huntsville, Alabama. Braun's *Explorer* satellite, carried aloft by the *Juno I* booster rocket, finally got the U.S. back in the game with a successful launch from Cape Canaveral, Florida, at 10 p.m. on January 31, 1958. Ironically, Braun's proposal had been passed over in favor of Vanguard because Ike wanted to keep the military out of the space program.

You see, Khrushchev kept accusing the Americans of using the IGY race as an excuse to spy on his country. *Vanguard I* did finally make it into space two months later on March 17 and has remained there longer than any man-made object since the *Sputniks* fell out of orbit years ago. (Yeah! Go U.S.! We're #1 . . . or 2, or something.)

Interesting Tidbit: The Soviets didn't initially realize the full impact *Sputnik I* had on the world and that day *Pravda* only ran a small story on the event. It wasn't until they became aware of the global reaction that the launch became propaganda article number one.

Ways to Bring Up *Sputnik* in Conversation

- *Sputnik* was nicer and roomier than my first car.
- I don't think you realize what big news this is . . . you're like the Russians the day after they launched *Sputnik* into space.
- Let's hope she treats her dog better than the Soviets treated their astro-dog, Layka.

The Big Deal with Smallpox

When Are We Talking About: October 1977

Why Are We Even Talking About This: The eradication of smallpox was a demonstration of how humanity can accomplish great things when united behind a common cause.

What You Need to Know to Sound Smart: Smallpox used to be one of the world's most deadly diseases, claiming the lives of more than 300 million people in the twentieth century alone, more than all the wars up to that time combined. Smallpox is believed to date back as early as the mid-1100s BC, to ancient Egypt, where a heinous rash was discovered on the mummy of Pharaoh Rameses V, which probably didn't make him the pharaohist of them all. From the dawn of civilization, the disease has been spread by traders, conquering armies, and Jehovah's Witnesses, as these groups traveled throughout the world. Like a nymphomaniac bisexual with herpes, smallpox infected whoever it touched, often ravaging entire populaces. Experts believe that the disease's infectious itinerary began in India (possibly attending the convention of *every* other disease in the world that seems to flourish there), followed by a slaughter safari in Africa before heading to Greece on Alexander the Great's "Bug Boat," courtesy of his exploits at the end of the first millennium BC. Somewhere in the first century, smallpox hopped a slow junk to China, and over the next few hundred years did the sickness circuit of the entire Far East. Occidentally hopping a ride with European traders, this contagion cargo ran rampant through the Continent, before the Spaniards sent smallpox via special deadly delivery to the untouched peoples of South America (who, because they were all autumns, looked great in red), where the virus eighty-sixed far more Incans and Aztecs than even Hernando Cortés and his cohorts did in the 1500s, not that they didn't give it the old Conquistador try. By the 1700s, smallpox was being used as a weapon by British soldiers who handed out disease-ridden blankets to an unwitting Native American populace ("these blankets will keep you warm . . . about 107 degrees to be exact"), destroying entire tribes without the Brits ever firing a single shot.

A little over a week after one contracts smallpox (*variola* in Latin, meaning "speckled" or "sayonara, sucker"), the victim experiences flu-like symptoms (muscular aches, high fever, an addiction to watching daytime TV), and is therefore often misdiagnosed. However, as the fever subsides ("Whew, I thought I was a goner . . ."), a red rash breaks out across the body, with dozens of hard pus-filled bumps. Now comes the fun part, as the rash spreads under the skin, it separates layers and makes the skin vulnerable to stripping away from even a casual touch.

For the lucky few, the rash can also spread internally, causing unbelievable agony, making swallowing and even breathing nearly impossible, bringing death within a couple of weeks.

There are two main variola variations: major and minor. Don't worry about the minor, since he can't even drive; it's the major that causes all the annoying dying stuff. Variola major comes in four distressing flavors: *ordinary*, which makes up 90 percent of the cases; *modified*, which is found only in those who've been immunized; the frequently fatal *flat*, where the pustules stay under the skin and form sheets; and *hemorrhagic*, where your blood vessels burst with excitement, bringing death from massive internal bleeding.

Throughout history, man had made heroic attempts to ward off smallpox through a variety of backward and somewhat hilarious remedies. In the tenth century, the Far and Near East experimented with a cure called *variolation*, trying to build immunity by deliberately infecting folks with a dead sample of the disease which, generally speaking, was *veriunhelpful*, since one in three still bought the farm (not to mention the fact that it created a nation of hosts ready to spread disease faster than a Times Square hooker during Fleet Week). It wasn't until 1796 that a British doctor named Edward Jenner made an incredible discovery (sadly, it wasn't that beer should be drunk cold). Jenner had taken note of a rural legend that farmhands who'd contracted the much milder cowpox were never plagued by its more deadly cousin. How the farmhands contracted the cow version, we don't feel comfortable discussing. Building on the concept of inoculating against a disease with the disease itself, Jenner milked pus from a cowpox rash on a local milkmaid (we'll never think of them in an erotic sense again) and injected it into the bloodstream of eight-year-old James Phipps, because let's face it, kids are expendable.

By 1801, through these and other clinical studies (i.e., raiding the local orphanage for "volunteers"), Jenner proved that the rumors were true and actually created a cure for the disease he had dubbed the "speckled monster." Jenner named his discovery *Vaccinia* from *vacca*, meaning cow (but perhaps he was referring to the milkmaid he was udderly smitten with), from which we get the word *vaccine*. Yet astoundingly, this was *not* the end of smallpox.

While vaccination immunized people in most developed countries, smallpox continued to incubate and spread in undeveloped countries, every so often rearing its pockmarked head and spreading chaos and panic, kind of like old-school Qaddafi. Not until more than a century and a half after Jenner's cure would the World Health Organization, or WHO ("The World Health Organization." "Who?" "Yes, that's what I said." "No, who are you talking about?" "Exactly."), established in 1948 to promote world health, finally resolve to eradicate smallpox from the face of the earth by 1959. Though it would still be another seven years before real action was finally taken. It was American epidemiologist Donald Ainslie Henderson (D.A. to friends) who would spearhead the eleven-year campaign, adopting a strategy of tracking down the disease like a renegade criminal. Rewards were offered for sightings, and following any reported outbreaks, a special team (with full diplomatic immunity) would systematically isolate the infection, inoculating everyone living around the exposure.

Smallpox was finally eradicated from the planet when a cook named Ali Maow Maalin caused an outbreak in Somalia in October 1977. ("Stay away from the chili.") The WHO team descended on the town of Merca and over the following two weeks performed 54,777 vaccinations in the surrounding area. With no eligible hosts to attack, the disease was defeated, and the lives of the citizens of Merca were saved so they could later be taken by bloodthirsty warlords.

Well, not quite. Unfortunately, the Superpowers, in their infinite wisdom (or is it infinitesimal?) cultivated smallpox as a weapon, storing it in not-so-secret locations around the world. In fact, in 1978, a medical photographer named Janet Parker contracted the disease from stores held at the University of Birmingham and died. NOTE TO GOVERN-MENTS: We're comfortable you've got plenty of crap to kill us with, and you have our permission to destroy this one. No, seriously, we're good. WHO has pressured governments to destroy their stores (". . . I don't know, that's what I keep asking!!!") and today, only two remain: one at the State Research Center of Virology and Biotechnology (Vector) in Koltsovo, Russia, most of which was probably sold on the black market for a box of chocolate Zingers and the May issue of *Playboy's Girls of the Big Ten*, while the other resides at the Centers for Disease Control and Prevention (CDC) in Atlanta, under the watchful eye of federal employees (think postal carriers only not as bright).

In 1980, after years of careful surveillance, victory was finally declared over the disease. That is until 1989, when during his defection to England, Soviet scientist Vladimir Pasechnik outed Ken Alibek and Russia's Biopreparat (bio-weapons program). A true humanitarian, Alibek, who'd been improving the anthrax bacteria (like giving it better gas mileage and a roomier interior), was now working on a small-pox weapon. Interestingly, 143 countries, including Russia and the United States, had already signed a pact agreeing *not* to develop bioweapons. (What? Russians violating treaties?) Luckily, the USSR, then in the throws of Mikhail Gorbachev's perestroika (you know, the guy with the smudge on his forehead who melted the Iron Curtain) were surprisingly receptive to an exchange of scientific teams (a joint U.S./British and a Soviet one led by Alibek) who inspected each other's labs. By 1992 it was clear the Americans had in fact abandoned their research, and the Soviets complied soon after (riiiiiiiight). However, the damage had already been done, with the Reds developing smallpox, among a plethora of other nasty bioagents, in both liquid and dry form, like a deodorant of death, that could be discharged by warheads flying overhead.

D. A. Henderson still heads the Center for Civilian Biodefense Studies at Johns Hopkins University and probably hasn't had a decent night's sleep in the last forty-five years.

Interesting Tidbit: WHO keeps calling for the United States and Russia to destroy their smallpox stores, but the Superpowers keep finding ways to weasel out of it. With the disease having been out of circulation for so long, the world's immunities have vanished. As if this wasn't chilling enough, consider the rumors that North Korea's Kim Jong Il ("this guy makes us" Il) has also developed the virus into a bioweapon. To round out this horror story is the fact that only 60 million vaccinations (called Dryvax) are available for the world's populace, and that in our modern culture smallpox could cover the entire planet in only one or two days.

Ways to Bring Up Smallpox in Conversation

☀ Agh! I've got this thing on my face that makes me look like I've got variola major.

☀ It's not that hard. You're acting like we're trying to eradicate smallpox.

☀ Don't tell Stacy anything. That woman spreads gossip faster than smallpox.

☀ **3** ☀

The Political Conversation

*T*he political conversation, while among the most important for sounding smart, can be like wrestling with a rabid alligator while on codeine which, come on, admit it, we've all done at least once. Like religion, this talk is full of partisan pitfalls. When it comes to politics, it's plain to see that ideological rivers run deep. So if you're going to drift into this conversation, it's best to consider just how hard you want to have to paddle through the rapids ahead. If you're among like-minded political party folk, this conversation can be a pleasure cruise full of good-natured scoffing and ridiculing of the ignorance and impotence of your rivals. However, if you are among a crowd with mixed beliefs, pull the pin and dive for cover, man, because tossing this pineapple into the crowd is sure to cause some explosions. If you're attending a political party, dress for success. No one pays much attention to the political opinions of the guy wearing an "I'm with Stupid" T-shirt.

Franz Ferdinand Rocked the World

When Are We Talking About: 1863–1914

Why Are We Even Talking About This: Ferdinand was the aloof, incompetent heir to the throne of the Austrio-Hungarian Empire, whose seemingly insignificant assassination sparked World War I.

What You Need to Know to Sound Smart: Destiny had a bullet with Franz Ferdinand's name on it from day one, that is, July 18, 1863, in Graz, Austria. Ferdinand accidentally became the heir to the Hapsburg throne when the two more competent successors died off, these being the Crown Prince and Ferdinand's father. Blessed with a magical, bigoted, hot-tempered, and uncouth personality, Ferdinand was shockingly detested by nearly everyone who knew him. Franzy was especially hated by the Serbs since in 1908 Austria had annexed Bosnia and Herzegovina, two Slavic nations Serbia wanted as part of its envisioned Slav empire. To make matters worse, Ferdinand proposed to establish Slavic equality when he became emperor, thus making it unlikely that the Bosnians would ever want to revolt and join the Serbian cause.

In June 1914, Ferdinand accepted an invitation to tour his troops in Sarajevo with his wife, Sophie. The Black Hand, a Serbian extremist group (as if there's any other kind), was looking to assassinate someone in protest of the annexation and a royal idiot in a convertible seemed like their best shot, or at the very least an easy one. On this fateful day in history, June 28, 1914, one of several Black Hand assassins lining the route threw a bomb at Ferdinand's car, which missed and exploded under the vehicle behind him, wounding several passengers. Despite the bumpy ride, the motorcade managed to arrive at city hall, where the archduke railed at the mayor about his explosive welcome.

In an unprecedented moment of good-heartedness, Ferdinand decided to check on the injured members of his entourage. His driver, seemingly Fate's own chauffeur, took a seriously wrong turn on the way to the hospital, and when informed of his mistake, backed the car up. While fortune may favor the foolish, it evidently had little love for Ferdinand, whose car miraculously reversed and stopped in front of the last assassin, Gavrilo Princip, who by pure luck happened to be sitting at a curbside café just a few feet away. Princip fired twice, striking the archduke and his wife, who, not being of royal blood, was usually forbidden to ride with her husband. However, in Bosnia she was allowed to do so as a gift for their wedding anniversary. Apparently her husband had forgotten that the fourteenth is supposed to be ivory, not lead.

They were both dead by eleven-thirty that morning. Shortly thereafter, Austria declared war on Serbia. Other nations around Europe, being bound by various alliances, were drawn into the largest war in the history of the world, which ultimately killed more than 10 million people.

Interesting Tidbit: The three Serbian assassins all suffered from tuberculosis (a death sentence in the early 1900s) and were issued vials of cyanide to drink after completing their mission so their connection to the Serbian government would not be discovered. Unfortunately for the world, the poison didn't work on any of them, thus beginning five years of trench warfare.

Ways to Bring Up Franz Ferdinand in Conversation

☀ You're screwed. You have about as much chance of escaping your fate as Franz Ferdinand did.

☀ Yeah, she's more popular than Franz Ferdinand at a Serbian firing range.

☀ Our anniversary was a mess. Franz Ferdinand had a better time on his.

Hitler 101
When Are We Talking About: 1889–1945
Why Are We Even Talking About This: An obscure starving artist by the name of Adolf Hitler clawed his way up the political ladder and nearly conquered most of Europe.

What You Need to Sound Smart: Everyone knows enough about most of the major events of World War II to bluff their way through a conversation. Just turn on the History Channel for an hour and you can pick up the highlights. What most people *don't* know are the events that turned a creepy Shmendrick into a planetary conqueror. Adolf Hitler took his first goosestep into the world in Braunau, Austria, on April 20, 1889 (oddly the same day as Carmen Electra in 1972). Hitler was reportedly a terrible student and had to repeat the sixth grade (forced to read *Where the Red Fern Grows*, yet again). When his old man died, sixteen-year-old Adolf dropped out of school, living off of the nation's "dead dad pension plan." At this point, the fatherless führer decided to try his hand at becoming a painter because, being an ugly runt, he had to find some way to see girls in the nude. Unfortunately for the entire world, Hitler's application to the Academy of Arts in Vienna was rejected in both 1907 and '08, due to his promising "lack of talent," and he was told to consider a career running the drive-thru at the local Weinerschnitzel. Just think, a few watercolor classes might have saved the lives of countless millions.

The German dropout continued to hang out in Vienna, trying to sell his paintings to tourists, but his *Final Solution with Daisies* never fetched much attention. In 1909, the historic hit man was out of cash and moved into a homeless shelter, enjoying his third helping of bitterness. At some point during this period, Adolf began developing his hatred for Jews (it was either them or himself), though some research suggests that previously he'd actually been *against* anti-Semitism and may even have had some Jewish acquaintances. Hitler was influenced by circulating racist propaganda and his own observation that Jews had a distinctly non-German appearance, combined with the fact that they had everything he didn't, that is, jobs, money, and friends.

In 1913, an angry Adolf moved to Munich, Germany, to dodge military service (wow, uneducated and a draft dodger . . . no wonder he got elected to rule his country), but was arrested and returned to his homeland to do his duty. However, after they got a good look at him with his shirt off, he was marked as unfit.

Let's recap: failed six grade, fatherless in the fatherland, rejected from art class, homeless, a coward, discarded by military . . . must we call in a social worker to puzzle this one out? When World War I began, Adolf joined a Bavarian outfit for some action in Belgium and France but spent most of his time running messages back and forth and drawing cartoons for a military publication. ("Hey Hitler, what's with all the characters with big noses?") Hitler twice received the Iron Cross for bravery, reaching the rank of lance corporal, although he was extremely unpopular with his fellow soldiers. Go figure. In October 1918, Hitler was hospitalized after a gas attack (the mess hall had been serving chili con carne) and a psychological evaluation evidently gave him less than glowing reviews. ("My report states that this man is definitely crazy and should never be allowed to rule the country.")

When the Treaty of Versailles was signed at the Paris Peace Conference in 1919, Hitler was one of many who blamed German politicos for what they termed *Dolchstosslegende*, or the stab-in-the-back that killed the army (apparently forgetting about the bullet-in-the-front and the bayonet-in-the-side that'd been doing a pretty good job of it for the past few years). The severe regulations of the treaty limited Germany to 100,000 soldiers, giving the once proud nation about as much chance to rise again as the Confederacy.

Hitler returned to Munich in 1919, working for the governing Weimar Republic as a spy. He helped to keep tabs on various socialist and nationalist organizations that were springing up around the country, one of which he ended up joining.

Hitler began hanging out with members of the German Workers Party where he met one of its founders, Dietrich Eckart, the man who would eventually coin the term the "Third Reich." The men bonded on their fierce nationalism, hatred of Jews, and bad choices in facial hair. Hitler claimed Eckart as a father figure (please, won't someone just love this boy?) and would later dedicate his manifesto of hate, *Mein Kampf*, to the man. ("For all those summer ball games and sunshiny picnics where you showed me the true meaning of love . . . this death sentence for thousands is for you.")

By the early 1920s, Adolf was really coming into his own as a public speaker, drawing more and more people to party functions, like the Workers Hatemongering Accordion Jamboree. In the middle of 1921, while Hitler was racisting around the region meeting like-minded misanthropes, Adolf's buddies back in Munich decided they didn't like him anymore and staged a coup of sorts. When Hitler told them he was taking what was left of his marbles and going home, group members realized that even though he was a weasel, he did draw a crowd (certainly better than he drew a bowl of fruit), and so they begrudgingly asked him to stay. Hitler accepted, under the condition that he be allowed to run the show and pick what movies they rented. This workers group would morph into the Nazi party, eventually dubbed the National Socialist German Workers Party.

Hitler's charisma and his ability to stir up an audience began to cement his destiny. On July 29, 1921, Hitler was declared the Nazi's führer with his nifty slogan, "One people, one country, one leader," which was way better than his old one, "I'm two, two, two freaks in one!" The big event that would elevate Adolf to the top floors of power was just a putsch of a button away. A collection of politicos, army officers, and wealthy socialites, who'd become increasingly dissatisfied with the whiners running the Weimar, began meeting in bars (known as

beer halls), where Hitler's crew encouraged them to do something about it. What became known as the Beer Hall Putsch
began on November 9, at the Burgerbrau beer hall, with a
planned march on the local Bavarian government offices as the
first step in capturing Berlin. "He who controls the pretzels,
controls the world!" But, as is often the case, plans that are
made when *certain* individuals have downed one too many
Mickey's Widemouths look a lot better on bar napkins than
when actually put into practice. It seems the Nazis forgot that
one of the benefits of being a government was that you got to
tell the guys holding the guns which way to shoot them, and in
this case, they were aimed straight at Adolf's mob. Several
Nazis were killed, and Hitler did a twenty-three skidoo, hiding
out and contemplating suicide.

Much to our chagrin, Adolf didn't have the guts to blow
his brains out and instead was tried for treason in April 1924.
He used the proceedings as a pulpit to blame the price of tea
in China on the Jews and Communists and blah-de-blah, all
of which made him very popular with the German people.
The fact that they were all now broke and miserable had
nothing to do with their instigating a massive world war just
a few years back . . . nahhh. Hitler served a cushy five-year
stint, and his personality cult continued to grow. While in
prison Adolf wrote *Mein Kampf,* which sold 1.5 million
copies in one year alone. The book indicted the Jewish race
(which if you want to get technical, isn't really a race at all),
as the source of all the problems in the world with not even
one nice word at least admitting how delicious bagels are.

Hitler was released early in December of the same year
he was sentenced, and over the next few years he led the
Nazis to power by helping them win seats in the Reichstag,
the German parliament. He finally ran for president in
1932 . . . but came in second. ("*Scheisse!* It's like art school
all over again!") However, the floundering government, obvi-

ously desperate, appointed the popular little man (and we mean this phrase in all its possible insinuations) German Chancellor on January 30, 1933.

Hitler began proving that he was the *only* man for the job by consolidating his power and eliminating any political enemies. On February 27, 1933, the Reichstag was set on fire, and Hitler and his stooge, Hermann Göring (head of the German Air Force and Adolf's right hand man), happened to pop up nearby shortly after. A mentally challenged Dutch former communist was found hiding behind the building by police (how do you say "plant" in German?), and the communists were put on trial. They were later acquitted, and Hitler, mad as a wet hen, used this as an excuse to suspend habeas corpus, leading to an untold number of deaths as the years rolled on. Hitler then assassinated anyone in the Nazi Party whom he felt had any amount of moral decency on the evening of June 29, 1934, in what became known as the Night of the Long Knives, which was just as bloody as it sounds. Seventy-seven left-leaning party members were officially killed that night, though many believe three or four hundred is a more accurate number.

But hungry people will tolerate anything if they think it'll get some food in their bellies, perhaps explaining the long lines people are willing to endure at the Cheesecake Factory, and so the German leadership applauded the move. In 1935, Hitler pushed the Nuremberg Laws through, removing citizenship from all German Jews, causing thousands to wisely flee the country. Three years later, on the night of November 9, 1938, he launched Kristallnacht, where his government made their anti-Semitic message crystal clear by destroying thousands of Jewish-owned businesses, while also killing a couple hundred people over the ensuing days. The Nazi war machine began revving its engine and preparing to launch the Third Reich into fifth gear but the rest, as they say, is history.

Interesting Tidbit: Many years after the event, Göring let it slip that he was actually the one who set the Reichstag fire. Shocking.

Ways to Bring Up Hitler in Conversation

☼ Just mention WWII or someone who you hate and you're off and running.

The Red, White, and Blue Scare

When Are We Talking About: 1945–1975

Why Are We Even Talking About This: The Red Scare and the resulting actions of the House Un-American Activities Committee (HUAC) as well as the crusade led by Senator Joseph McCarthy were some of the most flagrant violations of personal freedoms in the history of the United States.

What You Need to Know to Sound Smart: To set the tone for the witch-hunts that transpired during the 1950s, we have to look back to the little known *first* Red Scare (not to be confused with Kathy Griffin, who is just a scary redhead) of the early 1900s, a response to President Woodrow Wilson's effort to drag America into World War I ("Come on, they can't have a war without *us!*"). Left-wing socialists (anyone know any *right-wing* socialists?) and communist organizations protesting the war were being unconstitutionally harassed by government agencies, and when extremist radicals (. . . as opposed to *moderate* radicals?) struck back through a series of bombings in 1919, public opinion rallied behind Wilson. FACT: The fastest way to damn your cause in the eyes of the public is bombing . . . unless you're part of a fanatic religious cult that considers this a team sport. This violence sparked irrational hatred of all leftists and foreigners, in addition to the fact that they were leftists and foreigners.

While anticommunist fears subsided over the 1920s and

'30s, by the end of World War II, the world had polarized be-hind the two cold war powers, and by 1948, commie-phobia was back and redder than ever. The stage for the *second* Red Scare was set in 1938 when the House Un-American Activities Committee (HUAC) was created to root out anarchists. Congress's highly unconstitutional Alien Registration Act, which made it illegal to preach rebellion against the United States (uh, wasn't that the very thing that led to the creation of the United States way back in the 1700s?), forced all immigrants, age fourteen and older, to register their name, occupation, and political orientation with the government (Max Schweitzer. Tailor. Bent Over In Front Of).

Though the Soviets had been America's allies during the war, now under Joseph "I'm just giddy for gulags" Stalin, they'd become a dangerous nuclear powered enemy whose communist ways (wearing big fuzzy hats, playing chess, having parades) were spreading like wildfire across the globe, converting other nations to their nondemocratic cause. In this prizefight, the United States didn't like the idea of sharing its world heavyweight title. When Julius and Ethel Rosenberg were arrested on charges of espionage for passing nuclear secrets to the Russians, Americans became terrified of an "enemy" among them, like Erica from *All My Children*. The globe had just nearly fallen to fascism, and having paid a dear price for democracy to emerge triumphant (though it'd been a close game that could have gone either way), Americans felt sure as shinola that they didn't give the people of the world freedom so they could choose to be commies. Back then Americans were a far simpler, gentler folk (well, simpler), who believed what their government told them (Wonder Bread is good for you, women like wearing aprons, there was only one shooter . . .), while the media was full of sci-fi stories about wars between worlds and aliens taking over our bodies and minds.

In June 1947, HUAC, chaired by Senator J. Parnell Thomas, began its attacks on the Hollywood film industry, a known haven for leftists, socialists, and communists ("Bring me the head of Ed Begley, Jr.!"), many of whom had fled the political oppression of Europe and whose only true crime had been their more socially liberal philosophies, which according to this silly little document called the Constitution, they were freely allowed to hold. Forty-one "cooperative witnesses" ratted out nineteen of their associates as members of the Communist Party, and ten of the accused refused to speak before the House, standing on their First Amendment rights. (Ahhh, the classic defense for the *guilty*!) They were sentenced to up to a year in prison for their contemptible contempt. Others, through intimidation (threats of jail, deportation, no more television), answered the inquisition . . . er, we mean committee. Among them was famed playwright Bertolt Brecht (who then fled back to Soviet East Berlin, where it was safe!) and an actor of some note, Larry Parks. Parks admitted he'd once been in the Communist Party but had cut off affiliations four years before when they cut the musical theater category from their Charades games. HUAC demanded Parks name others he knew in the party, and though he pleaded not to be turned into a rat, when threatened with imprisonment, he realized he'd rather be a rodent than a "rough rider," and complied.

A "domino effect" ensued as each newly named person, cowed or coerced by the committee, turned on their red-fellows. While many held their high ground, others, such as director Elia Kazan, actor Lee J. Cobb, and writers Budd Schulberg and Leo Townsend, used their years of theatrical training to sing, sing, sing. In the years following McCarthyism, many of them found themselves scorned and derided as traitors by their peers. ("Commie? I thought they asked if he enjoyed origami!")

By June 1950, the FBI had released 151 names from the

HUAC sessions, all of which wound up on the "Hollywood blacklist," effectively making anyone on it persona non-Goldwyn in L.A., unable to work and financially ruined. The only way off the list was to inform on one's friends (or more accurately, ex-friends, since you probably wouldn't be invited to the Super Bowl party). Within no time, the list doubled in size, including such personalities as actors Stella Adler, Charlie Chaplin, and John Garfield; writers Arthur Miller and Clifford Odets; composer Leonard Bernstein; and director Orson Welles.

It was amid this milieu that Joseph McCarthy, a thirty-nine-year-old senator from Grand Chute, Wisconsin (the youngest judge in the state's history), feeding on the naiveté and anxiety of his shaky nation to seize power, leapt into the spotlight as Democracy's own caped crusader. In February 1950, McCarthy, backed by info fed from his good pal and FBI director, J. Edgar Hoover, made a six-hour speech to the Senate (the orchestra started playing but he kept talking anyway), claiming that a Soviet spy ring had infiltrated the U.S. government and that he had a list of names of dozens of possible security leaks. According to Joe, the folks on these lists were all card-carrying commies, rumheads, or "sexual deviants," that is, homosexuals. He believed that these evildoers were using their high-level positions to leak secrets to the enemy.

McCarthy became chair of the Government Committee on Operations of the Senate and over the next two years carried on his interrogations with impunity, chasing many left-wing thinkers and artists out of the country. McCarthy used his political clout to attack Democrats and liberal opponents (i.e., Democrats), bashing them publicly, and his influence on the masses helped put Eisenhower in the White House in 1952. While recent evidence suggests that communist spies actually *had* infiltrated the government, it seems none of *them*

were on McCarthy's list, which contained only political enemies, movie and media personalities, and military officials.

McCarthy's right-hand man and chief counsel was a
young favorite of Hoover's (and we do mean favorite), a
lawyer named Roy Cohn. Cohn was a famously ruthless, notorious (though not publicly out) homosexual, and had been
the driving force behind the Rosenberg prosecution and execution. He, in turn, brought David Schine (you might say
Cohn's "behind the scenes" guy) on board as his "consul-
tant." McCarthy and his team helped to ban (and even burn)
some 30,000 books (hmm, where did we see that last? Oh
yes, right . . . Communist Russia). When *Las Vegas Sun* reporter Hank Greenspun accused McCarthy of being a homosexual, the sinister senator fought back by marrying his
secretary, Jeannie Kerr, in 1953, and *adopting* a daughter
four years later. (Oh, right, you *adopted* a kid. We're *sure*
you're straight now!)

McCarthy remained bulletproof until he fired a fatal vol-
ley at a respected soldier named Robert Stevens, who was the
secretary of the army and a favorite of Ike's. Since war was
what the army did best, they battled back, releasing secret information on McCarthy to the press. Journalist hero Edward
R. Murrow, who'd been personally attacked and slandered by
McCarthy, was all too glad to take his shot on his *See It Now*
in 1954, which showed film clips of manipulative McCarthy
at work. While McCarthy appeared in person three weeks
later to "defend himself," he proved no match for Murrow's
poise and professionalism, coming across like an outraged
sixth grader, and only further deflating his now sagging reputation (much like his sizable "man cans").

Eisenhower also sicced VP Richard Nixon (known as
the pitbull of the executive branch) on the salacious senator,
and Tricky Dick blew the battlehorn, calling all to a crusade

to oust McCarthy from power. To make matters worse for Mr. Better Dead Than Red, the McCarthy hearings themselves were televised by ABC in 1954 ("This is Dick Clark from *American Bandstand* saying good night! Stay tuned for the *McCarthy Hour*, as Joe browbeats women and makes men cry"), further exposing his bullying and intimidation tactics to the American public, along with his nasty comb-over.

Finally, in an especially poignant and historical moment during the trials, McCarthy accused Joseph Welch, the army's attorney general, of contact with *some* guy who knew *some* lawyer who might have once worked for *some* group that might have once had communist connections . . . *some*time. Welch looked McCarthy straight in the eye and asked him, "Have you no sense of decency, sir? At long last, have you left no sense of decency?" America agreed. McCarthy, who'd become an embarrassment to the Senate, was condemned for "conduct that tends to bring the Senate into dishonor and disrepute" (other than the usual stuff, that is) and censured him in a 67–22 vote (shut up, shut down, and shut out), an initiative introduced by his longtime opponent Ralph E. Flanders (Doh! Flanders!), on December 2, 1954.

McCarthy faded from the public eye and fell into drinking (as well as fell *while* drinking), ultimately dying of cirrhosis of the liver in Bethesda Naval Hospital in 1957. Roy Cohn would die of AIDS in 1987, and his final days are fictionalized in the show *Angels in America*. The term "McCarthyism," coined by cartoonist Herbert Block of the *Washington Post*, remains an epithet for institutional actions that attack a specific group based on fear or paranoia.

Interesting Tidbit: In 1953, playwright Arthur Miller wrote *The Crucible*, an allegory for McCarthyism. This was probably the primary cause for Miller being brought before HUAC in 1956.

Ways to Bring Up the Red Scare in Conversation

- ☀ What's up with the third degree? Where am I, at the HUAC hearings?

- ☀ I totally lost my cool . . . it was like McCarthy vs. Murrow.

- ☀ Have you no sense of decency, Rob? At long last, have you left no sense of decency?

"Che" Guevara: More Than a Cool T-Shirt

When Are We Talking About: 1928–1967

Why Are We Even Talking About This: Communist revolutionary and expert in guerrilla war tactics, Che became a highly respected official under Fidel Castro in the newly created government of Cuba in the 1960s.

What You Need to Know to Sound Smart: Ernesto "Che" Guevara was born a willful boy on June 14, 1928, into a middle-class family in Rosario, Argentina. At an early age, Che became interested in the writings of Karl Marx, Friedrich Engels, and Sigmund Freud (before adolescent boys discovered *STUFF* magazine), all of whose philosophies would shape his revolutionary political ideals. After earning his degree in medicine from the University of Buenos Aires in 1953, in part to please his parents but also because he was fascinated with leprosy (hey, who isn't?), Che traveled throughout South and Central America. Zipping around the jungles on his motorcycle, Che dabbled in different revolutionary causes while learning, like the rest of the world, to despise the CIA and all other forces of imperialism.

In 1954, while passing through Mexico City, Che began practicing medicine at the General Hospital where he met a young Fidel Castro. The two men shared much in common, including an overwhelming desire to blow things up, and Che trained for an invasion of Cuba under Castro at a farm with a band of ex-patriots who soon left for Cuba. After setting up camp in the dense Sierra Maestra mountain jungles, they soon began to recruit disgruntled villagers from across the country. As a rebel leader, Che found his true calling, earning renown as a military leader and vicious killer, being a little hypocritical with his Hippocratic oath. The good doctor could on any given day be found executing his own men or innocent civilians who challenged his authority. Still, Che and Castro led a successful coup, only two years later ousting Cuba's president Fulgensio Batiste on New Year's Eve, 1958. Che celebrated the following year with a bit of revisionist history and declared himself Cuban-born.

Guevara toured China, Czechoslovakia, and the Soviet Union in 1960, and after gleaning all there was to learn from those wizards of finance, returned to Cuba to have Castro appoint him Minister of Industry, a position he held from 1961 to 1965. A charismatic speaker, Che's public outcries against imperialism (his most famous was in 1964, at the United Nations) transformed him into the iconic quintessential revolutionary. Guevara persuaded Castro to form a communist state that was not tied to Moscow, though he still encouraged trade with the Russians. As time passed, Che's extremist views caused him to lump their Soviet allies with the United States and other world powers, calling them cowards and imperialistic enemies of subjugated people everywhere. His big mouth and reckless economic practices drove a wedge between him and Castro, and in April 1965, he "gave up" his position in the government, which suited Guevara just fine since he longed for the action of a revolutinary's life.

Undaunted, Che took his gun and pony show on the road, and while rumors of his imprisonment and death circulated throughout Cuba, they were greatly exaggerated. Che reemerged in Bolivia in 1966, leading rebel forces there, but he overestimated Bolivian enthusiasm for blowing up government buildings. This oversight cost him his life on October 9, 1967, when he was captured and executed by the U.S.-trained Bolivian armed forces. Guess he never watched *Butch Cassidy and the Sundance Kid.*

Interesting Tidbit: Ernesto's famous nickname of "Che" is an Italian slang word for chum or buddy and was probably not used by the people he shot.

Ways to Bring Up Che Guevara in Conversation

☼ That guy's so repulsive only Che Guevara would want to hang out with him.

☼ Danny and I used to be close until he kicked me out of his party—like Castro did to Che Guevara.

☼ Omar's the Che Guevara of football: he always fights for the underdog.

Me Thinks the Chicago Seven Protested Too Much

When Are We Talking About: 1968–1970

Why Are We Even Talking About This: The trial of these seven counterculture icons illustrated gross abuses of big government and made America aware of the dangers of corruption in the system.

What You Need to Know to Sound Smart: The year was 1968. Tricornered hats and buckled shoes were all the rage . . . sorry, that was 1768, but revolution *was* in the air. The nightly news was full of reports on social turbulence, political activism, and seemingly unending global violence (disturbingly, just like . . . last week). Americans were still dying in Vietnam, two beloved leaders, MLK and RFK, had both been assassinated, racial unrest, as well as unarrested sexual liberation, and upsetting amounts of facial hair lurked around every corner. Let's face it, everyone in 1968 looked like they were part of some terrorist cell.

It also happened to be the year the Democratic National Convention would be held in Chicago, back in the day when those jackasses actually had candidates with half a chance of getting elected. The city's Mayor Richard Daley saw this as an opportunity to show off his kinda town. Activist groups, on the other hand, saw it as a chance to get public attention by protesting their various causes (Stop the Weed, Save the War, Free the Whales, whatever). Tom Hayden's peace movement, the National Mobilization to End the War in Vietnam, MOBE (which really should have been called NMEWV, but everyone was too stoned to make a fuss), met at a Chicago YMCA five months before the convention, in March, and Rennie Davis and David Dellinger handed out two hundred copies of their twenty-one-page *nonviolent* protest plan.

Elsewhere, the Youth International Party (YIPPIES) leaders, Abbie Hoffman and Jerry Rubin (think the guys from the *Freedom Rock* commercial), took a more confrontational approach, calling all "rebels, youth spirits, rock minstrels, truth-seekers, peacock-freaks, poets, barricade-jumpers, dancers, lovers and artists!" to join their "Festival of Life." Folks were instructed to bring their draft cards (for the campfire), tents, sleeping bags, and handkerchiefs for Pig Spray (tear gas), see-through blouses (even the guys), and food to share. Among the music, poetry, and political speech reading, was to be the nominating of "Pigasus," an actual pig, as president, who looked a little like U.S. prez number twenty-seven, William Taft. Worst of all, Hoffman bragged that a corps of some two hundred "cocksmen" would be organized to bed the wives and daughters of the convention delegates. Why they weren't harassing the Republicans was anyone's guess. Maybe their convention was too far away.

But Daley was not about to let a bunch of long-haired loud-mouths stink up (literally) his fine city and thwarted protestors by initiating an 11 p.m. curfew, denying their right to sleep in the parks and urinate on the azaleas. He also doubled police shifts and brought in more than 10,000 National Guard soldiers, who, unfortunately, forgot *their* see-through blouses. As convention time approached, 10,000 to 15,000 protestors, just a little shy of the 50,000 to 100,000 they hoped for, converged on the city, from August 25 to 28. They held rallies by day and battled police by night, who, in turn, employed excessive force against the unarmed students. ("He's got a *Trapper Keeper*. Get him!") Outraged, Hoffman and other ring leaders called for retaliation, including an attempt to take down the American flag and raise a communist one in its place (a loaf of bread with a big "X" over it). Stirring speeches were made by Black Panther Bobby Seale, who called for violent action against the oppressive police (or really, anyone who was white). There were threats to bomb city structures in retaliation for police brutality ("Death to all fountains!!!").

By the time the convention ended, Hubert Humphrey was nominated. He became known as the "Happy Warrior" and was subjected to a chocolate Jell-O assault by irate "peace-loving" hippies, later dubbed the "pudding assassination."

For their part in the political process, eight men, Hoffman, Rubin, Hayden, Dellinger, Davis, and Seale, plus John Froines and Lee Weiner (who allegedly suggested to undercover cop Irwin Block that the group should make Molotov cocktails). They had been arrested for violation of the 1968 Riot Act, a new federal law created to respond to the rising number of protests. Hence, the cops tried to "read them the Riot Act," but it was really hard to hear when they were being beaten with billyclubs.

Despite the false claims made by undercover cops, the protestors never rioted or carried out their idle threats even after being bludgeoned and brutalized by police. After all, who had time for violence when there was sex in the park? The Justice Department felt the city stood more to lose than gain by prosecuting, but an indignant Mayor Daley didn't agree and arranged for his buddy William Campbell, who happened to be a federal judge, to press charges against the group, proving once and for all it's not who you know . . . well, actually, it *is* who you know.

All eight men were indicted around the time President Nixon was sworn in, and John Mitchell, Nixon's new gung-ho attorney general, was all about grabbing those longhairs by the shorthairs and clipping their left wings. During the ensuing five-month trial the defendents would be dubbed the "Chicago Seven" by the papers. Bobby Seale's off-color color commentary had already got him bound, gagged, and four years for contempt: eight minus one equals seven.

Officially begun on September 24, the trial was an instant media circus, and as the stormy battle for justice raged in the courtroom, the radical underground group the Weatherman called for "Days of Rage," showering cops with stones during violent street protests. The trial was held in the courtroom of Justice Julius Hoffman (unfortunately for Abbie, no relation), with the prosecution represented by DA Thomas Foran, and the defense led by William Kunstler and Leonard Weinglass. While their lawyers and Hayden pleaded with the boys to stay cool, Hoffman and Rubin told Tom not to be a MOBE dick, seeing this as a golden opportunity to carry their antiwar message far wider than their Yippie flyers could fly. Unable to beat them (the cops had already done that), Hayden joined them, and the Seven began fighting back against the system that had falsely accused them by transforming the proceedings into a performance about injustice. They refused to rise for the judge (even saluting him with a "Heil Hitler"), blew kisses to the jury of their "peers" (mostly George C. Scott look-alikes), dressed in judges robes, set bags of weed on the defense table, and hurled colorful colloquialisms at the judge (we'll give you a hint . . . rhymes with shmocktucker). The judge, in return, slapped back with continuous contempt charges (159, to be exact). Witnesses for the defense were like a left-wing celebrity benefit concert, including Pete Seeger, Judy Collins, Arlo Guthrie (who threatened to play all twenty-eight minutes of "Alice's Restaurant"), and Allen Ginsberg (who threatened to read all twenty-eight minutes of one of his poems), who all showed up to do their part to "stick it to the Man."

While the jury miraculously acquitted on all conspiracy charges, "the Seven" *were* found guilty on the riot count. Though, truth is, the jury had initially been split, only changing their minds after Judge Hoffman insisted ("Okay, good first try. I was thinking more like . . . guilty?"). Hangman Hoffman, who had already run a terribly biased trial, began sentencing even before the jury handed in their verdict, giving the group (and even their lawyers!) five years in prison and a $5,000 fine for their contempt charges. He just really liked the number five. Each defendant then made a statement. Rubin was grateful to the court for converting even more young people to his cause, and good old Hoffman (the hairy, funny one, not the judge) offered to hook "your Honor" up with some LSD to improve Julius's personality, or lack thereof. Some of the jurors commented that they felt the cops ought to have shot the defendants and saved everyone a lot of time, but since the trial was not held in Los Angeles, this didn't happen. On November 21, 1972, the ruling was overturned by the Seventh Circuit Court of Appeals, who it seemed had a better sense of humor.

Though bound together in protest, the group went its separate ways. Dellinger continued his efforts as a protestor but died in the early twenty-first century. Yippie turned yuppie when Rubin, protesting that he was tired of being broke, became a broker on Wall Street. Davis appeared on a panel at the 1996 Democratic National Convention where the entire delegation shamefully danced the Macarena, which was not his idea. Hayden married Jane Fonda, though they later divorced, like everyone else who marries Jane Fonda, and he became a California senator. Froines and Weiner did some stuff, but no one really cares what. Seale, however, currently runs a Web page where he sells books about the future, and videos on barbecuing. We're not making this stuff up folks. Its called *Bobby-Que Not Barbeque* and try the chicken marinade . . . it's Panther-licious.

Poor Abbie Hoffman, often viewed as the Chicago Seven's de facto leader, sadly remained hounded by the FBI and his own drug abuse. In 1973, he was arrested for selling coke. He would eventually be incarcerated more than forty times in his agitated life. Hoffman evaded jail by undergoing plastic surgery and "hiding out" as Barry Freed in upstate New York, where he blended in with soccer moms who had also undergone facial reconstruction. Even undercover, Hoffman couldn't lay still and rose up as a local environmental activist. Finally, unable to continue a life in hiding (and in the suburbs), Abbie surrendered to authorities in 1980. Hoffman was found dead in his home in 1989 from an "apparent" drug overdose (officially a suicide), though many friends suspected federal foul play.

Interesting Tidbit: Eight officers were also indicted during the proceedings for civil rights violations. All were acquitted or dismissed.

Ways to Bring Up the Chicago Seven in Conversation

☀ You should have seen the way those guys were carrying on. They were like the Chicago Seven of the company party.

☀ Hey Judge Hoffman, it's a free country. I can say whatever I want.

☀ That guy's more contempt-able than the Chicago Seven.

4

The New Frontiers Conversation

*T*his conversation is likely to be among the least common at your modern party, unless you're hanging out with a lot of outdoorsy types. Generally speaking, few people really care anymore who discovered what place; they just want to know if there will be wifi when they get there. So, with no odds of getting a mountain range with your name on it (Mount Herman Greenblatt?), and space, the final frontier, proving to be like a flatulent, senile grandfather (boring and gaseous), society has lost its fascination with explorers and exploration in general. However, since the topic itself has become so unpopular, it is for most laymen uncharted waters, and therefore an excellent opportunity for you, having now unearthed its forgotten secrets, to sound smart. There isn't really a hard-core new frontiers crowd, so your standard wardrobe will do just fine (yeah, you can go return that coonskin cap now).

Around the World in 1,122 Days:
The Journey of Ferdinand Magellan

When Are We Talking About: 1519–1522

Why Are We Even Talking About This: Often considered the leader of the first expedition to circumnavigate the globe, although the man himself didn't quite make it that far.

What You Need to Know to Sound Smart: Portugal, 1480. Ferdinand Magellan disembarked from his nine-month "maiden voyage" and arrived in the world. His padre was the town mayor of Saborosa, in the province of Traz os Montes, and his madre came from a family of petty nobles (as if there were any other kind). However, both his parents had died by the time he was ten, and Magellan grew up in the Portuguese court, learning about astronomy, seafaring, and *culo* kissing. But Ferdinand was different. He didn't go in for that pacifist bull and flowered in the military, setting sail on his first expedition in 1505 to India. Within three years, he was a captain, fighting for the conquest of Malacca in the name of his queen. (She's into Malaccas, Dino!) By 1512, Magellan was fighting in Morocco, where he would explore a world of pain when he was badly wounded and maimed, and, after a falling out with his commander, he went AWOL, leading to his disfavor with the crown.

Bad timing since Ferdinand, who'd become convinced he'd found a shortcut to the Moluccas (not to be confused with Malacca), or Spice Islands, wanted backing for an expedition to prove his theory. You see, as Europe's demand for foreign spices increased, so did the competition to finder faster routes to the lands that supplied them. ("Bring me some marjoram, Ludwig, and I mean pronto!") To this end, Spain and its rival Portugal signed the Treaty of Tordesillas (which was not nearly as tasty as the Treaty of Tortillas) on June 7, 1494 (the same fateful day that Graceland opened for public tours in

1982). This document effectively divided the Atlantic, with Portugal taking the east (including Brazil, the eastern part of Africa, and India), and Spain taking the rest and not leaving a whole heck of a lot for the other countries to fight over.

The problem was that Magellan's pal, Serrao, who'd discovered the Moluccas, had slightly exaggerated their proximity. ("Dude, it's like five minutes past Sicily. We'll be back in an hour.") Without hope of local sponsorship, Magellan turned to neighboring Spain, where he was tight with Juan de Aranda, a courtier in the service of the nineteen-year-old Spanish monarch, Charles I (aka Holy Roman Emperor Charles V). De Aranda wanted the Moluccas for the glory of Spain (jealous that Antonio Banderas had been hogging it all) and arranged Ferdinand's pitch meeting. The young sovereign thought the idea had sea legs, and so Magellan swore allegiance to his new patron and renounced his Portugeseyness . . . Portugaity?

Magellan was outfitted with five ships and made fleet commander. He set sail from San Lucar de Barameda on September 20, 1519, commanding the *Concepción*. His other vessels, the *San Antonio*, the *Santiago*, the *Trinidad*, and the *Victoria*, were all captained by Spaniards (who loved serving under a Portuguese commander about as much as a man loves shoe shopping), and a total of 270 crew members, including a Genoese crewman named Antonio Pigafetta, whose diary is the only surviving account of the voyage. ("Day I—Captain is despised. We're all doomed. More later.") First stop was the Canary Islands (which actually taste just like chicken), before heading toward Brazil, because they had just finished watching *Blame It on Rio* and figured if Michael Caine could score with hot young chicas, surely they could too. Spanish Captain Juan de Cartagena soon tried to lead the others into a mutiny but was arrested by Ferdinand and imprisoned on his ship. The fleet crossed the equator (sending everyone running into the bathrooms so they could watch the toilets flush in the opposite direction), and a few weeks later Brazil was spotted, though wisely avoided since it was Portuguese-controlled land. The fleet instead stopped to resupply in the Bay of Rio de Janeiro.

Magellan had planned on sailing south around the Cape of St. Mary, but unforgivably cold weather and two months of stormy Antarctic waters forced them back. The group made camp in Patagonia, Argentina, in the port of San Julian in March 1520, where (upon learning that Ferdinand had left the marshmallows for S'mores in Spain) his three remaining captains also mutinied. It was only the loyalty of the crews that kept him in control of the ships. Two of the traitorous captains were executed, along with a few of their posse, while a third was marooned on the mainland, leaving him with only a volleyball named "Wil-sohn!" After waiting out the winter, Magellan sent the *Santiago* scouting for a western passage in May, but the ship failed in its mission grounded by shallow reefs.

In the latter half of August, sailing south again, Magellan discovered a way through to the Pacific on October 21, 1520, along Cape Virgenes. At the mouth of the straits, he found three channels, and sent his captains a few days ahead into each to investigate. Unfortunately, the *San Antonio*'s captain, Alvaro de Mesquita, secretly turned around and sailed back home absconding with much of the fleet's food stores ("Mesquita, you bloodsucker!"). By late November, Magellan and the remains of his fleet crossed the 373-mile Canal de Todos los Santos, the "All Saints Straits" (later renamed the Straits of Magellan), carefully navigating between banks that burned with Indian campfires ("Magellan, rowwww your boat ashore . . . and we'll kiiiiiill you"), which the crew consequently dubbed Tierra del Fuego ("the land of fire"). By November, Magellan was heading northwest across a vast body of open water that he named the Mar Pacifico, or Pacific Ocean (after Mar Plácido Domingo was voted down), which is really

kind of weird, since that's what we call it too. Magellan believed he was only a few days from the Moluccas but would
soon discover his guesstimation was a little off.

Months later, starving and scurvy-ridden, subsisting on
rat flesh (they apparently had found a Taco Bell sail-through)
or boiled leather from the sails (mmm, Spanish cookin')
washed down with sawdust (always important to get plenty
of fiber), the expedition finally sighted land in March 1521.
The crew spent the day fishing, eating, and trading favorite
rat-cipes. By the sixteenth, they were in the Archipelago of
San Lazaro (the modern-day Philippines), and while resupplying and refitting their vessels, Magellan became friendly
with the king of Cebú, whom he convinced to be baptized
along with eight hundred members of his tribe. Playing with
fire, Magellan burned any village that wouldn't get in the
holy water, maybe showing that he was a touch cranky from
his long trip. When the island of Matam refused to receive
the Catholic captain's aquatic anointment, a furious Ferdinand led an attack force of sixty men against the natives,
who are believed to have numbered between 1,500 and
3,000. Self-defense tip: When attacking angry villagers, it's
best not to be outnumbered six-trillion-to-one. While Magellan bravely stood his ground, all but eight of his men fled,
and Magellan was brutally cut down after an hour of fighting
on April 27, 1521. When word of this loss spread, the other
natives attacked the remaining Europeans.

Unable to fully crew all three remaining vessels, acting
commander Gonzalo Vaz d'Espinosa (who, with the death of
so many officers, might well have been the cook) burned the
Concepción and headed for the Spice Islands with the 115 surviving sick or wounded crewmen. Nearly a year later on November 8, 1521, they arrived at the Moluccas where they were
welcomed warmly by the king. ("From the Pacific? Why'd you
go the long way?") With their holds full of the precious spices

(and Kyle MacLachlan leading the Fremen against Baron Harkonen in *Dune*), D'Espinosa fled the islands. However, the young captain decided what was left of the expedition had a better chance of actually making it back home if they split up. The *Trinidad*, which headed back the way they came, was ironically captured by the Portuguese and her crew slain, captured, or forced to listen to Euro-pop. The *Victoria* made its way across the Indian Ocean and around the Cape of Good Hope, named by white people who'd had "good" hopes of subjugating black people for about 350 years. Nearly three years from the day it left, the last surviving ship of Magellan's expedition returned home. The eighteen men on board had sailed 42,000 miles (half of which was over uncharted waters) and were the first to travel around the world.

Interesting Tidbit: Magellan was a crafty tactician. When dealing with his mutineers, he sent six armed men to summon Mendoza to a meeting with orders to execute him on the spot if he refused. He simultaneously sent an armed crew of fifteen in a longboat to pull up alongside the ship and board should they hear a fight break out.

Ways to Bring Up Ferdinand Magellan in Conversation

☀ I think the theater is farther away than you think, Mrs. Magellan!

☀ Stop telling everyone what to believe like you're Ferdinand Magellan.

☀ Can we stop at the next restaurant? You're worse than Ferdinand Magellan.

What Was Walter Raleigh Smoking?
When Are We Talking About: c. 1552–1618
Why Are We Even Talking About This: Raleigh was the dashing British adventurer to whom history has been overly

kind, crediting him with numerous acts of courage and creativity, many of which he did not do, did not finish, or that never actually happened.

What You Need to Know to Sound Smart: History couldn't have chosen a better name for Sir Walter Raleigh, actually pronounced "Raw-Lie," whose date of birth in Hayes, Devonshire, England, is as erroneous as his claims to fame. What is certain is that, boy, did Raleigh hate him some Catholics, because those crazy mackerel snappers had persecuted his Protestant family during the reign of Queen "Bloody" Mary. Raleigh's first stroke of luck was the ascension of Protestant Elizabeth I to the throne in 1558. Now on the winning team, Raleigh, age fifteen (who reputedly spelled his name sixty-five different ways), crossed the channel to join the French Protestant Huguenots for a major-league slaughter-filled season, where he proved his courage by massacring Catholic soldiers while fleeing any pitched battles against organized armies. Raleigh idolized his half-brother, Sir John Gilbert, and at twenty-three, joined him on an expedition to bring civilization to ungodly savages (i.e. non-Europeans), though sadly, they were never able to reach Texas.

Captaining *The Falcon* in 1578, Raleigh proved a maritime moron, wrecking his ship off the coast of North Africa and killing half his crew. After limping their way back to their home port a year later, both he and the Gilster were forbidden from ever sailing again, somewhat hampering his employability as an explorer. Determined to rebuild his reputation, Raleigh spent the ensuing months getting drunk, getting into fights, and getting sent to prison. Finally finding his niche, the regal ex-con put his murdering and drinking skills to work as a military commander and was sent to Ireland with Gil-bro, where he massacred innocents and bred with the locals. Despite the glorious weather and delectable boiled cuisine, Raleigh soon grew weary of the Emerald Isle and, bravely abandoning his new Irish wife and daughter, sailed home to seek his fortune at the royal court in London.

Standing well over six feet (in a time when Gary Coleman would have been considered NBA material), it's no small wonder that this handsome Renaissance man (a title awarded to noble, courageous, cultured gentlemen, and mysteriously, also to Raleigh) quickly captured the attentions of the forty-eight-year-old "virgin" queen. The "privateer playa" is said to have schmoozed his way into power by chivalrously throwing his cloak on a mud puddle so that the queen could walk safely over it, though most historians refute the veracity of this event despite Thomas Fuller's "accurate eyewitness account" written some eighty years later. Raleigh was also reputed to have written poetry for the queen on a windowpane with a diamond. In return for his ten-karat tagging, Elizabeth made Raleigh the highest paid escort in her personal guard. Raleigh's was lucky enough to be part of the right plan at the right time, and helped uncover the Babington Plot. This was a plan to dethrone Elizabeth and install her cousin, Mary, Queen of Scots, in her place, which led to Mary's execution in 1586. For this the royal kiss-arse garnered himself a massive Irish estate surrounded by neighbors whose relatives he had slaughtered in his youth.

However, Raleigh's dumb luck ran out when he sponsored a number of expeditions to the Americas, the most disastrous of which was the colony at Roanoke (off the coast of North Carolina) in 1587, whose poorly provisioned inhabitants starved like the cast of The O.C. before disappearing without a trace. These voyages brought Raleigh fame for introducing both tobacco and the potato to Western civilization (his final revenge on the Irish), though in truth, he never left the comfort of his courtly couch. It was Thomas Hariot, the regal brown noser's right-hand man with a green thumb, who did the actual dirty work. In Raleigh's defense, though

Cortés had introduced tobacco to Spain in 1518, it was Raleigh who made sparking up fashionable in the English court, giving Raleigh his *first* authentic claim to fame as the father of emphysema.

Raleigh fell from favor in 1592, when the queen discovered her beloved Wally had married (technically making him a polygamist) and knocked up Bessie Throckmorton, one of her royal maids of "honor." Thin Lizzie tossed Raleigh into the Tower of London, think Holiday Inn but with thumb screws and an iron maiden. However, later that year, one of his more successful expeditions returned to England loaded with plundered Portuguese treasure, and Raleigh was able to "win" his freedom by giving the queen a whole lot of booty (no, not that kind). Free again, Raleigh busied himself as a civil servant, speaking in Parliament and executing Catholic priests. Raleigh spent the next few years looting and burning villages in South America while searching for the fabled golden city of El Dorado (and the summer home of the Easter Bunny).

In 1603, James of Scotland became king, and as thanks for Walter's help in executing his mother Mary, stripped Raleigh of his wealth and command and ultimately framed him for allegedly conspiring with the Spanish. Following a mockery of a mock trial, Raleigh found himself back in his spacious two-room cell in the tower, where he remained for over a decade. With no access to chatrooms, the shackled charlatan turned to writing and penned several works, his most famous being the incomplete *History of the World* in 1614, of which, in true Raleigh form, he wrote only two of his intended five volumes. In exchange for his release, King James (hurting for gold) sent Raleigh on a mission impossible to rob a Spanish garrison without killing anyone. Then in a royal change of heart, Jimmy sent Raleigh's itinerary directly to the king of Spain. Needless to say, the mission was a disaster, even by Raleigh's standards, with its crowning achievement being the death of his idiot son, Wat, who recklessly went along for the ride. Upon returning to England, Raleigh was arrested, yet again, for attacking the Spanish and thanked for years of loyal disservice by being sent on an exploration of the afterlife when his head was lopped off in the Old Palace Yard at Westminster on October 29, 1618. His melon was embalmed and presented to his English wife as a creepy parting gift, one which she carried everywhere for the rest of her life.

Interesting Tidbit: When Raleigh's first expedition in the New World landed, the crew asked the local Indians the name of the country. The answer was jotted down and soon a petition appeared before Parliament to confirm Raleigh's rights to the area translated as "You've got good clothes."

Ways to Bring Up Sir Walter Raleigh in Conversation

- ☀ Yeah, poor guy's got Sir Walter Raleigh luck.
- ☀ You never know what the real story is with her. She's like Walter Raleigh.
- ☀ Girl, I can't believe you took credit for that. You totally just pulled a Raleigh.

Amelia Earhart Flew in the Face of Chauvinism

When Are We Talking About: 1897–1937

Why Are We Even Talking About This: Earhart was the great female aviator who set a myriad of flight records and advanced not only the field of aviation but also the cause of equality for women.

What You Need to Know to Sound Smart: Listen up, all you gut-sporting melon-heads disparaging the courage and ability of women. It's time to lean back in your La-Z Boy, because Amelia Earhart, whose puissant aviation skills propelled women's equality into the skies, will leave you sputtering in your brewksi. Named after her grandmothers, Amelia Mary Earhart was born on top of the world July 24, 1897, at her stinking rich grandfather's estate in Atchison, Kansas. Living with Mom and younger sister, Muriel, in the lap of luxury (with all the prairie chickens they could eat), Amelia didn't see much of her black sheep dad who, having never lived up to his father-in-law's expectations, spent most of his time in Kansas City (which is oddly found in Missouri . . . a fact we feel gives us carte blanche to mock the Midwest) failing as a lawyer. In 1905, Amelia's parents moved to Des Moines, Iowa, in search of new opportunities (and perhaps to visit the legendary National Balloon Museum in Indianola), leaving the kids with the grandparents.

Little "Millie" was a tree-climbing tomboy obsessed with adventure who excelled at very unladylike activities such as baseball, bicycling, and belly-sledding, and at age nine hunted rats with a .22 rifle, which no one seemed to have a problem with in Kansas. Acutely aware of the limitations society imposed on her gender (well, they weren't limitations, so much as soul-stifling prison cells of despair), Amelia kept a scrapbook of women who had broken the rules by making achievements in male-dominated fields, such as pole-dancing and baby making. In the seventh grade, Earhart enjoyed a teary reunion with her folks in Iowa, not from joy, but because she was in Iowa . . . hey, this is the place where Winnebagos were created! At a state fair the young girl was legendarily unimpressed upon seeing her first plane, referring to it as a thing of "rusty wire and wood." It wasn't until ten years later, when watching a stunt flier swooping overhead, that Earhart's calling to the clouds took flight. However, family fortunes had taken a nosedive since Dad's high flying on booze lost him his job, right around the same time Grandpa's fortune went into a tailspin. Tired of letting men pilot their lives, Amelia's mom decided to wing it with the kids, landing in Chicago where she stayed with friends.

After graduation from high school, Earhart moved around a bit, working with the Red Cross in Canada as a WWI nurse's aide from 1917 to 1918, and trying to do the premed thing at Columbia University, but ultimately ended up with her parents, now reunited in California. On December 28, 1920, at an "aerial meet" in Long Beach, Earhart took her first plane ride, sealing the cabin door on her future. Her first flight lessons were with Anita "Neta" Snook. Over the next six months, she saved up enough to buy a secondhand, bright yellow Kinner Airster, which she christened *Canary*. Amelia crashed her new plane several times (though never blamed the paparazzi), drawing scoffs from peers who thought the idea of women flying was for the birds. Yet sexist skepticism couldn't deny Earhart's destiny, and on October 22, 1922, she set her first record by becoming the first woman to fly to 14,000 feet, where she did *not* serve sodas or bags of dry-roasted almonds.

In 1926, Earhart's growing notoriety attracted the attention of publisher George P. Putnam, who was looking for the first woman to make a transatlantic flight. After interviewing her in New York, Putnam was so smitten by Amelia's character that he married her years later. ("I just have some standard questions here . . . let's see, oh, yes. Does the thought of my naked body excite you? Answer however you like.") On June 17, though Amelia was only a passenger, Putnam promoted the flying feminist as the "Commander" (not even married yet and she's already wearing the aviator's pants in the family) of the *Friendship*, a German-made Fokker F7, which departed from Trepassey-Harbor in Newfoundland with two pilots. Less than twenty-one hours (20:40) later, they touched down in Bury Port, South Wales—their original Irish destination had been scrapped due to bad weather (Foggy weather? In Ireland? Unheard of)—taxiing Earhart into history.

Backed by Putnam's publicity machine (and sometimes backed by his "love machine"), Earhart returned to the States a conquering hero. Over the next two years, the sky siren continued to set flight records and became the aviation editor of *Cosmopolitan* magazine writing such articles as "How to please your man without crash landing your relationship." Amelia also published a book on her transatlantic flight called *Twenty Hours, Forty Minutes,* and worked in PR for the newly burgeoning commercial airline industry, all the while preaching that members of her gender must have the courage to do anything men do, regardless of the danger. In 1929, the forthright fly-girl organized an all-female air race from L.A. to Cleveland that Will Rogers dubbed the "Powder Puff Derby," which was a putzy chauvinist comment for an otherwise nice guy to say. In 1931, after having previously turned down several of his proposals, Amelia married Putnam, even though thoroughly modern Millie told the press they were in a "partnership," and Putnam was given custody of his "manhood" only on weekends.

Earhart soon decided to cross the Atlantic solo before another woman beat her to it (think, the first catfight meets dogfight) and on May 20, 1932, the fifth anniversary of Charles Lindbergh's historic transatlantic flight, Amelia took off from Newfoundland in a modified Lockheed Vega. Using smelling salts to keep awake and as seasoning for her disgusting in-flight meal, and fighting freezing weather, Earhart succeeded once again and became a worldwide media sensation. She was awarded the Distinguished Flying Cross, the first woman and only civilian ever to receive it, and a gold medal from the National Geographic Society presented by President Herbert Hoover. In August 1932, Earhart became the first woman to solo nonstop from coast to coast, set the woman's nonstop transcontinental speed record (17 hours, 7 minutes), formed the Ninety-nines, an international women pilot's club, and with the nation gripped by Earhart-mania, she even had her own aviator-style clothing line "for the woman who lives actively." On January 11, 1935, Earhart broke the sex barrier when she soloed 2,408 miles across the Pacific, from Honolulu to Oakland, California, an attempt that resulted in the deaths of ten other *male* pilots . . . some of them even *before* they got to Oakland.

At age thirty-nine, Earhart set her sights on a flight around the world (29,000 miles) in a twin-engine Lockheed Electra 10E, an incredible feat considering that most charts were as useless as an orange level "terror alert," and navigation was primarily conducted using the stars. While her first attempt resulted in a crash, on June 1, 1937, with navigator, Fred Noonan, the determined daredevil dame took her second shot at the world title, departing from Miami, loaded with blow . . . errr, we mean fuel. The aerodynamic duo got as far as Lae, New Guinea, fighting dysentery and fatigue. Planes were basically flying convertibles (thank goodness, considering the in-flight diarrhea), not the luxurious jets of today with their three cubic inches of leg room. With only 7,000 miles remaining, already setting the record as the first person to fly from the Red Sea to India, Earhart began the most difficult leg of her journey, landing on Howland Island, a pinprick in the Pacific, just over a mile in diameter. ("Let's see . . . Guam? Too easy. Hawaii? Nahh. Hey, how about this island I thought was a crumb from my danish?") Earhart's plane had been stripped down of nonessential equipment, such as parachutes, survival gear, and Mad Libs, to make extra room for fuel and booze for Noonan (a rumored alcoholic, and what better choice for the guy handling the directions?), and ships in the flight path were ordered to burn lights to act as beacons for the fliers. With clear skies ahead, the team took off at midnight on July 2 but was soon dogged by rain and overcast weather. As of 8 a.m. that morning, they had lost radio contact. The Coast Guard cutter *Itasca*, having received intermittent low-fuel reports, made black smoke for ten miles to hopefully help Earhart track the island, but she was never found.

The ensuing $4 million rescue operation was the largest in history, with nine ships and more than sixty aircraft scouring 250,000 square miles of ocean over the next few weeks. In 1938, a lighthouse was built on Howland Island in Amelia's memory. A year later, as a tribute to his lost beloved, Putnam published Earhart's biography, *Soaring Wings*. Eventually archeological expeditions to neighboring Nikumaroro, formerly Gardner Island, in the Bikini Atoll, believed they uncovered evidence that Amelia may have landed there on July 2, 1937. But the International Group for Historic Aircraft Recovery (TIGHAR—but not part of the Hundred Acre Woods), who worked the Earhart Project in 1988, disagree with that conclusion.

Interesting Tidbit: Earhart was a girl with a vivid imagination. She invented imaginary playmates, imaginary horses, and imaginary creatures she called "Dee-Jays" that she blamed for the naughty things she did. Plus she took imaginary trips around an imaginary world called Bogie in an old broken-down carriage in her shed.

Ways to Bring Up Amelia Earhart in Conversation

- ☼ You can do anything you set your mind to. Just look at Amelia Earhart.
- ☼ That girl breaks hearts like Amelia Earhart broke flight records.
- ☼ She's a little lost, but let's hope it's not an Amelia Earhart situation.

Charles Lindbergh: Flying Fascist

When Are We Talking About: 1902–1974

Why Are We Even Talking About This: Lindbergh was the first man to fly solo across the Atlantic Ocean, from New York to Paris.

What You Need to Know to Sound Smart: While Lindbergh was in many ways a supercool American icon, few have bothered to look up Chuck's spew of acidic Nazi propaganda that scarred his name late in life. He was born Charles Augustus Lindbergh in his grandmother's home in Detroit, Michigan, on February 4, 1902, to a father who was a lawyer and congressman. Growing up on his family's farm in Little Falls, Minnesota, Lindbergh's destiny was decided one fateful day after he saw an airplane fly overhead, luckily distracting him from the carload of transsexual circus clowns simultaneously cruising by. He immediately exclaimed, "Fi-diddly-dee, the pilot's life for me." In 1922, Charles dropped out of the University of Wisconsin engineering program to enroll at Lincoln Flight School in Nebraska. The following year, he sold his motorcycle to scrape together $500 to buy his first plane, a World War I–surplus Jenny. Lindbergh was soon earning a living as a daredevil flier, barnstorming for country fairs. In the days before Skinemax, watching a man fly a papier-mâché lawnmower through a manure-filled shack was considered high entertainment.

In 1924, Lindbergh enlisted in the Army Air Force reserves at San Antonio, Texas, guarding against invasion from the infamous pilots of the legendary Mexican Air Force. He graduated the top pilot in his class and two years later became one of the first airmail pilots, which was a risky business in a time when 75 percent of these fliers bought the farm. Lindbergh landed in crop fields at night with nothing but a flashlight and even survived two crashes, risking life and limb for *Us Weekly* and perfume samples.

In the fall of 1926, French ace Rene Fonck got all foncked up trying to make the first flight across the Atlantic and crashed, resulting in the death of two of his crew. This was the most recent in a string of fatalities since Raymond Orteig, a New York City hotel magnate, had put up $25,000 in 1919 for the first aviator who could fly nonstop from New York to Paris, having already lost fifteen bucks to a guy in a bar who could put his elbow in his ear. Lindbergh decided that a lone pilot in a single-engine plane stood a better chance than one flying with a crew and, using his life's savings supplemented by local St. Louis merchants, had an extralight plane built to his specifications: with no radio, sextant, or parachute. Most remarkable were the large gas tanks positioned directly in front of the cockpit, effectively blinding Lindbergh while he was flying. Though "Sky Coffin" seemed an apt name for the 220-horsepower modified Wright Whirlwind, he ultimately chose *The Spirit of St. Louis* in order to please his backers.

On the first leg of his flight, Lindy hopped from San Diego to St. Louis in record time. By the time he reached the East Coast, four other pilots had attempted the transatlantic flight and failed, raising the body count by three. After he arrived in New York, newspapers mocked Lindbergh as "The Flying Fool," but on May 20, 1927, Chuckles had the last laugh and, undaunted, he took off from Roosevelt Airfield in New York carrying a quart of water, five sandwiches, and maps and charts (but unfortunately forgot his headphones and was thus unable to watch the in-flight movie, *Turner & Hooch*). Defying rain, fog, ice, and drowsiness, Lindbergh set down thirty-three and a half hours later at Le Bourget Field near Paris where throngs of French fans gave him much props. Switching sides faster than the Italians in a world war, the press was quickly whistling a new tune, singing the praises of "Lucky Lindy," who had instantly become a worldwide celebrity.

When he returned home, 4.5 million people (4.2 million more than the Million Man March) attended a parade up Broadway in Lindbergh's honor, half of whom were probably mugged on the way home. Mr. Transatlantic was awarded the Congressional Medal of Honor, the Distinguished Flying Cross, received 100,000 telegrams and cables, 14,000 packages, and 3.5 million letters, including numerous proposals of marriage, uncountable commendations from governments across the globe, the Silver Buffalo from the Boy Scouts, a lifetime pass from the National Association of Professional Baseball Leagues, and a German shepherd. Remember the dog. It's foreshadowing.

While in Mexico working as a goodwill ambassador for the U.S. government, Charlie met Anne Morrow, daughter of the American ambassador, and married her in 1929. Three years later, tragedy struck when their twenty-month-old baby, Charles Jr., was kidnapped on March 1, 1932, in what would become "the crime of the century," resulting in a media circus that would haunt the family for years. The kidnappers left a ransom note demanding $50,000 and their homemade getaway ladder leaning against the open windowsill. Though the Lindberghs paid the ransom, their child was later found dead in the woods just a few miles from their Hopewell, New Jersey, estate. Bruno Hauptmann, a thirty-five-year-old German-born carpenter from the Bronx, was accused, convicted, and quickly executed for the crime, though Hauptmann never admitted to the kidnapping and his guilt remains uncertain to this day. Soon after, the U.S. Congress passed the Lindbergh Law, making kidnapping a federal offense. To escape the media and their dark memories, the Lindberghs moved to England and then France.

While most hobbyists spend hours cramming ships into bottles, Lindbergh's new pet project would revolutionize the medical industry. Working with a doctor, he created a perfusion pump, the first "artificial heart" that kept blood circulating during operations. This miraculous invention opened the way for organ transplants, open-heart surgeries, and athletic footwear. Lindbergh also inspected aviation development in various European countries, reporting his observations to U.S. intelligence, but he became so enamored with Germany and their superior air power that, upon returning to the states in 1939, he became spokesperson for the isolationist America First Committee, which opposed U.S. involvement in World War II. However, the "Lone Eagle's" hawkish pro-Nazi position caused such a public outcry that he was forced to resign from the Army Air Corps.

Ber-Lindbergh considered a move to Germany, obviously unmoved by their vicious attacks on the Jews. He argued that Russia, Asia, and Africa posed far greater threats, reminding Americans these were, after all, the birthplaces of King Kong *and* Godzilla! But the bratwurst was yet to come, when a *Reader's Digest* article quoted the aerial Aryan supporter as saying, "Only a Western wall of race and arms can hold back the infiltration of inferior blood and permit the white race to live at all in a pressing sea of yellow, black and brown." But how did he *really* feel? While family members feared the prevailing prowar winds would blow this hero from his cloudy perch, they failed to dissuade Charles from making public flights of racist fancy. In a speech on September 11, 1941, Charlie's mouth became a chocolate factory as he announced that American Jews ought to oppose the war "for they will be the first to feel its consequences" and then aimed his turrets at the Jewish media conspiracy. Like who? Ohhh, obviously, those famous Jewish media moguls Joseph Pulitzer-stein and William Randolph Silver-Hearst. Denounced by the press, the public, and the president, Lindbergh was branded a Nazi, and this "sunshine patriot" was grounded from public life.

Pearl Harbor threw Lindbergh for a loop-de-loop, and he changed his flight plan, working with Henry Ford on bomber production. He also served as a technical adviser and test pilot for United Aircraft, not to mention personally flying fifty combat missions over Japan as a civilian since Roosevelt's cabinet refused him reentry into the armed forces. After the war, Lindbergh was recommissioned a brigadier general in the air force where he championed early rocket research and chaired the National Advisory Committee for Aeronautics, the predecessor to NASA. Lindbergh was also a writer, and of his seven books, he is best known for the 1954 Pulitzer Prize winner, *The Spirit of St. Louis*, an account of his transatlantic flight. In the early 1960s, he began working on environmental causes in the Philippines and Africa and supported the establishment of national parks there, possibly an unspoken apology for never recanting his racist doctrine.

The Lindberghs eventually moved to Hawaii where Charles wore flowered shirts and was diagnosed with terminal cancer. The great aviator took his final flight in 1974, checking himself out of a New York hospital and returning home to Hawaii. He soared into the great beyond on August 26 of that same year, surrounded by friends and family.

Interesting Tidbit: In 2003, genetic testing proved that Lindbergh had fathered three children with a woman in Germany after the war.

Ways to Bring Up Charles Lindbergh in Conversation

- ☀ The hard thing when you're popular is not to pull a Charles Lindbergh so that suddenly everyone hates you.
- ☀ No thanks, I'm gonna go it solo, like Charles Lindbergh.
- ☀ Come on let's take a drive up the coast, it'll be an adventure . . . like we're riding in *The Spirit of St. Louis.*

Sir Edmund Hillary Was on Top of the World

When Are We Talking About: 1919–???

Why Are We Even Talking About This: Known by many as "the world's greatest living explorer," together with his Sherpa assistant Tenzing Norgay, Hillary was the first climber to successfully scale Mount Everest, the highest point on the planet.

What You Need to Know to Sound Smart: Edmund Hillary made his first major climb out of his mum on July 20, 1919, in Tuakau, New Zealand. His father, Percival, was a fiercely strict man who had been wounded at Gallipoli in World War I. A two-hour trip each way by train was required of young Edmund to reach school, where he was a shy and reserved student, traits that would stay with him. In fact, when Hillary proposed to his first wife, Louise, he was so nervous he had her mother pop the question for him. Fortunately, he was able to handle the wedding night all on his own. Edmund was a notoriously uncoordinated youth and terrible athlete and so retreated into a world of adventure books, checking a new one out of the library *every day* for several years. This would all change at the age of sixteen during a class field trip to climb Mount Ruapehu (Ruah pay who? Ruah pay me? Ruah pay you? . . . keep it going . . .), located on the northern island of New Zealand and the tallest point in the country at a little over 9,000 feet (back in the days before overprotective parents encased their children in foam whenever they left the house). Here, Hillary's ascent to greatness began when he discovered that, while his gangly gawky frame might have been terrible for ballroom dancing, it was perfectly suited to scurrying up mountainsides, which he did most ably, leaving his allegedly more athletic classmates in the dust. Hillary continued to hone his climbing skills in the southern New Zealand Alps while working with his father and brother in the family beekeeping business ("Someday all this . . . *ow!* . . . will be yours!").

In the Pacific Theater during World War II, Hillary served as a navigator in the Royal New Zealand Air Force but was badly burned in a boating accident (while trying to make it fly?) and returned home. In 1951, Hillary, as part of a New Zealand team, would make a failed run for the summit of Mount Everest, called Chomolungma by the locals, which sounds like a breathing disorder but isn't. It wasn't until two years later, as a member of a British team, that he finally succeeded. Of the four hundred climbers, medics, and porters (the polite term for the natives paid a pittance to schlep all those tea sets on their backs) who made it to base camp (about halfway up) only Hillary, along with his Sherpa (meaning "People belonging to the East") guide, Tenzing Norgay, were chosen to set out for the summit. Chances are it was because over 150 people had already died trying, and they figured they'd send the friendless Kiwi up since no one would miss him.

On May 29, 1953, five hours after dawn, Hillary, who was leading at that point (because heaven forbid we let the minority get there before the white guy), set foot on the top of the planet, 29,035 feet above sea level. Hillary photographed Norgay, not letting the Sherpa take *his* picture because that guy *always* cut the heads off. Edmund then looked around for signs of George Mallory and Sandy Irvine, who many believed had reached the summit in 1924, but found nothing, or so he *says*. Norgay buried some small items of food to honor Everest, while Hillary paid his respects to the mountain by urinating on it. The two worked their way down the mountain and into history as pictures of the world's greatest climber and his partner were splashed across the front page of newspapers around the globe, rocketing the two men to international stardom. Queen Elizabeth II, who coincidentally had her coronation the same day, threw a big party to celebrate.

After befriending the indigenous peoples of the region, Hillary, troubled by their poverty, unhealthy living conditions, and yak breath, started the Himalayan Trust in 1960, a non-profit organization whose purpose is to improve the quality of life for the locals around Everest and open some decent Italian restaurants in the area. This trust has been used to construct more than thirty schools, twelve hospitals, and two airstrips.

Not content to leave further exploration to others, Hillary continued his adventures by joining the multinational British Commonwealth Trans-Antarctic Expedition, which planned to be the first group to reach the South Pole using mechanized equipment, making them lazier than the first two groups who had gotten there by walking. Edmund was in charge of creating a supply line for a second team led by Vivian Fuchs that was coming toward the pole from a different direction and that was supposed to arrive first. However, Mr. "I'm just an average bloke who is used to being on top of the world" rushed ahead, reaching the spot on January 4, 1958, the exact day that *Sputnik* fell to Earth. Vivian (nice name, no wonder he came in second) didn't arrive until January 20 (the same day Elvis Presley got his draft notice) and must have been Fuchs-ing pissed to see Edmund and his team with their feet up on the coffee table, eating Moon Pies and watching reruns of *Gunsmoke*.

In 1960, Hillary took another break from his ongoing humanitarian efforts to form an expedition to search the Himalayas for the Yeti, a mysterious pale-haired, wild-eyed simian-like creature, but since Gary Busey was only sixteen and living in Kansas at the time, it kind of flopped. Throughout the 1960s and '70s, and beyond, Hillary used his fame and charisma to draw attention to the plight of the Sherpa people, raising money through his foundations. His efforts came with great personal cost as his first wife and daughter were killed in a plane crash in Nepal while en route to meet him in 1975. Four years later, Edmund became honorary president of the American Himalayan Foundation, an organization that works to improve the environmental damage heaped on the mountain, much of it by the climbing community. ("Look at this beautiful mountain. Nature at its purest. Now, help me toss this garbage over the side.") Later that same year, Hillary narrowly escaped death when he canceled plans to take an Air New Zealand flight to Antarctica that slammed into Mount Erebus on November 28, killing all 257 people on board, including Edmund's good friend Peter Mulgrew, who had taken his place.

Though Tenzing Norgay died in 1986 at the age of seventy-one, Hillary is alive and well, and along with his new wife, Jane, continues his humanitarian efforts while holding a load of impressive-sounding titles. On July 16, 1953, Edmund was made a Knight Commander of the Order of the British Empire, joining dozens of actors, politicians, and anyone else the queen wants to have over for tea. In 1987, his lazy countrymen took a break from their busy schedules of (. . . what? Help us out, here) to *finally* honor Hillary as a member of the Order of New Zealand, as if they had *so* many other qualified applicants. In 1995, Sir Climb-a-lot was made a Knight of the Order of the Garter, which sounds like a bunch of rich guys who like strip clubs, but is actually the longest running order of knighthood in the world with no more than twenty-five active members. Hillary's autobiography is entitled *Nothing Venture–Nothing Win*, which makes you wonder just how much damage was done to his brain while he was breathing bottled oxygen on the summit. Hillary's son, Peter, carries on the explorer tradition and has completed treks to both Everest and the South Pole, just like his dear old dad.

Interesting Tidbit: Among his other accomplishments, Hillary also holds the honor of being the only living New

Zealander to appear on currency. His face can be found on the New Zealand five-dollar note.

Ways to Bring Up Sir Edmund Hillary in Conversation

☼   Wow, that was quite a climb up here. I feel like Sir Edmund Hillary.

☼   Come on let's explore a little. I'll be Sir Edmund Hillary and you can be Tenzing Norgay . . . okay *I'll* be Tenzing Norgay.

☼   Their prices are so high, only Sir Edmund Hillary shops there.

5

The Philosophy Conversation

When you really want to show off your intelligence, it's time to whip out the philosophy conversation. Luckily, there might be about twelve people who have actually studied philosophy (and most of them are manning the drive-thru at the local Burger Barn), so you'll rarely find yourself having to go brain to brain with a philosophy expert. The last time most party people dabbled in philosophy was college, and that was because there was someone hot taking the class. It's easy to sound fascinating during the philosophy conversation because even though you're speaking English, no one else can understand what the hell you're saying. The trick here is to smile warmly and go back and explain things using simplistic metaphors. People are thrilled to finally understand what Descartes thought before "he was" and why Confucius is so confusing. And don't think you Kant, because you can.

However, every man and woman is in some way a

philosopher, since we all have "sort of" examined or contemplated our existence and its meaning (yes, even asking "Why doesn't he love me?" counts). Granted, you may run into a few walking cantaloupes out there, who may have only contemplated their navel lint. Despite our ethnic, religious, class, or sexual differences, we are all essentially human, and through the bond of our opposable thumbs, we share a common experience, thus making the philosophy conversation the perfect bridge across any social gap.

Though this is a stimulating introduction to use with new groups of people, don't linger too long on the philosophy conversation, or folks may find you a little too heady for cocktail-swilling banter. It's best to intermingle this kind of talk with other more mindless fare like bass fishing and the films of Adam Sandler.

The Trial of Socrates Poisoned His Reputation

When Are We Talking About: c. 470–399 BC

Why Are We Even Talking About This: Socrates was a fifth-century BC Greek philosopher who set the standard for Western thought, education, and thinking.

What You Need to Know to Sound Smart: Though ancient dates aren't always carved in stone, as far as we can tell, nine months after he was conceived, Socrates' theoretical life became a reality on June 4, 470 BC. His father was the sculptor Sophroniscus, and his mother was a midwife. Socrates grew up during the ascension of the city-state of Athens under Pericles, the first recorded liberal (before that became a dirty word) politician and proponent of democracy in recorded history. Pericles shifted power from the wealthy nobility into the grubby hands of the common man, established a constitution, judicial courts with juries of citizens from all classes (to ensure that the actors and sports figures who killed their spouses were set free), financing for the arts, and funding for city structures, such as building the Parthenon and restoring the Acropolis. The meteoric rise of Athenian power alarmed its primarily feudal neighbors, who futilely prayed for Athens' demise. It was in this environment of freedom, creativity, and democracy that Socrates grew up.

Socrates was a pupil of Archelaus, the first Athenian philosopher, and was also a disciple of Anaxagoras, who came from the Ionian school of thought. Ionian thinkers explored the distinction between appearance (also called "subjective experience") and reality, and believed in early atomic theory (that objects are made by invisible atoms as opposed to today, where everything's made by the Chinese). As a young man, Socrates served as a hoplite (which sounds like a schoolyard game, but means an Athenian soldier) in the Peloponnesian War between the Athenians and warlike Spartans (think Klingons without the dorky language). Defying academic stereotypes during battle, Socrates reputedly courageously remained beside an injured man, though his unit was retreating from the charging enemy.

Although it's not entirely clear how the philosopher made a living (maybe writing a *Dear Soccy* column), some claim he was a stonemason while others say a mooch, living off wealthy friends (now there's a Greek philosopher we can get behind . . .). He raised three sons with his wife, Xanthippe, a much younger woman reputed to be the only one ever to win an argument with the famed philosopher (of course, when you argue with your wife, even when you win, you lose), and whose name colloquially means "nag" or "shrew," which tells you a whole lot about *that* relationship. Socrates received an inheritance, although it couldn't have been much since Dad was an artist, and began pursuing philosophy full-time, teaching the youth of Athens. It's unclear whether or not the students paid to listen to Socrates' rabble babble about their need to challenge everyday truths and conventions, provoke argument and new thought, and equally mystifying how Gilbert Gottfried continues to find work.

Socrates inspired fanatical devotion in his students, raising concerns among parents possibly because, like a latter-day Mary Kay Letourneau, the philosopher was schtuping his pupils, although he was never dumb enough to get pregnant by them (twice!). He was soon accused of being a Sophist, or a charlatan charging for his ability to twist truth (today referred to as a lawyer).

Amazingly, Socrates was anything but a democrat. He disagreed with self-rule (much like the founding fathers of the United States) and believed people were sheep in need of a shepherd, generally lacking *arete* (virtuousness) and the wisdom to properly distinguish right from wrong, the only possible explaination as to why *Freaks and Geeks* was canceled after just one season. According to the portrayals of contemporary Greek authors Aristophanes and Plutarch, Socrates became a semi-vagrant, roaming the city streets barefoot, ragging on the ignorance of his fellow townsfolk in their shops and market stalls, and enduring beatings from the occasional pissed-off fishmonger.

Socrates was the ultimate skeptic (Greek for "one who examines") and believed truth must be pursued, not assumed or stumbled upon, or buried, as many these days seem to prefer. To this end, he formulated the *elenchus*, better known as the Socratic method, whereby the teacher through question and answer cross-examines the student on his position, using common experiences as reference. Once discovering a contradiction, the teacher then demonstrates the inaccuracy of the original belief. For example, if you believe chicken parmigiana is authentic Italian food, we'll show you why you're a moron.

Socrates was primarily concerned with the nature and pursuit of a virtuous life, which apparently involves a bit of buggering. In his eyes, to do good, one must first know what "good" is (that's easy, chocolate chip cookies) and often debate whether this concept could *ever* be known. Only by looking past our assumptions and accepting the possibility of our ignorance, can we have the opportunity to learn something new (sure, we get it . . . he means like knitting or golf). Unfortunately, Socrates thought everybody was stupid and therefore prone to vice (and who would know better than he?).

The greatest criticism of Socrates was that he never offered an alternative position after tearing down the opinions of others, even though Socrates himself stated he knew nothing at all . . . except for the fact that he knew nothing, which sounds a lot like that junk Deepak Chopra spouts that sounds smart, but never actually makes sense. Socrates argued that no one ever knowingly does evil but is invariably doing what they believe best (a theory proven false by the tobacco industry), or more simply, ignorance is vice and has nothing to do with weakness of will, lack of decency, or being part of the Taliban.

While all his questioning, mocking, and molesting might've been tolerated by the egalitarian Athenians, when the students of the anarchic academic began overthrowing the democracy, it was time to take action. One such pupil, Alcibiades, allied himself with the Spartans and briefly gave them control of the city from 411 to 410. Another was the democracy-despising Critias (Plato's cousin), who led a revolt installing the Thirty Tyrants, from 404 to 403, an oligarchy of wealthy nobles who viciously butchered 1,500 of Athen's most famous liberals. (Stop. Noooo. It's *not* a good idea.) When democracy was again restored in 403, a general amnesty was declared. But by 399 BC, prominent Athenians theorized that their city had one philosopher too many.

Socrates was brought to trial in the royal *stoa* (Athenian courthouse) before the king archon (or judge) to answer for his crimes of corrupting the youth of the city. ("I didn't corrupt them, I slept with them. Thank you, Athens!") In a preliminary hearing, the judge listened to both cases and deeming good cause, decided to allow Meletus (leader of the "Put a sock in it, Socrates" movement) to press formal charges. A document was created stating that Socrates was "guilty of refusing to recognize the gods recognized by the state, and of introducing new divinities," as well as the whole corruption rap. The trial took place at the *agora* (the civic center) in the People's Court (but without that smarmy Doug Llewelyn), and lasted approximately ten hours. The prosecution made its case over the next three hours with the most damaging evidence being Socrates' part in the death of Leon of Salamis. ("With a name like Salamis, I'd want to date him not kill him.") It seems that back when Critias was butchering innocents, he had ordered Socrates to bring Salamis to him for execution. Though Socrates refused, he didn't warn or help Salamis either, instead going home to watch SportsCenter, which in their eyes made him even more guilty.

For his part, Socrates gave his impassioned, yet unrepentent *Apologia* (or *The Apology*, as later recorded by Plato and Xenophon). Socrates employed his own method of argument by not directly answering the charges against him but instead pointing out the contradictions and flaws in the arguments of his prosecutors. This might've worked if he hadn't finished off his little speech by saying he'd rather die than stop preaching his beliefs, to which 280 of the 500 members of the all-male Athenian jury answered, "Not a problem." Socrates did not appeal his death sentence and refused to let his family testify on his behalf, believing such piteous pleas denigrated the Athenian courts. (So he won't belittle the courts of the democracy he despises. Anyone want to Socratically point out those contradictions?) During sentencing, Socrates brazenly demanded he be rewarded with a lifetime supply of free meals for his service to the city, at which point the vote for his death swung to 360 vs. 140.

Socrates, seventy-nine, accepted his fate with unparalleled poise. Though friends tried to arrange his escape, he decided through philosophical debate that it was wrong for a citizen to disobey the law. So Socrates poisoned himself with a draught of hemlock, dying painfully in his jail cell as the cruel elixir slowly seized control of his nervous system on May 7, 399 BC.

Interesting Tidbit: It's widely held that Anytus, a politician and tanner, was the instigator of Socrates' trial, because the sage had encouraged his son not to follow in his father's footsteps.

Ways to Bring Up Socrates in Conversation

- ☼ This punch is awful, what's in here? The hemlock that killed Socrates?
- ☼ Becky's always debating everything. It's like hanging out with Socrates.
- ☼ There's a lot I can teach you. And I'm not talking the Socratic method.

Elizabeth Cady Stanton Refused to Sufferage in Silence

When Are We Talking About: 1815–1902

Why Are We Even Talking About This: Stanton was a woman's rights activist and abolitionist who helped put the suffrage movement on the map.

What You Need to Know to Sound Smart: Though "feminism" has become a four-letter word associated with stocky left-wing extremists barking outside the White House lawn, the word, and for that matter, the movement, actually represents a woman's equal rights in the workplace, the home, under the law . . . and in the bedroom, which, sorry guys, doesn't mean her right to please *you*. Born in a time when these ideas we take for granted did not exist, Elizabeth Cady Stanton first demanded her rights on November 12, 1815, in tranquil Jonestown, New York. Young Lizzy was the daughter of Daniel Cady, a lawyer, congressman, and New York Supreme Court judge, who supported women's education, perhaps because he was used to wigs and robes. When her younger sister was born, Betsy, age four, overheard a neighbor remark, "Too bad she's a girl." Even as she chucked her juice box at the cretin's head, Stanton understood for the first time that females were actually considered less desirable than males, which mind you has never been our experience. From that point forward, Stanton was troubled by the plight of women (especially since she was one) who, despite their mental or physical capacity, were treated like second-class citizens, prizes, or pets.

At age ten, upon reading the laws that oppressed women (like all of them), specifically those that robbed them of their right to property and protection from marital abuse, Stanton took a pair of scissors and removed the offensive members from her father's legal books, as opposed to Lorena Bobbitt, who prefers a knife when removing offending members. Stanton learned to ride horses like men (that is, astride the saddle, the way men rode not the other thing you were thinking) and studied Greek with a local clergyman (because all men . . . speak . . . Greek?) while attending Jonestown Academy, a co-ed school where she excelled in math, language, and debating. Though she was a top student, Stanton was unable to go to a proper college after her graduation in 1830 due to their no girl-cooties acceptance policies. Women in those times were relegated to special academies (i.e., Needlepoint U), which were far inferior to male schools. At the Troy Female Seminary in Troy, New York, Stanton was beyond bored, breezing through her courses. Two years later, her "schooling" completed, Stanton returned home to the sedentary routine of a woman's life at the time: cooking, sewing, plotting the overthrow of male-dominated society, cleaning, and baking, you know, the usual. Her sympathetic father, admiring his daughter's keen mind and hunger for knowledge, began home-schooling her in law, lending her books to study from. Lucky for her, since most dads schooled their daughters on little more than the laws of finding a husband.

While visiting a cousin's home nearby, Elizabeth met runaway slaves taking refuge there, as well as abolitionist Henry Brewster Stanton, who wasn't taking refuge but was just pitching in, being a damned liberal. Lizzy soon became an abolitionist herself, and the two married in 1840. She demanded the word "obey" be removed from the wedding ceremony and also from her husband's vocabulary, and you *know* he did it because judging from photos Stanton looked like she could put a gorilla in an effective sleeper hold. Because flights to Honolulu were so pricey, the newlyweds honeymooned in London and took part in the World's Anti-Slavery Convention. While the Brits may have hung on to their royalty a little too long, they did figure out that the whole slavery thing was bad way before the equality-loving Americans.

But when Lizzy and her dear friend Lucretia Mott, Quaker minister, teacher, and abolitionist, were refused recognition in the assembly, the two women realized that even if the slaves were freed, women would remain in servitude. Over the ensuing eight years, Stanton moved with her hubby to Seneca Falls, New York (we're pretty sure that she drove the car on the way there and slept on the left side of the bed), popped out three of her eventual *seven* kids, and experienced firsthand the endless, backbreaking difficulties of motherhood. Her eye ever on the prize, Stanton finally organized a local women's rights convention with Mott (incidentally, no relation to the apple juice) in

1848, where the two women, along with three other like-minded sock-er moms, penned their "Declaration of Sentiments," a sort of modified "Declaration of Independence" demanding rights for women, both socially and governmentally, and advocating the death sentence for any husband who told his wife she had to lose a few. The sophisticated ladies published their creation in several newspapers that, mistaking it for satire, eagerly printed the absurd feminist bill of rights. ("Get a load of this. Equal pay! Haw-haw! Hoooo, that's a good one.")

In 1851, Stanton teamed up with Susan Brownell Anthony, yet another Quaker (man, who was making the oatmeal?), suffragist, abolitionist (and saxophonist—not really but it sounds cool), who found nothing at all funny about Stanton and Mott's declaration, or anything else by the look of her. Little Suzie wanted America to wake up, and despite being insecure about her looks (and for good reason, with Marty Feldman eyes and a smile that resembled a bluegill choking on a feathered jig), agreed to team up with Stanton as spokeswoman for their movement. While raising her children, Stanton still found time to forge the fiery speeches that Anthony (who also had a public speaking phobia) toured the country delivering, even appearing before the New York legislature (in 1854, 1857, and 1860), passionately discussing divorce rights, though there couldn't have been a subject less pertinent to her.

In 1866, these dynamic dames founded the American Equal Rights Association and created the *Revolution* newspaper with Stanton as editor. *Revolution* served as a pulpit to demand equal education, equal guardianship of children, equal financial rights, but not the equal right to fart and blame it on the dog enjoyed by men the world over. When the Civil War finally ended in 1865 (started by *men*, by the way), the Fourteenth and Fifteenth Amendments to the

Constitution finally destroyed slavery but astoundingly took along with it abolitionist support for suffrage ("Oh, you gals were serious about that?"), giving Stanton and Anthony that not so fresh feeling that they had been left high and dry. Four years later the femme fighters founded the National Woman Suffrage Association (NWSA), since it was important to start a new group every few years, with Stanton as president. NWSA fought for a woman's right to wear low-cut clothing and perhaps a thong bikini if the mood struck her. Just kidding, it was the voting rights thing again, but we're trying to keep the guys involved.

In 1876, Stanton moved with her family to Tenafly, New Jersey, where she and Anthony compiled research from all over the country to write the first three volumes (of an eventual six) on the *History of Woman Suffrage*, a cookbook compilation of rights, each of which called for the pot to be stirred and the heat to be cranked. The two also wrote the *Declaration of Rights of the Women of the United States*, which Anthony, uninvited, read at the Centennial celebration in Washington in 1876, which totally pissed off Jackie Mason, who had to go up next. Two years later, backed by continued conviction (that is, her beliefs, not jail time), Stanton lobbied for a woman suffrage amendment to the Constitution and found a supporter in California senator Aaron A. Sargent.

In 1888, Lizzy, needing another acronym in her life, helped form the International Council of Women. Two years later, she oversaw the NWSA, which later joined forces with AWSA (American Woman Suffrage Association) to become the NAWSA or National American Woman Suffrage Association, reigning as president until 1892. Men would have been afraid of any or all of these groups had they been smart enough to keep track of which was which. Stanton's last work, *The*

Women's Bible (1895), attacked religion's treatment of women and went so far as to claim that God actually wore heels.

Stanton died of natural causes at age eighty-six in New York on October 26, 1902, and was buried at Woodlawn Cemetery in the Bronx in a man-sized coffin. Her home in Seneca Falls is now part of the Women's Rights National Historic Park, whose new thrill ride, "The Ovulator," is set to open in December 2007.

Interesting Tidbit: It wasn't until twenty years after Stanton's death that the United States granted women voting rights, although in 1872, claiming that the Constitution already entitled her to vote, Susan B. Anthony cast hers in Rochester, New York, in a presidential election. She was levied a fine, which she refused to pay.

Ways to Bring Up Elizabeth Cady Stanton in Conversation

- ❀ Elise says she's not going to vote. Elizabeth Cady Stanton would be pissed!
- ❀ She's independent, smart, educated . . . think Elizabeth Cady Stanton only hotter.
- ❀ I was just telling you I thought you were pretty. There's no need to go Elizabeth Cady Stanton on me!

How Marx Saw Red

When Are We Talking About: 1818–1883

Why Are We Even Talking About This: Marx was a political philosopher and revolutionary thinker who coauthored *The Communist Manifesto*, the foundation of scientific socialism and modern communism.

What You Need to Know to Sound Smart: Karl Marx was born on May 5, 1818, in Trier, Prussia (now Germany), to a long line of rabbis, who probably would have thrown a Torah-tantrum had they lived to hear his theory that religion was the opiate of the masses. Marx's father had converted to Lutheranism in order to keep his job as an attorney during the semiannual wave of anti-Semitism once again sweeping through Europe. Marx began his studies at the University of Bonn, but his drunken shenanigans forced his father to move him to school in Berlin, then a hotbed for leftist thinkers. Here Marx began to formulate his radical ideas in 1842, while editing a revolutionary newspaper entitled *Rheinische Zeitung*, which we can only imagine had a terrible comics section.

Seen as a threat by the kaiser, Marx was drop-kicked out of the country and so headed for France in 1843. Like most tourists, Karl got the cold shoulder in Paris (*quel surprise!*) and so moved to Brussels two years later, where he formed the German Workers Party. Banished from Belgium in 1848, Marx and his buddy the political philosopher Friedrich Engels published *The Communist Manifesto*, a Bible-sized laugh-a-minute gripe-a-thon about the plight of the working man. Marx and Engels proposed that the wealth and control of a nation should be in the hands of the people (what were they, commies? Oh, wait.). Arrested in Cologne for causing a stink, and exiled from Germany in May 1849 for trying to start an armed insurrection, Karl returned briefly to France but was banished from there too in June and so decided on an extended vacation off the European mainland, settling in London.

While in the land that Crest forgot, Marx eked out a living as a journalist for the *New York Daily Tribune* but only financial support from Engels kept his family from starving. During this period, Marx wrote *Das Kapital* (the first of four volumes was published in 1867 with the others coming out after his death), an analysis of capitalism and an exposition on how the lower classes, namely him, will always be exploited by the upper, namely everyone else. Less than a smash success, the book sold barely one thousand copies, and Marx sardonically remarked that it did not earn him enough money to pay for the cigars he smoked while writing it. In *The Gotha Program,* Marx explained how capitalist societies will naturally evolve into a communist state after workers unite, a process which history has shown involves pillaging and burning while singing patriotic folk songs.

The last decade of his life was a bit dicey with Marx suffering from toothaches, liver ailments, carbuncles that covered his entire body, headaches, coughs, eye problems, pleurisy, and last but not least, hemorrhoids. He died while sitting lightly in his armchair in London on March 14, 1883.

Interesting Tidbit: During his drunken college years, Marx was involved in a duel, resulting in a wound to his right eye, proving that he was not much of a Marx-man. (Ha-ha. Sorry.)

Ways to Bring Up Karl Marx in Conversation

☼ Ed is sick all the time. The guy has more ailments than Karl Marx!

☼ I'm tired of you telling me I shouldn't buy a nice car. Who are you, Karl Marx?

☼ The book was a little boring. *Das Kapital* had more plot twists.

God Is Dead and So Is Nietzsche

When Are We Talking About: 1844–1900

Why Are We Even Talking About This: Considered by many to be the founder of modern atheism, Nietzsche's nihilistic belief system denounced all religions as a tool of society and promoted the acquisition of power as the only worthwhile goal in life.

What You Need to Know to Sound Smart: Friedrich Nietzsche was born October 15, 1844, in Rocken, Germany, which is fitting considering his nonexistent sense of humor. Nietzsche's father, Karl, a Lutheran pastor and emphatically the *last* of a long line of clergymen, died when Nietzsche was just five, the *first* of a long line of severely traumatic events that would isolate Friedrich from every other human being in the universe. The young man was raised by his mother, grandmother, two aunts, and a sister. Nietzsche was sent to boarding school (event two) where he suffered from constant bouts of illness (numero tres), and though he was a top student (four!), young Friedrich was less than popular with his schoolmates (five, six, seven, ad infinitum). During his formal education at the university in Leipzig, Nietzsche was strongly influenced by Arthur Schopenhauer's philosophical theories on human will as well as his abilities to repulse women.

In 1867, Nietzsche enlisted in the Prussian army to fight the Austrians. The military being simply the perfect place for a sickly, moody, creative type, it was to no one's surprise that Nietzsche made a pathetic soldier—he severely injured himself while mounting a horse. Back at school, Nietzsche was offered a teaching position at the University of Basel (apparently a popular place for creepy German thinkers, just ask Carl Jung), which he accepted. Before he left, Friedrich met the legendary composer Richard Wagner, whom Nietzsche worshipped and who influenced his first work, *The Birth of Tragedy* (1872), which lauded Wagner's creative genius. However, by 1876 the symphony was over, and Nietzsche broke off contact due to Wagner's anti-Semitic beliefs and demand for mindless worship, two very popular traits among Germans in the halcyon days before World War II.

Before the end of his career, Nietzsche would publish over a dozen books on philosophy. In *Human, All Too Human* (1878), Nietzsche rejected Schopenhauer and wrote that the human will is rooted entirely in the pursuit of survival and pleasure. In *The Dawn: Thoughts on Moral Prejudice* (1880), Nietzsche stated that Christianity was created for no other purpose than as a tool of society for controlling the masses. Two years later, he went on to declare in *The Gay Science* (1882), that God was dead and truth did not exist (it's amazing that Pixar hasn't scooped up the rights). He continued expounding on these ideas in the four-volume yuck-fest, *Thus Spake Zarathustra* (1883), where he discussed that the man who wishes to be a "superman" must gain power and reject fear by overcoming his own failures and shortcomings. *Zarathustra* became the most popular of Nietzsche's many depressing works. In the subsequent *Beyond Good and Evil* (1886) and *On the Genealogy of Morals* (1887), Nietzsche continued to espouse his hatred of Christianity and his promotion of subjective morality, where *you* decide what's right and wrong (kind of like with your taxes), and outright nihilism, the wonderful belief that existence is meaningless. In *The Case for Wagner* (1888), Nietzsche affectionately referred to his former idol as a puppet of the German masses, a mouthpiece for hatred and idiocy, and a sickness released on the world.

By the early 1890s, with Nietzsche's mental and physical health in steep decline, he began working on his autobiography *Ecce Homo*, which included chapters with catchy titles like (and this is no joke), "Why Am I So Wise?," "Why Am I So Clever?," and the ever-modest "Why I Write Such Good Books." Nietzsche spent the next couple of years in a pool of delusional grandeur and psychotic paranoia. Shortly after learning to spell his own last name, he died from a stroke, his third, on August 25, 1900, in Weimar, Germany, only to have his sister give him a Christian burial and warp his writings into pro-Nazi propaganda.

Interesting Tidbit: Along with his myriad physical maladies, Nietzsche suffered from a recurring nightmare that his father would rise from the grave and kill him. Kind of makes you feel okay about your own life, doesn't it?

Ways to Bring Up Friedrich Nietzsche in Conversation

☀ You think you got problems? You should hang out with Nietzsche.

☀ What are you doing sitting here alone? Doing a Nietzsche impersonation?

☀ That guy's so moody he makes Nietzsche look like a cheerleader.

The Human Tragedy
Conversation

*I*f you're at a dinner party or United Nations mixer with people interested in discussing the state of the world, the human tragedies conversation is fine fare, but if you're at a frat party or swanky disco, unless you're trying to show off your "big heart" routine, talking about the massacre of innocent millions can be a bit of a downer. Yet the human tragedy conversation binds us together. There are few people who don't share compassion for those afflicted by the cruelties of our world. It taps into our core desire for justice and our instincts to cherish and protect our loved ones. Plus the human tragedies conversation is a good way to gauge how selfish the people you're talking to are. A person who becomes disinterested or has nothing but callous remarks for the victims of these tragedies will probably have little sympathy for you and the difficulties of your (hopefully) far less horrific life-trials. New Agers, self-helpers, psychologists, ecologists, patrons of the arts, pastors, history teachers, and Ricky Lakers are all people who will be happy to shake their heads mournfully with you during the human tragedy conversation.

Oh, Rats! It's the Black Plague

When Are We Talking About: 1347

Why Are We Even Talking About This: This contagious disease wiped out one-third of the European population in five years in the mid-fourteenth century and nearly destroyed modern civilization as we know it.

What You Need to Know to Sound Smart: The Black Plague, caused by a bacteria (*Yersinia pestis*, Latin for "kiss your butt good-bye") found inside infected fleas carried by black rats, made its pestilent debut in Europe in October 1347. It came to be known by a variety of names such as the Great Dying, the Black Death, or the sometimes overlooked Family Sleepy-Time Jamboree. The disease came in two delicious flavors. Those contracting the bubonic plague (named after buboes, the baseball-sized swollen glandular tumors that would appear on the victim's neck, armpit, or groin) would enjoy soaring fevers and a rash of red lesions that gradually turned a lovely shade of black—hence the whole Black Plague thing. The disease usually left one dead within a week. Well, actually a lot more than one. Folks who opted for the pneumonic variant, contracted by inhaling the bacteria from an infected person (aka by breathing anywhere in Europe), would come to know the joys of coughing up copious amounts of their own blood all over their friends and family. Thankfully, death from this version ordinarily came in only a day or so.

This plague originated in the East (some blame the Chinese, others the Tartars), as opposed to the plague of advertising, which began in the West. It was Italian traders returning from the Black Sea who imported this rare delicacy to the

Western world. When their ships docked in Sicily, many on board were already dead and dying, and yet they were still welcomed into the city with a kiss of death on both cheeks. The disease swiftly decimated the populace before you could say "ciao," causing Boccaccio, Renaissance poet and humanist, to comment on how its victims "ate lunch with their friends and dinner with their ancestors."

The plague was most effective against those with weak constitutions and therefore headed for France in 1348. The French highly recommended their buddies the Germans for the next stop on the plague's mega-death European tour, and after killing in city after city across the Rhineland, it journeyed north to the British Isles where it cut its newest record, decimating a third of the population within two and a half years, though sadly, enough Brits would still survive to produce *The Benny Hill Show* centuries later.

In many areas, chaos prevailed with fires, riots, and looting (basically, the city of Los Angeles on any given day) as there were not enough lords or watchmen left alive to keep the peace. Soon the bodies were piled so high that religious burial procedures were abandoned in favor of mass graves. Corpses filled the streets, often heaped in the middle of towns, where man's alleged best friend would snack on the Buboes-n-Bits before loyally bringing the disease back home to his master. Terror tore apart the very fabric of society as parents abandoned children, brother deserted brother, and husbands ran out on their wives. Did we mention Italians were responsible? Due to their close proximity to the dead while administering last rites, the plague was also taking out clergymen faster than an altar boy sex scandal, thus denying spiritual guidance to a troubled continent when it was needed the most.

"Doctors" specializing in potions, charms, and leeches were baffled when their highly scientific eye-of-newt concoctions failed to slow the plague, while the mythical elixir of *clean, running water* somehow escaped their vast medical wisdom. Other attempts to arrest the disease's proliferation included booting Italians from one's borders (which didn't help but made dying more pleasant without the constant soccer chatter), ringing of church bells (again, pretty much only good against the soccer chatter), applying dried toads to infected areas, stuffing pockets with bundles of flowers, or the tried and true cure-all, Blame It on the Jews. In Strasbourg in 1349, on Valentine's Day (that holiday of lovers), instead of a dozen roses two thousand Jews received a burning at the stake, which also conveniently enabled the locals to wipe out their debts and confiscate coveted Jewish property. Disappointingly, this did nothing to halt the progress of the plague, plus there was absolutely no decent theater in town for years.

Luckily, the Catholic Church was on top of things. Pope Clement VI, who up until then had bravely holed up in the Vatican, cowering on his throne between two large bonfires (which interestingly enough, kept him alive by purifying the air), gave his blessing to a rather gnarly group of ascetics formed in Germany known as the Flagellants, not to be confused with flatulence, though their scent was similar. These fanatical pilgrims had taken a vow to abstain from shaving, showering, washing their clothes, or having any contact with the opposite sex, the last of which was likely the result of the first three. Processions of these smell-ots marched around Europe in groups of fifty to three hundred, beating themselves with whips or canes in order to cleanse their souls of their sinful desires. Though initially the Flagellants were an amusing distraction from open sores and endless death, the papacy went into canon-iptions as the people began offering devotions (and more importantly, money) to this odorous order, and quickly deployed troops to have them disbanded. While their pilgrimages of thirty-three and one-third days (the number of years Christ walked the earth) had little effect on morale, their lousy hygiene may have actually contributed to the spread of the deadly disease.

By the time the death toll stopped ringing in 1352, the plague had spread nearly everywhere on the European continent, killing one-third of the population, over 25 million people.

Interesting Tidbit: The widespread carnage crippled the European economy and, with no peons to pee on, destroyed the feudal system. Since there were not enough workers to go around, those few who remained were able to demand higher wages and better working conditions (e.g., no beatings during lunch hour), forever changing the face of the Western world.

Ways to Bring Up the Plague in Conversation

☼ This party is deader than a European town in the 1340s.

☼ We should call Bruce *Yersinia pestis,* since he sucks the life out of any party he goes to.

☼ Are those plague-inflicted buboes in your pants, or are you just excited to see me?

Idi Amin Bites

When Are We Talking About: 1925–2003

Why Are We Even Talking About This: Amin was the president of Uganda and a notorious hatemonger who killed thousands of his own people while despotically ruling his country from 1971 to 1979.

What You Need to Know to Sound Smart: Though he celebrated his birthday on January 1, the actual day Amin slithered onto the planet is anyone's guess as his tribal village of Koboko, Uganda, kept no records in 1925. Born Idi Awo-Ongo Angoo, Amin was deserted by his father and raised by his mother, a local mystic . . . think a Ugandan Miss Cleo but without the 1–800 number. In 1946, at age twenty-one and with next to no schooling, he joined the King's African Rifles (part of the British Colonial Army) where he excelled as a brave, yet brutal, soldier. While fighting in Kenya, Somalia, and other holiday hot spots, Amin quickly rose through the ranks, earning a reputation as a remorseless killer, a tradition maintained to this day by certain modern-day African leaders. After honing his warcraft in England at the request of his best buddy Apolo Obote, head of the Uganda People's Congress, Amin returned in 1964 to help his pal work toward "Ugandan independence," i.e., the freedom to be murdered and oppressed by their own people.

In 1965, the two men were indicted for smuggling, allegedly to help their cause, but the money never got past their pockets, and deciding turnabout is *un*fair play, they staged a revolt. Forcing President Edward Mutebi Mutesa II (known 'round the way as King Freddie) into exile, they seized control of the nation with Obote as president. In 1971, while Obote was in Singapore (we assume for business *and* pleasure), Amin decided he needed a title to match his Mr. T–sized collection of medals. Amid rumors that his buddy was going to unjustly arrest him for some harmless embezzling, Amin threw friendship to the wind and staged his own coup, declaring himself (and we swear we're not making this up), "His Excellency President for Life, Field Marshal Al Hadji Doctor Idi Amin, VC, DSO, MC, Lord of All the Beasts of the Earth and Fishes of the Sea, and Conqueror of the British Empire in Africa in General and Uganda in Particular." It is unknown whether he was voted in by the fish or simply appointed by some sort of aquatic high council. Ever a man of the people, except of course for the 70,000 Asians he exiled (because he claimed God told him to) and the 300,000 Ugandans he murdered, Amin was an equal opportunity butcher, simultaneously calling for the murder of the chief justice, governor of banking, and the archbishop of the Ugandan Anglican Church.

In 1975, Amin was elected president of the Organization of African Unity, whose constituency must have been drinking heavily at the time. Idi also generously thought to expand his governing abilities by volunteering to assume the throne of Scotland, an offer that was oddly rejected. A savvy diplomat, Amin forged a lasting friendship with those explosive experts the PLO, not only training their troops, but also allowing a hijacked Air France jet loaded with Israeli hostages to land in Entebbe. Amin's elite military machine broke down, however, when duped by a small Israeli strike force that staged a daring rescue disguised as the fish king's personal entourage (sure, because Israelis look sooo much like Africans). The hostages were saved after a thirty-five-minute battle that decimated the Ugandan air force, while the Israelis lost only a single man.

Late in 1978, Amin, longing to spread his goodwill to the rest of the world, attempted to annex northern Tanzania. The Tanzanians weren't feelin' the love, and with the help of many of Amin's own people, they went a little coup-coup, forcing his Less-Than-Excellency to flee the country on April 13, 1979. Amin spent ten years hanging out in Libya with fellow lunatic Muammar al-Qaddafi before finally settling down in comfortable retirement among our beloved allies in Saudi Arabia. Amin died of heart failure, seventy-eight years too late, in Jeddah, Saudi Arabia, on August 16, 2003.

Interesting Tidbit: In his youth, Amin was an accomplished boxer and from 1951 to 1960, he held the Ugandan light heavyweight boxing title.

Ways to Bring Up Idi Amin in Conversation

✵ Idi Amin deserved his title more than that guy.

✵ Be friends with her? I'd rather hang out with Idi Amin.

✵ That woman's on an Idi Amin diet: She's a real man-eater.

Jonestown—Bad to the Last Drop

When Are We Talking About: November 18, 1978

Why Are We Even Talking About This: The death of Jim
Jones and the congregation of his People's Temple was one
of the largest murder/suicides in world history.

What You Need to Know to Sound Smart: The heavens
darkened on May 13, 1931, when James Warren Jones was
born in Crete, Indiana, during the not-so-Great Depression.
Psychosis begins in the home, as did the mixed messages that
would shape Jones's "divine" demeanor. While James's father,
James Jones Sr., a disabled veteran yet able Klan member,
worshipped at the church of segregation, his superstitious
mother, Lynetta, raised her son to pray for social equality
and avoid organized religion. But what set young Jimmy on
the path to wrong-tiousness was a neighbor's invitation to a
multicultural Pentecostal church service. As the preacher
aroused the initially humble congregation to fits of shrieking,
shaking, and barking like dogs, Jones's twisted soul heard "the
calling" . . . from whom, we have no idea. By age sixteen, he
was haranguing both blacks and whites alike from street cor-
ners with jug-fulls of his home-brewed spirits that mixed
equal parts charismatic doctrine with universal brotherhood.
After graduation, Jones married his high school sweetheart,
Marceline, and worked hard to keep up the passion in their
relationship by freaking out and throwing things at his young
bride if she so much as looked at another man.

Despite his strong moral code, Jimbo's patchwork faith
began to unravel as the poverty and suffering around him led
him to the conclusion that God did not exist. Unwilling to be
dissuaded from his unholy path by such silly incidentals,
Jones continued preaching at Methodist and Assemblies of
God churches, while probably keeping that whole "no God"
thing to himself. Still, his sermons were considered too con-

troversial (i.e., Black people were mentioned) and so he decided to start his own church (why not?) called Wings of Deliverance (sure) on April 4, 1955, but renamed it People's Temple (or, that works too) the following year. By the 1960s, Jones's church had been shepherded into a Christian denomination, the Disciples of Christ, and the charming rage-a-holic was ordained a pastor, despite having no formal religious education. Not long after, the man who would one day murder nearly one thousand people was elected president of the Indianapolis Human Rights Commission. Irony? Table for two?

In 1965, when Indianapolis proved too conservative for his mixed-race congregation, Jones and eighty devotees moved to Redwood Valley, California, to set up shop. The city was chosen for its liberal political philosophies, mixed-race populace, and survivability in the event of nuclear attack. It's true, look it up. After building a new compound (Cult Warning Sign 1: Your church meets in a compound) at the site, the pawns of the paranoid pastor unleashed his dogma of social justice on an unsuspecting public. By the 1970s, the temple had expanded into San Francisco, and its socialist programs (feeding the homeless, caring for the elderly, blah-blah-blah) attracted many young upper-class whites—still suckers for that "peace, love, and harmony" garbage—to their ranks, swelling its coffers.

During this period, Reverend JJ had a dyn-o-mite idea to begin experimenting with drugs as well as "lifestyle choices." In 1973, two weeks before Christmas, he was arrested in a public restroom for offering to unwrap the "Yule Log" of an undercover police officer. In his altar-ed state, Jones grew more domineering, demanding that his flock donate their property to the church in exchange for endless hours of service and an allowance of $2 a week. Tired of his rantings and extramarital affairs, Jones's wife had a revelation of her own and threatened divorce, but unfortunately for her, she never made good on it.

Alas, nothing bad can last forever, and in 1977, Jones's theology of beatings, blackmail, and sexual abuse brought pressure from the IRS and ex-church members known as "concerned relatives," driving him and 1,100 deluded devotees to leave the United States for the church's agricultural cooperative in Guyana (Cult Warning Sign 2: Your church owns an agricultural cooperative). The three-hundred-acre farm, humbly dubbed Jonestown, was a veritable heaven on earth, overflowing with armed guards, torture devices, and a big dirt hole where naughty dissenters were thrown for days at a time.

While the *really* blind faithful toiled in the blazing sun for up to twelve hours a day, subsisting on meals of beans and rice, Jones lived high on the hog . . . and the hash. Reverend Jim began preaching that he was the reincarnation of Lenin, Buddha, and Jesus and demanded sex from anyone he wanted at any time, which must have been nice for Lenin, who didn't look like he got a lot his first time around. He also claimed to be "the only true heterosexual," even once going so far as to publicly sodomize a member to prove the guy was gay, which is kind of a long way to go to win a bet. Amazingly, some members still refused to admit that their buggering bishop might be a few pages short of a hymnal.

When a Democratic congressman from San Francisco, Leo Ryan, caught wind of the outlandish behavior at Jonestown, he flew to Guyana in November 1978 with members of the press and "concerned relatives." After a tough journey (the in-flight movie starred Lee Majors) and temple-sponsored harassment at the airport, the congressman's entourage entered the enclave, where their questions to cult members were answered with obviously prewritten responses. When about two-dozen members of the happy family quietly pleaded with

Ryan to cram them into his carry-on, "Father" (Jones's new nom-de-demagoguerre) flew into a rage, but then, as if by an act of God, he decided to let them go unharmed.

Soon after, however, God appeared to have changed his mind, because Jones dispatched his armed death squad (Cult Warning Sign 3: Your pastor has an armed death squad), known as the Red Brigade, to the Port Kaituma airstrip where, along with one of the defectors on the plane, they opened fire, killing the congressman and six others. Having murdered a U.S. government official, Jones became fearful that the Green Berets, rumored to be "in-country," might drop by for evening services to make some lead donations. Jones immediately called for a White Night, a ritual communion of death where the fellowship demonstrated their dying devotion by coming together to drink fake poison. Only this was not a drill. Although Kool-Aid got the bad rap, it was actually grape Flavor Aid mixed with cyanide that caused the deaths of 913 of the 1,100 inhabitants, including nearly three hundred children. Those who refused the poisonberry cup of trembling were either shot, injected, or had it forced down their throats.

The great prophet met his end on November 18, 1978, while sitting on his backside in a lawn chair . . . not unlike many other residents of Indiana. It is debated whether the bullet that parted his skull like the Red Sea as he directed the genocide was fired by a fleeing cultist or by Jones himself, in his first true act of Christian charity. To this day, the U.S. government has refused to release much of its information on the tragedy on grounds of "National Security."

Interesting Tidbit: In the early years, while trying to raise money for his ministry, the "Reverend" Jim Jones sold monkeys door-to-door.

Ways to Bring Up Jonestown in Conversation

- ☼ Stay away from the punch. I think it's left over from Jonestown.
- ☼ Dude, that party was totally Jonestown, nothing but a tragedy.
- ☼ Oh, I hate hanging out with that guy. I'd rather go drinking with Jim Jones.

A Dark Cloud Over Bhopal

When Are We Talking About: December 3, 1984

Why Are We Even Talking About This: The Bhopal incident, in which a cloud of toxic gas from a Union Carbide pesticide plant killed between 10,000 and 20,000 Indian citizens, was the deadliest industrial accident in world history.

What You Need to Know to Sound Smart: In 1969, the U.S.-based Union Carbide Corporation, one of the world's largest chemical manufacturers, allowed an Indian (dots not feathers) subsidiary to build a pesticide plant in Bhopal, India, out of a rising fear that somewhere on the planet was a square inch of soil not routinely hosed down with liquid carcinogens. Early advertisements for the plant boasted the "vast scientific resources" U.C. had employed during construction to ensure "the promise of a bright future" for the citizens of Bhopal, all brought to you by the people who gave us asbestos!

However, all those business-degree-wielding execs back in corporate America must have slept through their econ classes, since no one questioned how those funny little farmers, who could barely afford curry for their families, would purchase expensive pesticides for their crops. Consequently, the Bhopal plant was about as successful as a pork chop vendor in Tel Aviv, which really disappointed all those U.C. guys who thought India, with its loose legal system, would be an ideal place to sell their poison. During the early 1980s, Bhopal sales dropped so low (down to three guys all named Patel) that the company ceased all production and began using the facility for storage.

The night of December 2, 1984, a runaway exothermic reaction (which, by the way, is bad) caused a massive explosion, sending a deadly cloud of methyl isocyanate (and let's face it, anything with the word "methyl" in it already sounds like a reaming in the making) over the city. Officially, the exact cause of the accident remains uncertain. Union Carbide claimed sabotage by a disgruntled employee (tired of Fish 'n' Sticks Tuesdays), while the Indian government blamed corroded pipes and a lack of proper maintenance. What *is* known is that all seven safety systems at the plant had either been disengaged or were as useless as the U.S. electoral college.

While the cause of the disaster can be debated, there is no questioning the deadliness of its results. As the giant milky cloud billowed inexorably across the city, like the plague of insects over Egypt, it awakened residents to a burning sensation. Described as breathing fire, the gas scorched lungs and eyes, causing blindness and vomiting, and sending panic-driven thousands stampeding into streets, much like the Kathy Bates full-frontal nude scene in *About Schmidt*, and ultimately resulting in the deaths of over 10,000 people. Those unfortunate enough to survive would enjoy years of breathing, vision, and gynecological problems (even the men). Somewhere in the neighborhood of a half-million people had received a dose of Union Carbide's early Christmas/Ramadan gift (hey, U.C. does not discriminate and is an equal opportunity destroyer), a noxious cocktail, which continues to claim innocent lives to this day since the chemicals have never been properly cleaned up.

"A hand in things to come," is the company motto, and

their commitment to this philosophy was truly demonstrated immediately following the accident. U.C. executives sprang into action by sending *no* relief team, and refusing to reveal the exact chemicals released (claiming they were a "trade secret"), while the dead (termed by U.C. execs as "existence challenged") were still being counted. Like a noble leader, Union Carbide's chairman, Warren Anderson, gallantly promised his company would fairly compensate the victims of the disaster. Later, just like a world leader, he reversed himself entirely, stating that U.C. America bore no responsibility since the plant was owned and operated by Indians. He then bravely dropped out of sight, ducking the Indian government's charges of manslaughter and an international warrant for his arrest.

It wasn't until 2002 that those buttinski Greenpeaceniks, with their whole annoying stop-destroying-the-planet-I-live-on agenda (Man! What's their deal?), tracked down Warren. Apparently, the poor fellow had been enduring agonizing hardship and suffering soul-wrenching remorse poolside at his mansion in the luxurious Hamptons, driven, in his madness, to join a country club with a paltry nine-hole golf course. We like to think of him as the kind of guy who spends his time torturing puppies with car batteries and blaming it on his Dominican gardener.

The Indian Government also charged the corporation itself with manslaughter, but U.C. has never faced a jury, simply refusing to appear in court. Who knew the "I don't want to go" defense would actually work for grown-ups? Someone call Alan Dershowitz. Not only has no action ever been taken to extradite Anderson or compel Union Carbide to face the charges against them, but they're not even banned from ordering chicken vindaloo at their local Indian takeaway.

In 1989, despite Warren's amoral conscience, Union Carbide finally agreed to pay the people of Bhopal a whopping $470 million in compensation . . . which roughly works out to a nifty *three hundred dollars* per person. Today, about 50,000 of these "early retirees" are enjoying their newfound "fortune" living in tent slums in the shadow of the rotting carcass of the abandoned plant, which continues to keep insects at bay by cutting short the lifespan of every living thing in the area. ("Respect! Does this stuff work, or what?") What's more, soil and water samples recently taken show the contamination is continuing (cleanup, shmeanup, it's fine!), guaranteeing generations of new recruits for anti-American organizations everywhere.

In 2001, Union Carbide was purchased by the much more humane Dow Chemical, renowned for consumer-friendly products such as DDT, napalm, and the ever popular Agent Orange. While Dow has paid off various outstanding claims against U.C., it has refused to accept culpability for Bhopal, once again flagrantly defying the law (go big business!).

Interesting Tidbit: Shockingly, the Indian government, renowned the world over for its fair and incorruptible nature, has yet to pay out over $300 million in reparations promised to its own people for the horrors unleashed upon them. Of course, once divided among the affected families, this might cover a single lease payment on a Nissan Sentra.

Ways to Bring Up Bhopal in Conversation

☼ Kelly's as irresponsible as Union Carbide was at Bhopal.

☼ Don't you hate people who make empty promises like Union Carbide at Bhopal?

☼ Something's burning my eyes. I just hope it's onions and not that stuff that exploded over Bhopal.

☀ 7 ☀

The Art Conversation

Get ready for black outfits and people who are authorities on the history of espresso. Besides the handful of liberal arts majors who took art history in college and boorish art critics, few people are armed with hard art facts. Some educated people know to match Picasso with cubism and Dali with surrealists, but few can name a painting. ("You know, the flower one by what's-his-face who cut off his ear.") At an art party, bold fashion statements and eccentric behavior are hallmarks of genius, and even blatant rudeness will earn you some respect. Generally speaking, art party people are fascinated with symbolism and are capable of finding cultural, philosophical, or sexual meaning in a milk carton nailed to the wall. For the rest of the world, the arts seem like a cloudy realm where only the truly intellectual elite dare to tread. These days, new names in art are as fleeting as boy bands, so don't worry too much if you haven't heard of Christo until now. The trick in the art conversation is to insist that your favorite artist is the best. After all, art appreciation is subjective, so screw those idiots.

Michelangelo Had a Brush with God While Painting the Sistine Chapel

When Are We Talking About: 1508–1512

Why Are We Even Talking About This: The ceiling of the Sistine Chapel is considered by many to be the single greatest artistic work of all time.

What You Need to Know to Sound Smart: Johann Wolfgang von Goethe, the German writer-philosopher, once said, "Without having seen the Sistine Chapel, one can form no appreciable idea of what one man is capable of achieving." Anyone who has seen this marvel in Rome knows that truer words were never spoken. What makes the work all the more astounding is the nigh-unbelievable fact that it was reputedly completed by a single man, Michelangelo Buonarroti. In 1506, Michelangelo was called before Pope Julius II, where the Godfather of the Church made him an offer he couldn't refuse: to paint the ceiling of the holiest of sepulchers in Christendom, the Sistine Chapel.

Buonarroti had told friends and colleagues that he was no painter; sculpting was his true calling. He had already completed the amazing works the *Pietà* (1499) and *David* (1504—you know, the famous statue with the marble set of massive marbles), as well as numerous others, all of which possessed an uncanny realism that made one expect them to just open their alabaster eyes and say, "Are you gonna do something about these pigeons, or what?" Michelangelo had no desire to stop his current work on the pope's tomb, figuring the faster he finished, the faster the creepy old bugger might croak. But since this was the guy writing the checks, he really didn't have a whole lot of choice. Keep in mind that the measurements for the "canvas" were 131 feet long by 43 feet wide.

Although notoriously arrogant (ain't braggin' if it's true), this classical artist knew this was a Herculean project. So he decided to get a little advice from his peers, meeting with a passel of painters for suggestions on the best way to proceed, especially since he was to complete the work in *fresco* ("fresh" in Italian), painting in moist plaster, and was a little clueless about how it all was supposed to work (sort of like that guy Brownie, who they had "running" FEMA).

After hiring several assistants to mix paints and schlep crap into the chapel from the trunk of his car, in July 1508, the work began . . . along with a lot of neck craning. Famed architect Donato Bramante suggested hanging scaffolding from the ceiling, leaving a series of large holes where Mike and his mechanics would be painting. The painter quickly rejected the lame-o idea, choosing to bolt his scaffolding into the walls, but was kind enough to mount it above the Peruginos and Botticellis painted there so as not to disfigure these lesser works. (Just kidding, their stuff is great, too . . . but seriously, when was the last time you heard, "The ceiling was nice, but did you see the *walls*?") There's a common misconception that Michelangelo painted on his back, but the truth is, he used a scaffold that was curved like the ceiling, though he often had to paint over his head, which pissed him off like crazy and made him think about quitting and maybe becoming a dentist or something. Buonarroti hired a mess of pretty, young boys as his models, even for the female figures, because the boys were cheaper . . . and for *some* reason, women just didn't *inspire* him.

Things sort of got off to a slow start since his first fresco cocktails left the plaster too moist, which caused his work to mold and fall apart . . . and you just *know* someone got reamed for that one, and not in the good way, though Michelangelo was renowned for often sleeping with his models. However, he was even more infamous for firing his assistants, constantly rotating fresh meat into the roster, so that even those who'd helped with the painting (usually just sky or background figures) could never take any real credit. The one exception was his chief assistant Jacopo l'Indaco, who had the special honor of applying the plaster to the workspace every morning. ("Oh, big honor. Thanks soooo much. And please, let me know when your butt needs scratching.")

Having figured out his plaster plan, Buonarroti painted the fake architecture that separated the ceiling into its different sections and then really began to "figure" things out. Every day after the plaster was applied, the cartoon (the thin canvas that held the rough drawing of the figures) was laid over the top, and the shape of the image was transferred to the wall by poking tiny holes through it into the moist plaster (think Lite-Brite unplugged). There were supposed to be only twelve figures in the entire painting, but, you know, for Michelangelo, the more half-naked men around the better, and so he wound up painting around three hundred instead. The ceiling is roughly divided into four sections. In the middle are the nine central Bible stories, running from Creation to the Flood. The corner pieces, called the pendentives, display the eventual miraculous salvation of Israel, while the series of little triangles that frame the work are known as the webs and possibly show relatives of Christ (but no one's really sure, because that guy kept saying *everyone* was his brother), and finally the Old Testament prophets are strung along the outside. Some of the most legendary images are *The Creation of Adam* (where it kind of looks like God is telling Adam to "pull My finger") and *The Separation of the Light from the Darkness*.

Buonarroti's sculpting experience served the artist, enabling him to paint all the ceiling characters in perfect perspective, unaltered by the curved surface of the ceiling 60 feet from the ground. All things considered, it's a bit of a divine miracle that one man (well, sort of one man) was able to finish over 5,000 *square feet* of fresco in only four years. Pope Julius II (also known as *Il papa terribile*) thankfully didn't micro-Michelangelo-manage, being more preoccupied with political machinations and warfare in the name of God. He apparently never *quite* got on board with the Apostle Paul's "our struggle is not against flesh and blood" thing, since his conflicts tore up plenty of the former, resulting in mucho spilling of the latter.

The ceiling was unveiled on October 31, 1512, at the big Halloween Party, where the pope dressed up pretending to be God . . . at least everyone *hoped* he was pretending.

Interesting Tidbit: Between 1535 and 1541, Michelangelo worked on the area behind the altar in the Sistine Chapel, painting *The Last Judgment*. There was a huge scandal when it was revealed because many of the figures sentenced to hell had exposed genitalia. A movement known as the Fig-Leaf Campaign sought to have them covered, to which the pope replied that he had no jurisdiction in hell so could change nothing. They were eventually painted over by Daniele da Volterra, who has gone down in the books as "the breeches painter."

Ways to Bring Up Michelangelo and the Sistine Chapel in Conversation

☀ You did a great job painting your apartment. Michelangelo would be jealous.

☀ Karen goes through more assistants than Michelangelo at the Sistine Chapel.

☀ Look, just tell me the story without doing the entire ceiling of the Sistine Chapel.

For Toulouse-Lautrec, Life Was a Cabaret

When Are We Talking About: 1864–1901

Why Are We Even Talking About This: This French artist is renowned for his paintings and lithographs of the Monmarte district of Paris, which was the center of Parisian bohemian life.

What You Need to Know to Sound Smart: Henri Marie Raymond de Toulouse-Lautrec-Montfa (who must have cursed his parents every time he was forced to sign a stack of mortgage papers) was born November 24, 1864, in Albi, France, the last child of an aristocratic family dating back over a thousand years. His parents divorced when H.M.R.T.L.M. was only four, shortly after the death of his younger brother. In 1872, the little guy and his *mére* moved to Paris, where Lautrec received his first painting lesson from a deaf mute who was a friend of his father's. At least he thought the guy was a friend of his father's, but since Toulouse didn't understand sign language, he may have actually been a Jehovah's Witness named Kathy. Toulouse was a petite and rather sickly boy (which historically speaking appears to be *the* prerequisite for genius), and his mother had to call Phil Rizzuto at the Money Store to finance the small fortune she spent on treatments to help him grow (obviously missing the whole "Got milk?" campaign), but still came up a little short.

During his early teens Henri Tou-lost his hope for a normal life after breaking both his legs, in separate incidents, which the Hoboken Waste Disposal Historical Society speculates concerned an unpaid debt and a guy named Guido. Though the bones would eventually heal, they failed to mature with the rest of Henri's body. Possessing a normal torso, Lautrec's legs were "carnival length" in a time when being handicapped meant public derision and humiliation, not convenient parking. In the first half of 1880 Toulouse hid out at his uncle's nice pad in Nice (which was nice). It was this uncle who persuaded the lad to pursue painting and drawing. In the following year, Henri announced to his mother that his only happiness in life would be in becoming a professional painter and argued his case by pointing out example after example of what a stable, financially sound, trouble-free life most painters enjoyed throughout history.

In 1882, Henri made his return Le-trek to Paris where he studied drawing with Leon Bonnat, an artist of some note at the time, whose constructive criticisms encouraged his student with words like, "revolting," "hopeless" and "crap burger," which we assure you sounds much better in French. Undiscouraged, Toulouse began studies at the famed studio of Ferdon Cormon, where he met future legends Emile Bernard and Vincent van Gogh. Sadly it wasn't the studio of *Roger* Corman, where he would have met future has-beens David Carradine and Richard Grieco. Henri first got to use the only part of his lower body that *would* grow with Marie Charlet, a seventeen-year-old "model" (the term used here is the less commonly employed definition of "a female paid to have sex with lonely men"), who certainly earned her money that day.

In 1884, Lautrec moved to the Montmartre section of Paris, which was the center of the new bohemian artistic lifestyle, one filled with dancing, drinking, the pursuit of love, drinking, art, drinking, and vomiting, followed by more drinking. Finally feeling at home amid this society of wackos, he became chummy with his neighbor Edgar Degas and asked him, "Dude, what's the deal with all the pictures of little girls in tutus?" Shortly after his arrival, Lautrec was disappointed to find the bohemian "live and let live" mantra apparently didn't exclude midget mocking. To calm his sorrowful soul, lil' man drowned himself in his art as well as absinthe, a wormwood cocktail that was the Red Bull of its day.

In 1886, Henri met Suzanne Valadon, whom he painted and who would become his lover until she came to her senses and attempted suicide two years later, which must have done wonders for his pocket-sized ego. Fortunately, his career was picking up the slack from his personal life as Henri's work began gathering attention at art shows all over Europe, including Paris, where he shared a wall with Van Gogh.

On October 5, 1889, the Moulin Rouge, what would someday become the most famous nightclub in all of France, opened its doors for business. Over the next twelve years, Lautrec would seldom leave the club while the sun was down. The Moulin Rouge, and more specifically, the women who danced there, became some of Henri's favorite subjects. One of his most famous paintings, *Moulin Rouge—La Goulue*, depicts the originator of the French Can-Can (or in the case of Henri, the "Can't-Can't"), Louise Weber, with his friend Jacques Renaudin, who unlike Lautrec, never had people accidentally set drinks on his head while they were talking to him. Locals refer to Toulouse as "The Soul of Montmartre" for his skill at capturing its "joie de vivre" as well as its "joie de syphilis" since many experts believed he suffered from the disease toward the end of his life.

By then, Lautrec was making bank on his work, almost enough to cover Pint-Diddy's costs for booze and broads. However, even French hookers have to draw the line somewhere, and in February 1899, suddenly Tou-losing his mind, Lautrec crossed it. After pitching a fit inside a brothel, Henri got tossed into the sanitarium. Dropping from public view in August 1901, while visiting Taussat, France, Henri had a stroke that paralyzed one side of his body. His mom took him back home, which had to look bad in front of the guys. Lautrec's routine had finally gotten the best of him and his short (c'mon, we had to get one more in) life ended on September 9, 1901, at the age of thirty-six, in his ancestral home in Malrome.

Interesting Tidbit: Henri's father, the wealthy Count Alphonse, was quite eccentric, and today might be referred to as a "moron." He spent much of his time hunting while wearing idiotic costumes and was such a bother at Lautrec's deathbed that some of his final words were, "Old fool."

Ways to Bring Up Toulouse-Lautrec in Conversation

☀ Allen's short but he's not Toulouse-Lautrec short or anything.

☀ Are you kidding? Toulouse-Lautrec had better luck with girls than I do.

☀ That guy's more hammered than Toulouse-Lautrec at the Moulin Rouge.

What a Woman Wants . . . to Wear: According to Coco Chanel

When Are We Talking About: 1883–1971

Why Are We Even Talking About This: The most influential fashion designer of the twentieth century, Coco Chanel transformed women's fashion from restriction and confinement to comfortable elegance. Her creations include women's trousers, the pullover sweater, the cardigan suit, the blazer, the little black dress, costume jewelry, and much more.

What You Need to Know to Sound Smart: Though she claimed to have been born August 19, 1893, like many women, Gabrielle Bonheur Chanel lied about her age, having actually arrived ten years earlier in a poorhouse in Saumur, France. Chanel's mother died when she was only six, and not long after, Papa said "au revoir" and left her and four siblings in the care of two aunts. While working as a cafe singer from 1905 to 1908, Chanel adopted the name Coco, meaning "little pet," derived from the song "Qui qu'a vu Coco," a standard of hers. She met a millionaire cavalry officer who brought her to Paris, giving the sixteen-year-old (French for eighteen) her first taste of the finer things in life.

Backed by her wealthy admirers, such as her lover, textile heir Etienne Balsan, Chanel opened a shop in Paris in 1910 where she offered her new "simple hats," simplicity, in her words, being the key to elegance. Sales started slow, but within three years Chanel's designs became a smash among society women. While living out of the swanky Hotel Ritz, Chanel opened her fashion house in Biarritz in 1915 and expanded into every facet of the design world. Within five years she was a leader in French couture, while also taking a break during the Great War to help apply stylish bandages as a nurse for the Frenchies in the trenchies.

By the 1920s, Chanel, who almost never sketched her outfits before their creation, was setting trends by introducing men's style into women's wear, as opposed to the organ-crushing corset vogue of the previous century. Unlike her many male competitors who suffered from pattern envy, Chanel enjoyed having her styles "knocked off" and once said, "A fashion that does not reach the streets is not a fashion." Though wooed by the most powerful men in the world, Chanel remained her own woman, reminding her suitors (among them were European royalty, politicians, and sports figures) that "There are a lot of duchesses, but only one Coco Chanel."

In 1922, Chanel introduced her signature perfume, Chanel No. 5, and when asked by a young woman, "Where should one use perfume?" Coco replied, "Wherever one wants to be kissed." During the Nazi occupation of France, Chanel's affair with a German officer was ill received by even the "Adolfanatics" of WWII Paris, resulting in an impromptu "vacation" to Switzerland (Germany Minor) and an early "retirement." By 1954, however, Chanel was back on the scene and once again taking the fashion world by storm.

After years of overwork, her grueling schedule finally caught up with her and Chanel died in Paris on January 10, 1971 (making her somewhere between seventy-six and eighty-six), from natural causes. Her fashion empire, known as the House of Chanel, is now fronted by Karl Lagerfeld and continues to bring in over $160 million a year.

Interesting Tidbit: In 1969, Katharine Hepburn starred in a musical based on Chanel's life entitled *Coco.* Needless to say, it was not nearly as interesting or successful as the woman herself.

Ways to Bring Up Coco Chanel in Conversation

❂ That girl's got more designs than Chanel.

❂ She's a real original. Coco Chanel would be put to shame!

❂ She's very Chanel about her boyfriends—it's all about their bankbooks.

Georgia O'Keeffe Had Great Bone Structure

When Are We Talking About: 1887–1986

Why Are We Even Talking About This: O'Keeffe's abstract desert wildlife paintings of the American West are some of the most recognizable images in art history.

What You Need to Know to Sound Smart: The woman who was once quoted as saying, "I hate flowers. I paint them because they're cheaper than models and they don't move," saw her first sunset on November 15, 1887, in Sun Prairie, which sounds like it might be a lovely place, were it not located in Wisconsin. Her parents, Francis Calyxtus and Ida Totto, having both suffered through life with unfortunate names, decided to give one to their daughter. While living with milk and milk by-products, since Wisconsin state law required all citizens to be dairy farmers, Georgia learned to draw thanks to a local schoolteacher staying in her family's home, and was shown the wonder of watercolors by a local artist who resided nearby. ("Now, let's get our green and make some happy trees, because this cloud needs a friend.") After icy winters claimed the lives of three of her uncles in 1902, the family moved to Virginia (quite possibly at the request of the fourth uncle) where O'Keeffe's art flourished at Chatham Episcopal Institute in 1905 and where she was voted "Most Likely to Paint Flowers and Bull Skulls in the Desert."

Missing the thrills and chills of frostbitten winters, Georgia furthered her education at the Art Institute in Chicago, but after only one year, found herself majoring in a major case of typhoid and dropped out. After the painter survived this brush with death, she continued her studies at New York's Art Students League in 1907, where O'Keeffe dyed her hair blue, pierced her nipples, and experimented with being a lesbian. Well, not really, but that seems to be what happens to most girls who go to college in New York. O'Keeffe studied under famed painter William Meritt Chase, who taught her the techniques of the European masters. While developing her style, Georgia posed nude for artists, including painter Eugene Speicher, who told Georgia she'd never amount to anything more than a teacher at a girls school, which sounds awfully critical for someone named *Eugene* to say to any woman nice enough to be naked for him. The following year O'Keeffe decided not to return to New York, seeking commercial work in Chicago to help support her father and his failing business ventures, but in 1912, the measles forced her back to Virginia. Over the next few years Georgia took a variety of teaching jobs (probably pleasing Eugene to no end), while continuing to draw and paint.

Early in 1916, a friend of O'Keeffe's showed her drawings to famed photographer Alfred Stieglitz (who, despite being from New Jersey, was the driving force behind photography's recognition as a fine art), who owned the 291 Gallery, a place as famous as the artist himself. Trust us, in the art world it's like Studio 54. Stieglitz loved O'Keeffe's works and, unbeknownst to her, hung them in his studio. Georgia in the meantime accepted a teaching position at the West Texas State Normal College, having turned down an opportunity at West Texas State Criminally Insane College. During this time O'Keeffe made many trips into the local desert canyons to eat hallucinogenic mushrooms and talk to the ghosts of Indians. Sorry, that was Jim Morrison . . . um, let's see here . . . Oh, right! Georgia hiked around and painted about fifty watercolors. In April 1917, the young painter gained notoriety at her first official showing at Stieglitz's gallery but was struck down by an influenza epidemic. (Hey, crazy lady with no immune system, we got one word for you . . . inoculation.)

In the spring, Stieglitz encouraged O'Keeffe to return to New York, probably by sending her a surgical mask and oxygen tank, to pursue her career as well as a relationship with him. Stieglitz, fifty-four, left his wife and shacked up with O'Keeffe, finally ruining things by proposing in December 1924. Stieglitz took several nudes of O'Keefe, causing quite a stir by hanging pictures of the exhibitionist at his exhibition, while also selling her gargantuan flower abstracts for as much as $25,000. Not bad for 1928 . . . or now, for that matter, considering most painters work at Arby's to pay the rent.

O'Keeffe painted the cityscape from her penthouse apartment but felt her creative potential was limited there, and so she boarded a train for Taos, New Mexico, in May 1929, in search of inspiration. Georgia scoured the state for suitable subjects, even buying a Model A Ford and ripping out the backseat so she could drive to isolated areas to work. On her paint-about she met the famed writer D. H. Lawrence and stayed several weeks at his ranch, where we can only assume filthy things occurred. The New Mexican desert that Georgia referred to as "the faraway" became her true home, although she'd return to New York to see Stieglitz, and to get a decent slice of pizza, every winter until his death in 1946.

Now permanently at her place near Abiquiu, Ghost Ranch, O'Keeffe became obsessed with all aspects of desert life . . . and death. Her modernist abstract style blended the beauty of flowers and sunsets with the eeriness of bleached desert bones as seen in her *Cow Skull with Red* (1936), inspiring many designs for MegaDeth concert tees. Interestingly, Georgia didn't like signing her own works or naming them, usually painting a simple OK in a circle on the back. Despite her fame and growing notoriety—her *Sunset on Long Island* was chosen to represent New York at the 1939 World's Fair—O'Keeffe preferred solitude. In 1962, Georgia was nominated to join the American Academy of Arts and Letters, the most esteemed artist group in the country. By age eighty-four, she had begun to go blind but continued painting and doing other colorful activities with her very "handyman" Juan Hamilton. In 1977, President Gerald Ford awarded O'Keeffe with the Medal of Freedom (which is kind of weird, because she didn't free anybody), and she was given the National Medal of Arts by President Ronald Reagan almost ten years after that.

O'Keeffe died on March 6, 1986, at the age of ninety-nine, while staying at Hamilton's home in Santa Fe. Ten years after her passing the Georgia O'Keeffe Museum opened in New Mexico, on March 17, 1997. Today O'Keeffe is commonly acknowledged as the greatest female American painter of the century.

Interesting Tidbit: O'Keeffe left the vast majority of her estate to her lover Hamilton, sparking a fierce legal battle over her new will with museums and other groups mentioned in the original will. Hamilton, who acted as the first curator of her museum, amicably gave back a portion of his rightful inheritance. ("Yo, I had to sleep with her until she was like eighty! You think women in their *forties* want sex . . .")

Ways to Bring Up Georgia O'Keeffe in Conversation

☀ She's as pale and bony as a Georgia O'Keeffe painting.

☀ I'm from the Georgia O'Keeffe school of dating: younger men who wait on me hand and foot.

☀ I'm like Georgia O'Keeffe: I need space and time to be alone and create.

Christo and Jeanne-Claude Are More Than Just Wrap Stars

When Are We Talking About: 1935–

Why Are We Even Talking About This: Known by many as "those wrapping artists," a label they vehemently oppose, this husband and wife team has created many environmental art projects that are among the most expensive and expansive of this century.

What You Need to Know to Sound Smart: The artists formerly known as Christo Javacheff and Jeanne-Claude Denat de Guillebon were creepily born on the same day, June 13, 1935 (interestingly, the same day Steve-O from *Jackass* was born in 1974). Christo was unwrapped in Gabrova, Bulgaria, while Jeanne-Claude was born in French-controlled Casablanca, Morocco. Christo began his formal artistic instruction at the Fine Arts Academy in Sofia, Bulgaria, in 1953, and after tiring of painting for the Red Guard, joined the avant-garde at the Viennese Academy of Fine Arts in Austria four years later. Christo moved to Paris where, like every artist in the world, he eked out a meager existence painting portraits and subsisting on mac and fromage. Loveless in the City of Love, Christo struggled with bouts of loneliness. Hey, here's a crazy idea, how about you learn the language? Maybe then someone will talk to you. True to artist form, Christo channeled his pain into his work while visiting the city's many museums and galleries, seeing whatever he could of his favorite artist, Jean Dubuffet, who wasn't a French restaurant with all-you-can-eat crêpes, but a famous experimental painter and sculptor.

Realizing some of these guys passing themselves off as experimental "artists" were really just crap, Christo decided to try his hand at it. In his first foray, he wrapped an empty can in fabric and painted it, creating something a kindergartner might patch together so he could finish up and be first in line for kickball. Mental health professionals consider compulsive wrapping a sign of psychological instability, and it seems Christo's critics agreed since his art sold poorly.

Meanwhile across le monde, Jeanne-Claude premiered into a military family whose parents divorced shortly after her birth. Like Christo, Jeanne-Claude had her own instabilities and pain to deal with (besides being cursed with a man's name), having been "raised" by her mother, Precilda, who, when not busy divorcing four husbands, was off fighting with La Résistance during World War II. Leaving her daughter in the hands of an ex-husband's family, Precilda was stunned after the war to find Jeanne-Claude had been neglected and was in serious need of both mental and physical care. ("How dare you not take care of the little girl I abandoned!") In 1946, Jeanne-Claude's mother married a wealthy and influential French general, and the whole gang moved to Paris, where she at last got some decent TLC (tender loving and croissants). Jeanne-Claude excelled in school as well as social circles but lacked direction in her life. Her top three career goals being PR, pharmaceutical sales, or wrap crap around other crap . . . until one fateful day in 1958.

It was October. Christo had been hired for a portrait of Precilda, and though Jeanne-Claude was initially unimpressed by the vulgar Bulgar, she was soon taking art lessons from him, while she taught him French in return. Just when it looked like love was in the air, Christo blew it by dating Jeanne-Claude's stepsister Joyce. The Claude didn't help things much by marrying some cheesy French guy. But, shortly after the honeymoon, she left her husband, and shacked up with Sis's not-so-beau beau.

While Christo was covering household items in cloth and calling it art, the couple kept their relationship tightly under wraps, with Jeanne-Claude pretending she was bulking up for football season. However, on May 11, 1960, things became slightly difficult to hide when their baby, Cyril, was born. Jeanne-Claude's parents, ashamed, cut the creative kids off from all financial support—because her mom had been such a model young wife herself—forcing them to live like artists, which was pretty much . . . fine.

Christo's wraps finally began getting notice from the Parisian art community, and in 1961, he started work on his first large-scale project entitled *Wrapped Packages at Cologne Harbor*, which pretty much looked exactly how you're imagining it right now. The following year, his piece *The Iron Curtain* blocked off a street in Paris by stacking barrels across it to re-create the experience Berliners had of having their city cut in half. People in cars trying to get to work pointed out that this was the primary reason they didn't live in Berlin, but the work was allowed to stay in place for several hours before being dismantled (a word Jeanne-Claude hates, which is why, as a provocative artistic statement, we are using it here).

In February 1964, the couple illegally entered the United States. Give us your poor, your needy, your experimental wrapping artists. Because they had no money and no avenues to earn an income, they chose to reside in New York City, oh so famous for its reasonable cost of living. They rented a commercial studio, flagrantly violating housing ordinances (it's shocking we know, but even illegal immigrants break the law once in a while), and decorated the place to look like a children's photography studio to help explain the constant presence of their child. They managed to escape detection long enough to complete their first American works, a series of fake storefronts that Christo wrapped and sold to rich people, since most poor people use their wall space for normal things like a couch or bookshelf.

Over the next decade, the couple, who pretentiously dropped their last names, ran around the world raising money for their projects and wrapping everything from old buildings (*Wrapped Fountain and Wrapped Medieval Tower*, in Spoleto, Italy, 1968) to newer buildings (*Wrapped Museum of Contemporary Art*, in Chicago, 1969), to statues (*Wrapped Monument to Leonardo da Vinci*, 1970, Milan, Italy) to entire beachfronts (*Wrapped Coastline, Little Bay*, 1969, Sydney, Australia) . . . but DON'T YOU DARE call them "those wrapping artists." These projects consumed an unbelievable amount of material, money, and labor requiring long hours to make sure each was finished precisely to their specifications.

In 1972, the gifted wrappers shifted to bows by creating *Valley Curtain* in Rifle, Colorado, stringing 142,000 square feet of nylon material across a gorge for absolutely no apparent reason. True to artist form, the artists rarely explain their projects, leaving the interpretation up to the viewer. ("Looks like a bunch of cloth to me.") They believe the temporary nature of their works adds to their beauty and reinforces the brevity of our own lives, and isn't that something we all just love being reminded of? In 1976, the wonder-twins premiered *Running Fence*, an 18-foot-high, 24½-mile-long length of nylon fabric supported by a series of steel posts that ran through Sonoma and Marin counties in California for the enjoyment of the disgustingly wealthy residents of the area. But hey, in all fairness, three years earlier the poor folk in South Central LA got to enjoy their own highly interactive experimental art piece called the Watts Riots.

In May 1983, the artists unfurled *Surrounded Islands* in Biscayne Bay, off the coast of Miami. The ambitious work involved surrounding (if you use the word "wrapped" Jeanne-Claude will go postal on you) eleven small islands with a pink polypropylene material, making it look as if the land masses had been vandalized by a group of gay teenagers. The islands were "non-wrapped" with the material for two weeks before it was taken down. Christo-Claude were also nice enough to pay for the removal of forty-two tons of garbage from the area before beginning with their work, but since they claim to leave their areas just as they found them, they were probably furious when the garbage was never returned. ("I want that damn garbage put back!")

In 1986, Jeanne-Claude dyed her hair fire-engine red, and so it remains, giving the impression her scalp has been replaced with a science-fair volcano under a constant state of eruption.

In September 1991, the artists formerly known as people with last names unveiled *The Umbrellas,* a project which occurred simultaneously in California and Japan: 1,340 gigantic blue umbrellas, symbolizing shelter and probably something phallic, were opened in Ibaraki, Japan, while 1,760 equal-sized yellow umbrellas were opened in Tejon Ranch, California, where they stood for eighteen days, while chances are, in London, 350,000 umbrellas were simultaneously opened . . . because it was raining. In June 1995, you-know-who unveiled their strangest, and possibly most symbolic project (of what, they'll never tell) yet, *Wrapped*

Reichstag, covering the most famous building in Berlin in a silvery fireproof fabric, which was obviously unavailable when it was burned by the Nazis in 1933.

Their most recent, and perhaps grandest, adventure took place in New York, where in February 2005, they erected 7,503 small structures draped with orange fabric, called *The Gates*, that ran throughout Central Park. The flowing nylon sheets hung for sixteen days, transforming the park into a playground of breathtaking color that gave muggers hundreds of hiding places from which to pounce upon enthralled upward-glancing tourists. Today, the husband and wife team continue their work in Arkansas on a piece entitled *Over the River* and look forward to a future project *And Through the Woods* while wrangling the Big Bad Wolf for the sequel, *To Grandmother's House We Go*.

Interesting Tidbit: During the assembly and viewing of *The Umbrellas*, two people were actually killed. A workman in Japan was electrocuted while installing an umbrella in a river that was a little too close to a low-hanging power line and a woman was hit in the head when an umbrella in California fell over during a freak (but not nearly as freaky as the artists themselves) windstorm.

Ways to Bring Up Christo and Jeanne-Claude in Conversation

❀ My mom just loves wrapping presents. She thinks she's Christo and Jeanne-Claude.

❀ Do I like rap? You mean the music or the Christo and Jeanne-Claude kind?

❀ Nice hair. Do you use the same stylist as Jeanne-Claude?

☼ **8** ☼

The Crime and Punishment Conversation

*I*f season after season of uncountable cop and procedural law shows haven't convinced you of how many people are fascinated with crime and punishment, then perhaps twenty-four hours of Court TV and the fact that *COPS* is *still* in syndication finally will. Humankind is obsessed with how people commit crimes, why some get away with it, and what happens to those who don't. In our world, there's always someone on trial for something, somewhere, which means there's always a way for you to get into a crime and punishment conversation. What's great about this conversation is that everyone has ideas about justice and how it should be served. If you're going to a party full of lawyers (and these days it's hard to find a party without at least one in attendance), cops, or criminals (even gangsters admire smart people), this conversation is also going to be a big hit. Whether you're pro–death penalty, anti–three strikes rule, or still wondering why "the man" is bogarting your hemp stash (strictly for medicinal use, of course), this conversation will always attract a bevy of armchair barristers, ready to cross-examine your facts.

Since there is soooooo much case law, even the legally savvy can't possibly know everything, and equipped with the info below, you'll be able to kick any challengers right in their rebuttal. If you're in a room full of lawyers (suit and tie for evening gatherings, golf-wear for Sunday barbecues), it will be admittedly more difficult to prove the case of your smartness, and if you find this jury of your peers is beginning to find in favor of the defendant, you may want to prosecute a different line of questioning. By the way, be careful of that creepy guy from your office who eats lunch by himself and knows a little *too* much about serial killers.

Who Put the S in S&M? The Freak-Master Marquis de Sade

When Are We Talking About: 1740–1814

Why Are We Even Talking About This: Marquis de Sade was the French author and infamous womanizer whose deviant sexual exploits and perverse writings gave birth to the term "sadist."

What You Need to Know to Sound Smart: Donatien-Alphonse-François de Sade got his first taste of discipline when he was lovingly slapped into consciousness on June 2, 1740, in the Conde Palace in (where else?) Paris. He was the son of Count Jean Baptiste de Sade and his wife, Marie-Elonore, petty nobles in prerevolution Paris (a time when sexual experimentation made the 1960s free-love movement look like a Moral Majority mixer). Young de Sade was left with his mother, while Father was away on "royal business" (drinking and whoring). After beating his cousin, a young prince four years his senior, unconscious over a toy (and perhaps *with* the toy), de Sade was sent to live with his grandmother and a throng of creepy doting aunts, most of whom were nuns, which sounds like the making of a great sitcom.

Fearing his son would end up a girly-man, de Sade's father shipped him off to stay with his Uncle Abbe, a clergyman (seemed like a good idea), renowned for bedding anything with two legs and a pulse (or not), where he spent lazy Sundays paging through the lecherous liturgist's vast collection of erotic literature. Before de Sade could go blind, Dad moved him again, this time to a Jesuit prep school (talk about mixed messages!), where he learned firsthand the fine art of punitive whipping, a practice he would come to know, and love, and yes, master.

By fifteen, de Sade, who was odd as a codpiece, was a cavalryman, fighting in the Seven Years' War (Britain and Prussia vs. pretty much the rest of the European continent), earning a reputation as a skilled and heroic soldier and someone you wouldn't want dating your sister. At war's end, de Sade's father married him off to a wealthy noble family, though his curious boy had previously contracted gonorrhea from poking his head where it didn't belong. Trading martial trysts for marital bliss, de Sade spent most of his young manhood kissing up to his mother-in-law, Madame de Montreuil, who adored him and was oddly referred to as "Presidente." That is, until Donny went darko and was arrested for whipping a prostitute, a crime Presidente elected to keep hidden from her daughter.

In 1767, de Sade became de daddy, but not even the pleasure of fatherhood could keep him from his pursuit of pain. Less than a year later, he was arrested again for raping a local widow. However, like an Enron exec, he only served four months in jail, thanks to his high-level connections. In the summer of 1772, de Sade, believing you have to be cruel to be kind, finally went too far, sodomizing a group of prostitutes, and was forced to flee the country. Escaping bondage, the masochistic Marquis toured Europe like a rock star (he did like leather pants . . . and masks) until 1774, when he sneaked back home with the help of his wife (aka the doormat) . . . where he raped and tortured six young girls under his employ over a period of as many weeks.

Over the ensuing few years, de Sade was in and out of prison, doggedly pursued by Presidente, who wished to bury the embarrassment he'd become. In 1777, he was tossed into the dungeons of Vincennes in Paris. In 1784, the leash liege decided that he'd had enough punishment and escaped confinement, but authorities disagreed and chucked him into the Bastille. That is, until he incited a riot in July of 1789, by screaming to passersby that the inmates inside were being killed. Transferred now to the luxurious asylum for the criminally insane at Charenton, de Sade just missed the liberation of the Bastille on July 14, which marked the beginning of the French Revolution, by a week or so. Abandoned by his wife when he got out of the asylum, de Sade found work with the Libertine government but was appalled by the brutality of the Reign of Terror—where the French people butchered anyone remotely linked to the aristocracy. ("How can you kill people when you should be sodomizing and beating them!")

During his umpteen years of incarceration, de Sade wrote several heartwarming works detailing his myriad sadomasochistic sexual fetishes. Among them are *The Story of Juliette* (1797), *Philosophy in the Boudoir* (1795), and *Crimes of Love* (1800), immorality tales that so impressed Napoleon that he ordered the naughty novelist imprisoned again. Back at Charenton, de Sade passed his time putting on plays with his fellow inmates (though they never did *One Flew Over the Cuckoo's Nest*) and molesting a twelve-year-old girl. Grossly overweight, the Marquis de Sodomy died on December 2, 1814.

De Sade's final request was to be buried in an unmarked grave so that "all traces of my tomb may disappear from the face of the earth, just as I hope all traces of my memory will be erased from the memories of men." His eldest son helped fulfill this wish by torching his father's newest manuscripts. He also had phrenologists (guys who feel the funny bumps on your head to tell your future) examine his father's skull in the hope of finding an answer to what had gone so horribly wrong. In 1904, de Sade's magnum opus, *120 Days of Sodom*, which somehow escaped the purge of his progeny, was found and published posthumously for legions of lascivious literati to enjoy.

Interesting Tidbit: The philosopher Voltaire was a close family friend who not only encouraged the deviant behavior of de Sade's various members but also wrote poetry about it.

Ways to Bring Up Marquis De Sade in Conversation

- ☼ That's so sick, even the Marquis de Sade would be turned off.
- ☼ I think Helen likes the Marquis de Sade type, rich ones who always end up hurting her.
- ☼ Oww! Hey, Marquis de Sade, it's called a kiss, not a lip lunch.

Watching the Detectives by Allan and the Pinkertons

When Are We Talking About: 1819–1884

Why Are We Even Talking About This: This Scottish immigrant formed the first professional detective agency and established the foundation of modern crime investigation.

What You Need to Know to Sound Smart: The son of a

policeman, Allan Pinkerton was born in Glasgow, Scotland, August 25, 1819. Pinkerton grew up protesting the ugliness of English law (and perhaps their oral hygiene), and by adult-hood, with a crown of red hair to match his fiery temper, had become a notorious revolutionary. At age twenty-two, Pinker-ton wed and a day later surprised his young bride with an im-promptu honeymoon "getaway" to America to avoid arrest for insurrection. Arriving in Detroit (which suddenly made prison look like a viable option), the couple beelined for Chicago, where Pinkerton dove headlong into the danger-filled world of barrel making. The rush of assembling wooden slats into barrels at last grew cold when Pinkerton, too cheap to pay for his own lumber, decided to chop down local trees and in the process stumbled upon a campsite of counterfeit-ers, and subsequently assisted the police in their arrest.

Deducing this to be his true calling, Pinkerton followed in his father's kilt-steps, traded in his bagpipes for a badge, and by 1850, had become the first and only detective in Chicago, a city of 30,000. Two years later, Pinkerton said good-bye to the fellas on the force (all twelve of them) to form his own private agency. Unlike the U.S. Congress, Pinkerton elected to work with only respectable professionals, forbidding his detectives from smoking, drinking, gambling, or collecting rewards, set-ting them apart from the "We don't need no stinking badges" bounty hunters of the day. Pinkerton's advertisements de-picted an eye-framed by the slogan, "We Never Sleep," eventu-ally leading to the modern-day term "private eye" (and unfortunately the series *Baywatch Nights* starring David Has-selhoff).

In 1861, while President Lincoln was en route to his in-auguration, Pinkerton, a close friend and security adviser to Honest Abe, unearthed an assassination plot in Baltimore, and the Scot-cop sneaked the president-elect out of Harris-burg, Pennsylvania, saving him from certain death and the horrors of an Orioles home game. When Civil War broke out in 1861, Pinkerton focused his magnifying glass on the world of espionage, organizing the first Secret Service, sending his spies (including Kate Warne, the first female detective in American history) deep into Confederate territory to collect military secrets and spicy gumbo recipes. Tragically, due to political infighting, Pinkerton was relieved of duty before the end of the war and replaced with crack security specialists whose most notable accomplishment was their stunning performance at Ford's Theater.

Pinkerton returned to Chicago where he expanded his business and honed his crook-catching techniques, creating the mugshot and the first criminal database. In the late 1860s Pinkerton sent his agents West to arrest a rash of train robberies, and it was on the frontier that these "Pinks" gained a reputation as the most feared lawmen in the nation (despite the girly nickname), apprehending outlaws such as Jesse James and Butch Cassidy and the Sundance Kid.

Though Pinkerton died of an infection in Chicago on July 1, 1884, his legacy continued to influence law enforcement, and when the FBI was formed in 1908, the Pinkerton National Detective Agency was used as the template.

Interesting Tidbit: Just shy of his sixty-fifth birthday, Pinkerton slipped on the street and bit his tongue. Too busy with work, he neglected to properly care for the wound, and the simple cut eventually became gangrenous, leading to his death.

Ways to Bring Up Allan Pinkerton in Conversation

❋ Jordan notices *everything*. He's a regular Allan Pinkerton.

❋ I feel like she's always snooping around, like she's working for the Pinkertons.

❋ Debbie shoulda worked for the Pinkertons, since she always gets her man.

John Wayne Gacy Was No One to Clown Around With

When Are We Talking About: 1942–1994

Why Are We Even Talking About This: Known as the "clown killer," this serial murderer lured young boys back to his suburban home where they were raped, executed, and buried beneath the floorboards.

What You Need to Know to Sound Smart: John Wayne Gacy Jr. was born March 17, 1942, in Chicago, Illinois, and guess what? His dad was a violent alcoholic! I know, we're as surprised as you are. As if getting whacked around by his father wasn't bad enough, even his toys took a crack at him at the age of eleven when he was hit in the back of the head while on his swing set, causing a blood clot that resulted in chronic blinding headaches. In his late teens, J.W. was diagnosed with a heart ailment (like not having one) that brought him even more pain for the rest of his miserable life. In 1960, Gacy dropped out of his senior year of high school, so no one was able to sign his yearbook, "Don't ever change! Except maybe your homicidal tendencies!"

John Wayne moved to Las Vegas but had difficulty finding work in the city because he looked funny in tassels. He went through a variety of low-paying odd jobs (some that weren't odd until his arrival) such as janitor at a funeral parlor, which must have done loads to bring him out of his shell. Upon returning to Chi-town, Gacy went to business school and began working for the Nunn-Bush Shoe Company where he became a killer salesman (literally). John Wayne became the duke of sales with lines like, "Boy, those shoes look so good I'd like to hit you on the head and bury you under my kitchen floor," and was soon promoted to manage a store in nearby Springfield.

In his free time, Gacy was working with charities such as the Catholic Interclub Council, the Federal and Chicago

Civil Defense Leagues (oh, the irony), as well as the Holy Name Society, an organization that works to promote God "by acts of love and devotion to the most holy name of Jesus," though we've had a little trouble locating those passages on pedo-necro-sado-philia in the New Testament. He was even once voted "Man of the Year" by the chapter of his local Jaycees; subsequently, revised questionnaires now ask all possible candidates, "Have you ever killed a whole bunch of people and liked it?"

In September 1964 Gacy married Marlynn Myers, and the couple moved to Waterloo, Iowa, to manage a Kentucky Fried Chicken franchise owned by Gacy's father-in-law, before it was renamed KFC and pawned off as a *healthy* alternative to nasty *fried* foods. The couple settled down into domestic life with two kids, and by all accounts (except for those of his later victims), John was an upstanding member of the community. But alas, the good times were destined to disappear quicker than a bucket of the Colonel's Extra-Crispy at a family picnic.

Rumors about Gacy's questionable sexuality began to spread through young male employees at his chicken joint, and in the spring of 1968 he was brought up on charges of sodomy. Knowing immediately how to remedy the situation, Gacy paid a local thug ten dollars to beat up his accuser. Unfortunately, when it comes to low-end muscle, you apparently get what you pay for, since Gacy's tough proved anything but and was beat up by the boy he was sent to intimidate. Arrested, fowl John pleaded guilty to the charge of sodomy and, because he wasn't an NBA all-star, was sentenced to ten years in the Iowa State Reformatory where "shucking the corn" takes on an entirely new meaning. Strangely, his wife had little interest in remaining married to a convicted sodomite, and despite his pleas, left him, taking the children with her, apparently "a no butts about it" kind of gal. John's exemplary behavior in prison won his release after a mere eighteen months, cutting his sentence by eight and a half years, a shining moment in the history of the Iowa State Parole Board.

Gacy moved back home to Chicago and, with his mom's help, purchased a small house outside the city limits. Shortly after moving in Gacy was again charged with committing lewd acts with a minor, but charges were dropped when the kid failed to show up for the hearing. In 1972, John Look-I'm-Not-Gay-cy married divorcee Carole Hoff, who brought her two young daughters into the house of horrors.

When later interviewed, the couple next door described Gacy as a quiet and friendly sort of fellow, although they did recall his house tended to smell like a shallow grave on a hot day. Is it just us or do serial killers purposely move in next to clueless people? John again worked hard to make himself a pivotal member of society, throwing Hawaiian- and Western-themed block parties as well as volunteering as a clown for local charities, which right there should have been a big ol' red flag to anyone paying attention.

In 1974, John started his own contracting company and took jobs as a painter and handyman. Yesiree, nothing spells normal to us like a guy in clown shoes who's good with a saw. However, even as Krusty the Carpenter began building things around town, his relationship at home was falling apart. He had stopped sleeping with his new bride, which concerned her but not quite as much as the male pornography she found scattered around the house. ("It's research, honey! These guys are the masters of laying pipe!")

The Gacys divorced in March 1976, and John Wayne, free from familial responsibilities, was now able to do what any convicted sodomizing chicken-selling construction worker dreams of: run for public office. They say that the only thing that can kill a political career is being caught with a dead girl or a live boy, and Gacy knew he was home free in either case. He set to work making a name for himself as an active member of the Democratic Party, moving up through the local ranks, even once getting his picture taken with First Lady Rosalynn Carter, a photo she does *not* keep on her desk.

In the last few months of 1978, while Gacy's world was coming up roses, a rash of young boys were suddenly found pushing up daisies. While investigating the disappearance of a local teen, the police noticed a few things: there were a lot of missing young boys in the area, several of them worked for Gacy, and his house smelled like a mausoleum. ("Damn! If only we had a solid lead!") When the police stopped by to ask Bozo the rapist a few questions, they discovered enough suspicious objects to bring in the clown and were flabbergasted when further searches turned up a body in the crawl space of his stinky house. Just wait, the truly flabbergasting is still to come.

On December 22, 1978, Gacy confessed to the killing of more than thirty-three young men on his property. Twenty-eight bodies were removed from John Wayne's house and another five were found in a nearby river. Gacy described how he would lure the boys to his funhouse where they would be handcuffed, drugged, raped, and killed. Few cried tears for the clown when he was found guilty and sentenced to death by lethal injection on May 10, 1994, outside of Joliet, Illinois. His brain was later examined by "experts" and found to be perfectly fine; . . . for lawnbowling.

Interesting Tidbit: Awaiting his conjugal visit from the Grim Reaper while on Death Row, Gacy expressed his artistic side by oil painting. His collection of creepy clown paintings (is that redundant?) was auctioned off after his passing. The winning bidder reportedly then burned the lot to ensure no one had to look at them ever again.

Ways to Bring Up John Wayne Gacy in Conversation

☀ That guy's house stank so bad, I thought John Wayne Gacy was renting a room.

☀ That's about as funny as John Wayne Gacy's clown routine.

☀ There's something weird about Kevin. He's no John Wayne Gacy, but maybe he's a distant cousin.

Psycho-Killer, Qu'est que C'est— Fromme-Fromme-Fromme . . .

When Are We Talking About: 1948–

Why Are We Even Talking About This: Fromme is currently serving a life sentence for attempting to assassinate President Gerald Ford in 1975. She was a member of the Manson Family, self-proclaimed "wife" of Charles Manson, and is believed to have played a role in the grisly Tate-LaBianca murders.

What You Need to Know to Sound Smart: Lynette Fromme proved that bad things *can* come in small packages. Though seemingly innocent and sugary-sweet on the outside, Fromme was what sociologists refer to as a freak-o nutbag from Crazy-Town, USA (in this case Santa Monica, California). Born on October 22, 1948, little Lynney grew up in an *Ozzie and Harriet* middle-class family (Ozzy Osbourne, that is) with an emotionally bankrupt dad whose failure to invest time and bond with his daughter yielded an unhappy girl who searched in vain for fatherly love and instead found a gross prophet. Fromme's only childhood joy was performing with a local dance troop called the Westchester Lariats, lassoing hearts on the *Lawrence Welk Show* as well as at the White House, her first, but not last encounter with a U.S. president.

In the 1960s, now a teen living in Redondo Beach,

Fromme chose tripping over dancing, and with a roach clip in her Jazz-hands, finally found a way to get attention from her Franken-Father who, enraged at her acidic personality, unleashed his monstrous side. After a particularly vicious argument one fateful day in 1967, Fromme fled in tears to the beach where she met Charles Manson, whose obvious insanity must have been difficult to discern among the scores of local loons lounging on the Venice boardwalk. You know when they tell people to "go sell crazy somewhere else"? This is where they come. With her father-figure relationship so out of shape, Lynnette was desperate for some man-love, and instantly became Manson's gal Fromme-day, moving in with him and the other hippies living at his compound. Really, does anything good *ever* happen in a compound? This clubhouse of death was known as the Spahn Ranch. (Spahn of the Devil, perhaps?) Lynette adopted Manson's nickname for her, "Squeaky" for her high-pitched voice, and took on the role of the family's mama-bear in the grim scary-tale that was about to unfold. While Manson liked the sex and drugs part of hippieness, he had a little trouble getting with the whole "peace and love" thing, since his vision and ambition was to ignite an apocalyptic race war.

On August 9, 1969, two of the most gruesome nights in history, Manson and his followers gutted actress Sharon Tate (eight months pregnant) and the four others in her home. The following evening, August 10, they killed Leno and Rosemary LaBianca, a grocer and his wife, hoping to pin the murders on blacks. But the Bride of Chuckie was never linked to any of the crimes since at the time she was at home knitting butcher knife cozies. At Manson's trial Fromme camped out in front with the other two Charlie's Angels—Susan Atkins and Patricia Krenwinkel—all of whom passed the day carving swastikas into their foreheads, because everyone knows that if you're trying to win public sympathy, it's swastikas or nothing. Squeaky almost got off clean but was charged with contempt of court for failing to testify and obstruction of justice for trying to convince others to do likewise and so served a little time in the pokey.

Eventually back on the outside, Fromme grew bored without Manson's good-natured Helter-Skelter high jinks to cheer her up and so, looking for a pleasant change, moved to crime-ridden Stockton, California, which satisfied her nostalgia for prison. Squeaky hung out with two friends, James Craig and Michael Monfort, both of whom probably forgot to mention that they were ex-convicts when filling out their apartment applications. The trouble-trio moved in with an unsuspecting married couple, James and Lauren Willett, forming one big happy family, except for one small problem: the Willetts kept on dying. When their bodies were discovered in early November 1969, the local police thought it prudent to arrest any remaining nondead roommates.

Though her accomplices went back inside, Fromme squeakyed by without an indictment and moved to the suburban paradise of Sacramento. ("Hi, I'm Squeaky Fromme. I'm your new neighbor. Do you mind if I borrow a knife? Do you have a bigger one?") When cow-tipping proved anticlimactic, Fromme declared herself a nun of Manson's religion, even though he didn't really have one, and no one really cared. Going by the name of "Red" (fitting considering all the skeletons in her closet . . . and under her bed . . . and in the carport), Fromme decided she wanted to raise awareness and save the environment and that meant one thing . . . shoot the president.

On September 5, 1975, President Gerald Ford was crossing downtown Capitol Park from his hotel to meet with Governor Jerry "Moonbeam" Brown (mistake number one) when Fromme approached the president with a loaded .45 in hand and screamed, "The country is in a mess! This man is not your president!" To this day it is unclear whether Fromme was referring to the fact that Ford had never been elected to the presidency (he was Nixon's vice president when the president resigned after Watergate) or if she, like most of the country, simply thought Ford was kind of an idiot. Squeaky was wrestled to the ground by Secret Service agents (at last, some more man-love) before she could pull the trigger and end Ford's life and shame at only being a one-termer.

During her trial, Fromme claimed that although the gun was loaded, she never intended to shoot the president but was simply going to hand the gun to Ford and wait the three seconds necessary for him to accidentally do the job himself. She was found guilty of attempted murder of a bumbling dignitary and was sentenced to life in a correctional facility in West Virginia, which seems like being punished for the same thing twice. In 1987 the Red Menace escaped from jail but was rounded up two days later by authorities who happily added five more years to her life sentence. ("Damn it, Dad! Would one trip to the roller rink have killed you?") Fromme continues to reject release hearings, saving the parole board the trouble of listening to her.

Interesting Tidbit: Lynette Fromme goes into the record books as being the first woman to ever attempt to assassinate an American president, just beating out Sara Jane Moore, who tried to kill Ford only seventeen days later in San Francisco. Keep shooting for the stars, Lynette!

Ways to Bring Up Squeaky Fromme in Conversation

☀ I think that girl has Squeaky Fromme–sized father issues.

☀ She's got a killer smile. Squeaky Fromme would be jealous.

☀ Jeez, she has the highest voice. It's like talking to Squeaky Fromme.

There's No Business Like Coke Business with Pablo Escobar

When Are We Talking About: 1949–1993

Why Are We Even Talking About This: Escobar became ruler of one of the largest cocaine cartels on the planet, by consolidating all aspects of the drug trade—growing, refining, and smuggling—into one organization, and made himself the seventh wealthiest man in the world.

What You Need to Know to Sound Smart: Pablo Emilio Escobar Gaviria blew onto the Rionegro, Colombia, scene January 12, 1949, with a schoolteacher mama and a modest cattle rancher papa. But by adolescence Pablo was bored with school and yearned to sniff around for excitement on the streets of nearby Medellín (and being the murder capital of South America, it's easy to understand the allure). Pablo dropped out, and like many young people took the *high* road to education, studying botany, specifically as it relates to cannabis. If you don't know what we mean, you're probably one of the five kids who thought homework meant doing it at home not five minutes before class . . . he was getting stoned, people!

Pablo grew up a reflection of the country in which he lived—Colombia had eight major civil wars in the nineteenth century alone (that's almost one per decade); he knew fewer days of peace than Bobby Brown and Whitney Houston. In the 1950s, an uprising known as La Violencia (trans.: the violencia) swept the nation, with leftist guerrillas blowing up government facilities and federal troops slaughtering peasants, many of whom had no connection to the rebels. Consequently the outlaws who roamed the countryside raping, robbing, and murdering were viewed as heroes by the poor, because at least they didn't tax you while doing it. Pablo admired these *banditos*, telling his friends, "I want to be big"; if only his mother had simply bought him a pair of lifts.

Escobar, along with his cousin and partner in crime, Gustavo Gaviria, began boosting cars, dismantling them and selling the untraceable parts for cash. ("Pablito, what are all these bumpers doing in the basement?") Soon the boys were doing so well that they simply bought falsified deeds of ownership from corrupt officials. ("We cut out the middleman and pass the savings on to you!") The larger Escobar's organization grew, the greater became his need for a violent reputation to keep his enemies in check. He soon began ordering the kidnapping and death of anyone challenging his authority or who made fun of his double chin. The pudgy, pizza-pounding purveyor of pain (who, ironically, guzzled tons of Coke every day . . . the Cola, that is) officially moved into cocaine trafficking in 1975 when he murdered drug kingpin Fabio Restrepo.

The organization of El Doctor, as he was now known (his folks must have been so proud to have a doctor in the family), quickly grew by leaps and coke mounds for a variety of reasons. First, the late 1970s was the perfect time to be selling the white lady, since the white man (i.e., Americans and Europeans) was buying kilotons of the stuff to cram up his stuffy nostrils, perhaps in an effort to blank out the overwhelming horror of the clothes he was wearing. Second, Escobar was more ruthless than anyone had ever been in the business. Where his competitors might kill you if you muscled in on their territory, Pablo would kill you, your family, your neighbors, their baby-sitter, and that guy, Carl, who lives down the street with his mom and smells vaguely of warm cheese. While in public, Pablo appeared soft-spoken, well mannered, and genteel, but behind closed doors he ruled with an iron fist, actually a chubby one, but you know what we mean. One worker who was caught stealing was hog-tied and thrown into the pool to drown as a spectacle for party guests, while yelling, "This is what happens to those who steal from Pablo Escobar!" (and to those who forget to put *three* olives in his martini? . . . We shudder at the thought). Never one to be out of drug czar fashion, Escobar loved himself a nice Colombian necktie, which is cutting someone's throat and shoving their tongue through the slit, making it the perfect accessory for any drug-dealing outfit.

The beauty of his organization, el Cartel de Medellín, was that initially, none of Pablo's people did any actual growing, processing, or smuggling themselves. They simply took a large percentage of already existing operations in exchange for "protection," but as the money rolled in, Pablo began buying up controlling interests throughout South and Central America. Pablo adopted a business strategy known as *plato o plomo* (silver or lead), which meant either you accepted a bribe or you accepted a bullet in the head (decisions, decisions). Either way, his plan took care of any unwanted interference from either police or government officials.

With his newfound wealth, Escobar decided that it was time to start enjoying life, buying enormous houses, sports cars, and a bevy of beautiful babes who would jump through hoops naked (literally) with just a word from their boss, proving that you may not be able to buy love, but you sure can lease it for a while. In a grand gesture (well maybe a few hundred grand, it was all the same to him), Escobar improved the city of Medellín, building schools, helping the homeless, and sponsoring youth soccer leagues ("Today's game will be the eighth-grade Eightballs versus the Tiny Tootheads!"), making him a hero in the eyes of the Colombian peasants, but let's face it, these people had so little, a reliable microwave oven could look heroic.

Pa-blow married fifteen-year-old Maria Victoria (his preferred age for sexual partners, unless you know anyone younger), an act that cost him a bribe to the Catholic Church, because apparently, God is okay with statutory rape as long as you pay for the privilege.

Escobar became so popular by 1982, that he was elected substitute representative for the Colombian Congress and was perhaps the inspiration for the political career of D.C. mayor Marion Barry. Though possessing all requirements for a lengthy political career (tons of cash and a total lack of morals), Escobar's term was short-lived as his presence attracted the attention of the new justice minister, Rodrigo Lara. This Dudley Doomed Right publicly accused Pablo of drug trafficking, though Escobar claimed his fortune had come from the bicycle business, giving new meaning to the term "ten-speed." Pablo was forced out of office by Lara's relentless attacks in the Colombian press, but three months later the good justice was killed in a car accident when the vehicle he was riding in collided with seven bullets fired by one of Pablo's gunmen.

When Colombia adopted a new criminal extradition agreement with the United States, Escobar and his cartel comrades-in-harms decided to relocate somewhere less lawful and headed to Panama, run by coke-friendly General Manuel "I Should Have Layed Off the Chocolate as a Teen" Noriega. Mark Twain once quipped, "Fish and houseguests both stink after three days," and Noriega must have agreed, since he raided Escobar's headquarters, sending Pablo and his buddies scurrying back to Colombia with their enchiladas between their legs. ("You think you're bad? I'm CIA-trained, buddy!")

By the end of 1984, Pablo was back in his hometown, still living the "high" life, making public appearances everywhere from bullfights to bake sales and conducting a killing spree on everyone calling for his arrest. Escobar snorted at the authorities, as judges and legislators were targeted in his murder campaign to cow the entire country, even blowing up Avianca Flight 109 in 1989 to rid himself of an enemy, forgetting that he was also ridding the world of 149 innocent people. However, through this act Escobar moved up from kingpin to terrorist, and it's such a *fine* line between a terror and a terrorist. But it was his killing of Luis Galan, an antidrug crusader and presidential hopeful adored by the Colombian people, that sent tremors through Escobar's empire.

The first sign of real trouble was Nancy Reagan's appearance at Arnold's class on a *very special* episode of *Diff'rent Strokes*, warning American children to "Just say no!" The next was the ascendancy of George Bush Sr. to the presidency and his declaration of a war on drugs, which we're *still* "winning" . . . twenty years later. Bush labeled cocaine a "national security threat" and sent in the military. Escobar suddenly realized his extradition fears were about to come true and, after watching *Oz* on HBO, was terrified that he might wind up in a cell with Luke Perry.

Craftily, in June 1991, Pablo surrendered to Colombian authorities with the understanding that he would serve his time locally. Escobar was given a five-year sentence (we're sure no money changed hands during *that* trial) at La Catedral, a hilltop prison overlooking Medellín, which he'd personally renovated with saunas, pools, and a workout gym that made the Ritz Carlton look like a Motel 6. Pablo served his time swimming, eating, and hanging out with his buddies, that is when he wasn't leaving prison to attend parties, soccer games, and other social events.

In July 1992, when word came that Colombia might hand him over to the irate United States, Escobar esco-aped while the guards were counting their per diem. With the help of American Special Forces, the Colombians created an elite team known as Search Block, whose sole purpose was to hunt and kill anyone named Pablo Escobar. Pablo's enemies, in turn, organized an army of their own, Los Pepes, which murdered over three hundred members of Escobar's cartel, hobbling his organization. On December 2, 1993, the government of Colombia permanently ended Pablo's line when they shot him dead as he stood talking on his cell phone on the roof of a not-so-safe house in Medellín, possibly finding out if Dominos could deliver. Rest assured that anyone sniffing nearby was not crying.

Interesting Tidbit: One of Pablo's favorite leisure activities was nude foot races (which he thankfully did not take part in). A bevy of busty beauties would strip down and race toward an expensive sports car with the winner walking away with the keys.

Ways to Bring Up Pablo Escobar in Conversation

☀ I'll have a Coke, and not the Pablo Escobar kind.

☀ Naomi is so ruthless she makes Pablo Escobar look like Mr. Rogers.

☀ Please, no ultimatums. The whole *plato o plomo* tactic just doesn't fly with me.

☀ 9 ☀

The Sports Conversation

*T*he sports conversation is the ultimate icebreaker, because there's pretty much no social setting in the world where you can't find someone more than willing to slip into a little color commentary. While traditionally this has been a male-dominated topic, in these modern times there are an increasing number of women sports fans (most notably, NBA basketball has seen quite a jump in female enthusiasts), as well as dozens of women's professional sports leagues and stars. So if you're off to a sports bar, Super Bowl party, or watching the big fight on Pay-Per-View with a group of colleagues, you'll be right at home if you brush up on your sports conversation skills. *Note:* If you know your party will have one or more non-Americans be sure to study your soccer.

Sports enthusiasts are the only nerds in society who receive instant approval for their nigh-fanatical obsessions with statistical facts, outdated player information, and historic game dates. Don't panic, there's no way you can know everything about every sport, and even the most devout sports fans aren't experts. The majority of these party players have one or two particular games that they specialize in with only a rudimentary knowledge of the others. The key here is to shift the conversation to a sport you know something about. As long as you can hit a few conversational pitches, the essential information and key superstars, you'll stay in the game. Sports fans love to argue about who was the best: DiMaggio vs. Ruth, Ali vs. Louis, Spreewell vs. The Boston Strangler. Like so many conversations, there's no winning the sports argument. Everyone has their favorite team, all of whom have been champs at one time or another (unless you're a New Orleans Saints, or "Aints," fan).

Eventually, you'll find that all sports conversations are eerily similar, no matter where you are having them. They usually begin with the score of that week's game, drift to the state of a favorite team's offensive and defensive capabilities, and then head to the likelihood of the team's "going all the way," which has nothing to do with sex, unless it's a party cruise sponsored by the Minnesota Vikings.

Mind you, some sports fans are so devoted that their entire mood can be depressed or elated based on the state of their team's most recent performance. If you're at a party where people have been watching a game, you may be surprised to observe a once perfectly normal person reduced to abject depression or irate fury if their team loses. Likewise, from fans of winning teams, expect lots of raucous screaming and rosy cheeks and maybe even a few tears of joy. All because of the outcome of a game played by a group of men (or women) that the fan doesn't even know and that will be played again next week. While no one is telling you not to root for your favorite franchise, there is a time to pick your battles. And, if you're trying to win friends or impress socially, this might be an occasion to take one for the team.

You Have to Use a Husky Voice in the Iditarod

When Are We Talking About: 1908–

Why Are We Even Talking About This: Also known as the Last Great Race, the Iditarod is a 1,000-mile trek through Alaskan wilderness and some of the harshest environments on the face of the planet.

What You Need to Know to Sound Smart: The core of Iditarod is the relationship between a man and his best friend . . . well, no, we're actually talking about his *other* best friend, the dog. For centuries, people living in the frozen Arctic tundra, such as trappers, traders, miners, and anyone longing for a life of permanently erect nipples, have traveled from town to miserable town via dogsled (and still do to this day) carrying supplies, goods, or booze to help keep them from blowing their brains out until next week. In 1908, the All-Alaskan Sweepstakes was created, as a 408-mile journey between Nome, also called Anvil City (because if you ever move there, you'll pray one falls on your head) and Candle, not quite hell, but just a sleigh ride away. In 1910, racers brought the first Siberian huskies to Alaska, which despite their Bolshevik political leanings, made amazing sled dogs.

In 1925, an event that became known as the Serum Run to Nome, or the Great Race of Mercy, helped popularize this pastime. A diphtheria epidemic was threatening the Inuit children, who had no immunity from this gift that white settlers had brought them. ("Wow, disease, pollution *and* alcoholism . . . and we didn't get you anything.") A supply of antitoxin left Nennana on January 27 and was rushed to the children 674 miles across the ice in –50 degree weather (cold enough to freeze even Tommy Lee's libido) via twenty dogsled teams in a sort of "relay race for life." They arrived in Nome in just five and a half days, saving hundreds of lives. The lead dog on the last team was Balto, an enormous black husky who was immortalized with a statue in New York's Central Park, although what that city has to do with a bunch of Eskimo kids is anyone's guess.

The modern race was started in 1967 by Dorothy G. Page, "Mother of the Iditarod," with fifty-eight racers participating in the 25-mile trek. Originally, the Iditarod was sponsored as a way to celebrate the hundredth anniversary of our screwing the Russians out of Alaska. ("Tell you what, you give us this oil-soaked land nearly half the size of our country and we'll give you . . . ohhhhh, how's $7 million sound?") At the time, the deal was mocked as Seward's Folly after Secretary of State William Seward, who pushed for the purchase and got a ton of crap from everyone, but now it looks like we all owe him an apology, except for those lucky residents who are being paid by the government to live there . . . yeah, you heard that right. At any rate, no one really cared about celebrating *Alaska* anything, so instead they changed the race to loosely follow the Serum Run of 1925, because everyone knows how the whole sick kids thing can always draw a crowd.

The first real Iditarod (which, in Inuit can be translated either as "far, distant place" or "I can't feel my nuts") was in 1973, and was about 1,049 miles long as a tip of the hat to Alaska being the 1049th state, with thirty-four mushers (racers) competing. Today, the Iditarod starts on the first Saturday of March in Anchorage, with a northern route used on even numbered years and a southern one on odd. Why? We have *no* idea. Must be an Alaska thing. The trail leads musher and dog through towering forests and over featureless tundra, while braving the blasting winds, subfreezing cold, driving snow and . . . well, that pretty much covers it. On their way to Nome, racers pass through twenty checkpoints, where they periodically stop to rest their dogs and take on supplies, with teams made up of between seven and twenty hounds.

Great lengths are taken to ensure the health and safety of the dog teams, so you can all stop fretting about the poor widdle puppies . . . since only a *few* dogs have died during the race! The dogs even get to wear cute little booties to protect their little piggies, and an average team will go through 1,500 to 2,000 booties in a race. Just imagine entire factories of grandmas knitting furiously weeks before the event.

The Iditarod is the most popular sporting event in the state. Actually, it's the *only* sporting event in the state because gin-chugging isn't technically a sport. For a while the speed record was held by a woman named Susan Butcher, who won the race *four times* through the 1980s and '90s, even though one year two of her dogs were killed by a moose (don't let their dopey faces fool you, they're killing machines). Rick Swenson won the contest an unbelievable five times and is the only person to win it in *three different decades*, proving you're never too old to do something stupid. While it used to take around eleven to twelve days to finish the course, Martin Buser set the current record in 2002 of 8 days, 22 hours, 46 minutes and 2 seconds. It's all the steroid biscuits the dogs are using these days.

Everyone who finishes the Iditarod receives $1,049 as an "attaboy" (it doesn't even cover the $1,800 entrance fee), while the winner earns about $75,000 plus a big-ass pickup truck, but still less than what an NBA player spends on sneakers in a given year. The last musher in gets the Red Lantern Award, which says, "You suck. But we love you anyway because it's Alaska and we can't be all that choosey." There is also a Rookie of the Year Award and a Golden Harness Award for the best dog. With all this and plenty of frozen poo to boot, we suggest you buy your tickets today!

Interesting Tidbit: Balto, the heroic dog, was stuffed and mounted after his death and now hangs in the Cleveland Museum of Natural History, chasing cats for eternity.

Ways to Bring Up Iditarod in Conversation

☀ Wow, it's cold out there. I feel like I rode the Iditarod to get here.

☀ His girlfriend's not that cute. I think I saw her win the Iditarod last year.

☀ Spend the night with you? I'd rather run the Iditarod naked.

In Your Face, Master Race! Jesse Owens and the Berlin Games

When Are We Talking About: 1913–1980

Why Are We Even Talking About This: Jesse Owens was an Olympic sprinter whose four gold medal wins stood as a record for nearly fifty years.

What You Need to Know to Sound Smart: James Cleveland Owens certainly broke no records when he was born into a family of ten other kids September 12, 1913, in Oakville, Alabama. Owens's grandparents had been slaves and his parents were sharecroppers (aka slaves) who wantonly wasted their monthly birth control budget on frivolous things like bread, while topping the family out at thirteen. Owens was a reputedly thin and frail child with a poor constitution (not surprising since his ethnic group had only been given access to the document for a few years), who was often sick, barely surviving harsh winters and several bouts of pneumonia thanks to inadequate clothing, substandard housing, and a nine-mile trek every day to school. By age seven, Owens was expected to pull his weight by picking one hundred pounds of cotton a day, which had to weigh more than he did. When Jesse was nine, his family joined the

Great Migration north, along with hundreds of thousands of other African Americans fleeing the oppressive South (to the oppressive North), and wound up in Cleveland in the hopes of a better life, obviously forgetting they were in Cleveland. (They don't call the city "The Mistake by the Lake" for nothing.) When he was in elementary school, Owens's teacher misunderstood his southern drawl when he said "J.C.," and so called him Jesse. Owens was terrified of correcting his white teacher, so the name stuck. Still the family remained poor (again, Cleveland), and Jesse supplemented their income by delivering groceries (we bet *he* didn't put the dang milk on top of the bread), loading freight cars, and working in a shoe repair shop. Parents, let's recap: Kid with nine jobs, Olympic Gold Medal legend. Your kid, no job, award-winning idiot.

Owens's life changed in 1928 when he attended Fairmount Junior High School, where he met Ruth Soloman, who would eventually become his wife, and Coach Charles "Charlie" Riley (wonder how in the world he got *that* nickname), who the runner credited with his eventual success. Some say Riley spotted Owens on the playground while others say he noticed him during PE class. Wherever it happened, Riley saw just one thing (no, not that—why is it that people these days always assume a grown man cruising the playground and hanging out in the locker room is up to no good?) . . . he saw talent. Owens, whose work schedule meant he was unable to train after school, instead got up at the crack of dawn to practice with Riley before class began. While sweeping floors to earn a buck, Owens also swept local athletic events as a sprinter and jumper. With his mother's encouragement, Jesse finished junior high despite the fact that his entire family had lost their jobs in the Depression.

In 1930, Owens enrolled at East Technical High School,

where he became captain of the track team and was voted class president by the primarily white student body. However, his scholastic and athletic careers were nearly sidelined two years later when Ruth announced she was pregnant, proving that Jesse was not only a good runner and jumper but also a strong swimmer. The couple eloped to Erie, Pennsylvania, but Ruth's father, less than thrilled with the sprinter for running off with his little girl, decided to teach him a new field event called "Kicking the Ass of the Kid Who Knocked Up My Daughter."

That summer, 1932, Owens failed his first tryout for the U.S. Olympic team but had little time for regrets, since shortly thereafter, Ruth delivered their daughter, Gloria. While Jesse loved the sound of the starter's pistol, he feared the sound of the one carried by his father-in-law and so was forced to stay away from his wife and child, continuing instead to train (proving that hanging out with the boys isn't *always* a waste of time). In June 1933, at the National High School Championships in Chicago, Owens achieved national fame by tying the 100-yard dash world record (9.4 seconds) and breaking the high school long jump world record by leaping 24 feet, 9.5 inches (imagine leaping over a subway car . . . but not when it's in the tunnel). Returning to Cleveland a hero, Owens was honored with a parade and a meeting with the mayor and, *finally*, Ruth's folks let him see his kid but with the stipulation that he remain famous . . . pretty much forever.

Owens kept it real, going to Ohio State despite myriad offers from universities whose mascots were far cooler than the buckeye, a small inedible fruit. At nineteen, Owens was named to the Amateur Athletic Union (AAU) All-American Track Team and struggled to balance training, family, work, and school but broke no scholastic records, barely skirting expulsion and often on academic probation. But these minor hurdles did little to slow Owens's athletic stride as he won a record *eight* individual NCAA championships.

In 1935, at the Big Ten Conference Championship in Ann Arbor, Michigan (home of the Ann Arbor Folk Music Festival. Come, won't you? And bring your banjo.), over a period of forty-five minutes, Owens made athletic history. Despite injuring his tailbone during a college prank (slipping on a goldfish he was swallowing while streaking up the flagpole after binge drinking), Owens set three world records: the 220-yard dash in 20.3 seconds, 220 low hurdles in 20.6 seconds, and the long jump. Before his jump, Jesse boldly placed a handkerchief at the world record mark of 26 feet, 2.5 inches (the track and field equivalent of Babe Ruth calling his shot to the stands) and then proceeded to soar nearly six inches past it at 26 feet, 8.25 inches. Owens also tied the 100-yard world record of 9.4 seconds, and in fact, his performance as a sprinter was *so* incredible that in two races he was given medals for shorter races he hadn't run but whose time *he had beat in the longer ones!* ("Uhh, good job, Phil, but that Owens kid beat you by 3 seconds . . . while running twice as far.")

The next leg of Jesse's legacy was at the 1936 Olympic Games in Berlin. With the globe under the looming shadow of the brown-shirted, goose-stepping Nazis, Jesse scored a victory for humanity and proved, once and for all, that when it came to the human race, the "master" race placed dead last. Hitler had made it no secret that the games were to be a demonstration of Aryan superiority, though not necessarily *his*, since Adolf was a short, dark-haired weasel. The German authority even ridiculed Americans for using "subhumans" on their Olympic team, their endearing term for African Americans. But Owens stunned the world, running circles around the Teutonic team, winning even the hearts of Berliners as he blitzed through his events, plundering four gold medals. Owens ran the 100 meter (that's 330 feet, folks) in 10.3 seconds and beat Jackie Robinson's older brother (cousin's uncle . . . sorry), Mack, for the 200 in only 20.7 seconds.

Owens nearly fouled out of the long jump but qualified in his final attempt by getting a last-minute tip from, of all people, his German rival, Lutz Long (who sounds like a Gothic porn star, but isn't), which must have pleased Hitler to no end. ("Oh Lutzy . . . remember ze discussion we had vere ze Americans were supposed to *lose!*") Owens bested Long's long jump by sailing 26 feet, 5.5 inches, setting another world record while Hitler had a führer-fit watching the two athletes embrace as his German people masterfully chanted Jesse's name. Owens was so moved by Long's act of sportsmanship that he continued to correspond with the athlete's family long after Lutz was killed while fighting for the losing team in World War II.

Though Owens was technically finished with his Olympic events, at the behest of the German officials, he and another black athlete were subbed into the relay team to relieve the group's only Jews, Marty Glickman and Sam Stoller (because if, God forbid, the Jews *and* the blacks beat Germany, Hitler would have to go back to painting). Owens finished his leg of the 4×100-meter relay in 39.8 seconds, 15 yards ahead (that's 45 feet, or about the width of your average Burger King) of his competitors, earning his fourth gold and putting the finishing coat on their legendary shellacking. Owens's record would remain undisputed until Carl Lewis tied it in the 1984 games.

On the streets of Berlin, Owens was a superstar, but returning to "the land of the free" he found that he came in last when it came to racial justice. The man who had single-handedly carried the torch of American victory and received a NYC tickertape parade was forced to ride in the freight elevator to a reception in his honor at the Waldorf Astoria. Owens didn't re-

ceive the opportunities or endorsements available to white athletes (before Roy Camapanella in 1952, Wheaties should have
been called White-ies) and so turned to stunt appearances: running races against horses, motorcycles, cars, beating them all in
the 100-yard dash, but keep in mind that in the early 1940s
most cars were about as fast as your lawnmower.

In 1941, Owens was appointed head of the Office of
Civilian Defense's national physical fitness program, but he
still couldn't outrun his financial needs. Now in Chicago,
Jesse worked as a jazz DJ, a playground director, and even a
dry cleaner to put food on the table for his growing family,
eventually declaring bankruptcy. In 1950, an Associated
Press poll declared Owens the greatest track and field athlete
of the century, and the most broke one too. Despite the hardship and disrespect he faced, Owens found great reward
working with disadvantaged youth and through the 1950s
and '60s worked with the Chicago Boy's Club and was eventually named the U.S. Ambassador of Sports by the State Department, touring impoverished third world nations teaching
kids how to play sports.

As the times changed, thankfully, so finally did Jesse's
fortunes. In the 1960s, he toured the lecture circuit and did
PR for major American corporations. Charming and mag-
nanimous, Owens's modesty made him popular with whites,
though his racial conservatism didn't go over well with Black
activists. (Come on guys, Jesse's old school.) In 1976, President Gerald Ford presented Owens with the highly presti-
gious Medal of Freedom, and in 1979, President Jimmy
Carter presented him with the Living Legend Award.

At sixty-five, the sovereign of sprinting, who smoked a
pack a day, lost his race with pneumonia and died on March
31, 1980, in a hospital in Tucson, Arizona. He was buried in
Chicago, Illinois. In 1982, Berlin named the street leading to
the Olympic stadium Jesse Owens Allee. In 1990, President

George H. W. Bush posthumously honored Owens with the Congressional Gold Medal presented to his widow, Ruth.

Interesting Tidbit: Rumor has it that Hitler snubbed Owens at the games by refusing to acknowledge him. But Owens refutes this tale in his autobiography, stating that, in fact, it was Franklin D. Roosevelt who refused to receive Owens at the White House due to reelection concerns about Southern voters.

Ways to Bring Up Jesse Owens in Conversation
- ☀ That Kaycee is full of surprises. She's like Jesse Owens at the 1936 Olympics.
- ☀ I'll be back faster than Jesse Owens running the 100-meter dash.
- ☀ You shoulda seen the looks on their faces. It was like they were the Germans, and I was Jesse Owens sweeping the games in Berlin.

Billie Jean King Comes Out Swinging
When Are We Talking About: 1943–
Why Are We Even Talking About This: Billie Jean King was a tennis phenom and woman's rights advocate who is considered to be one of the top female athletes of all time.
What You Need to Know to Sound Smart: Billie Jean Moffit took her first swing at life on November 22, 1943, in Long Beach, California, and started her career in sports as a softball player but surprisingly switched teams (nudge-nudge, wink-wink) to tennis despite the frenzied popularity of professional women's softball. At age eighteen, she bested Margaret Smith Court, the world's reigning champion, at Wimbledon, asserting her presence in the professional arena. Billy Jean married lawyer Larry King (not the living skeleton of CNN fame) and though they eventually divorced, she kept his name

since BJ King is a much sexier nickname than Little Miss Moffit.

In 1967, King was enthroned as the queen of sports when she was crowned "Outstanding Female Athlete of the World." By 1971, she became the first woman sports figure to make over $100,000 dollars in a season. Unfortunately, that's probably what Jimmy Connors paid in taxes that same year. Two years later, in 1973, King was graced with the title "Sportsperson of the Year" by *Sports Illustrated* magazine (once again, the first woman to do so), and by the end of her career, she had set a world record by winning twenty Wimbledon championships.

King's most widely publicized victory, however, was the famous "Battle of the Sexes" on September 20, 1973. She dueled with male tennis hero and renowned chauvinist pig Bobby Riggs (twenty-six years her senior), who had won Wimbledon waaaaaaay back in 1939, before the use of penicillin. As part of the media circus, King was brought onto the court in the Houston Astrodome on a golden litter carried by musclebound men, while Riggs arrived via rickshaw pulled by scantily clad supermodels. Broadcast on television and watched by an estimated 50 million people worldwide, King beat Riggs handily (6–4, 6–3, 6–3, game, set, match), proving once and for all that young female athletes can stomp elderly male athletes far out of their prime.

However, King's reign was rocked by scandal in 1981 when it came out (no pun intended) that the champ had been "hitting from the other side of the court." Marilyn Barnett, King's *really* personal secretary, had slapped the star athlete with a palimony suit, which, though ultimately dismissed, enabled Billy Jean to speak out as an advocate of both gay rights and women in sports. King has helped to create the Women's Sports Foundation and the Women's Tennis Association, the premier tour for female players.

Interesting Tidbit: King's accomplishments are all the more amazing when you take into account that she has played her entire career with severe breathing problems and 20/400 eyesight.

Ways to Bring Up Billie Jean King in Conversation

☀ He had no chance with that girl. It was like Billy Jean King versus Bobby Riggs.

☀ Did you see those Coke bottles? She made Billie Jean King look like 20/20.

☀ Watch out for her backhanded compliments. She's the Billy Jean King of the party scene.

Driving in Circles Is Fun: The Birth of NASCAR

When Are We Talking About: 1947–

Why Are We Even Talking About This: The National Association of Stock Car Auto Racing (NASCAR) is one of the fastest growing entertainment arenas in the United States.

What You Need to Know to Sound Smart: Say what you will, but NASCAR racing has slowly climbed from a regional entertainment oddity to the second most popular televised sporting event in the United States, beaten only by the sultan of spectator sports, the NFL. NASCAR drivers are considered athletes of the highest caliber (we know, *we're* surprised too), whose images adorn everything from the front of Wheaties to the sides of buses. While the sport's original audience was essentially people who had cars up on cement blocks in their front yard, it is now enjoyed across the country (28 percent of Americans proudly call themselves fans) by folks from all walks of life. But NASCAR began not with a checkered flag, but with a checkered past.

The sport began with the illegal bootlegging industry in

the southern United States during the Prohibition era, from 1919 to 1933. In an attempt to meet the demand for supply, drivers were needed to outrun Officer Rosco P. Coltrane and his dog, Flash, while transporting trunkloads of hootch to their customers in northern states. To this end, moonshiners began souping up their cars with larger engines, better handling, and fuel with just slightly more chemical additives than the wood-grain alcohol they were hawking. Many of these good ole boys contrabanded together on Sunday afternoons (right after church), forming loose racing organizations to see who had the hottest hotrods and the heaviest lead foot, with much of the action gravitating toward Wilkes County, North Carolina.

In the summer of 1938, William H. G. "Bill" France Sr. (bet his kid was really thrilled he passed *that* one on) decided to put on a little stock car race in Daytona Beach, Florida, now the official capital of NASCAR. The cars were called "stock" because participants were not allowed to make any changes to the factory specifications on them (except to install a beer cooler, naturally), in order to ensure that the competition would be fair with the winners receiving booze, stogies, and oil as rewards. France realized that there needed to be a parent organization to ensure that rules and safety were upheld. On December 12, 1947, he met with sponsors and enthusiasts at the Ebony Bar in Daytona, and while employees were doing business up front, he and his associates were having a party in the back, drawing up terms for their organization over the next three days.

On June 19, 1949, the first official outing for the group took place in North Carolina (the state now called "NASCAR Valley") at the Charlotte Speedway, or "that place I knocked up your ma under the bleachers." The cars were from the "strictly stock" division, which meant they had to be American factory-made passenger cars. Glenn Dunnaway won the day in a 1947 Ford, but as the roars faded, race authorities found a non-spec piece of equipment on his car. Following a legal battle, Jim Roper (no relation to Mr. and Mrs.) piloted his 1949 Lincoln into the history books as the winner of the event. By season's close, Red Byron had become NASCAR's first national champ. On September 4, 1950, the first "Superspeedway" event was held when the Southern 500 was run in Darlington, South Carolina, with Johnny Mantz taking the checkered flag in a 1950 Plymouth.

During the 1950s, the sport built up speed as corporate executives realized the untapped advertising potential that was theirs for the taking with the oil, tire, and Big Three automotive companies—sponsoring drivers to shill their products. Men like Junior Johnson, Smokey Yunick (possibly earning that name after burning his nads in a bad fire), and Glenn "Fireball" Roberts would become household names throughout the South. Roberts was the sport's first superstar, winning thirty-two races over the course of his career. Unfortunately, he lived up to his nickname on July 2, 1964, when he died from injuries received in a crash during the World 600 at Charlotte.

The next leg of French's race to success was the opening of the Daytona International Speedway in 1959, whose Daytona 500 (named for the race's length in miles) has become the World Series of the sport. The first official race was one of the most exciting in the history of the sport with a photo finish that took over sixty hours of analysis before officials announced that the Oldsmobile driven by Lee Petty had just barely bested Johnny Beauchamp's Ford.

For logistical reasons, most races took place at fairgrounds (and other hick-friendly locales) around the southeast, with the exception of Riverside International Raceway in Riverside, California (mullet capital of the world), which opened in 1957 to give folks in the 909 area code something to do besides stab each other with homemade knives. Episodes of *CHiPs, Knight*

Rider, and *The Rockford Files*, as well as the movie *The Killers* (the crappy one with Ronald Reagan, not the cool one with Burt Lancaster), were all filmed at the raceway before it was closed in 1989.

Due to controversy in the mid-1960s, NASCAR hit the skids just as it was ready to move into first place. In 1964, Chrysler entered a car with a hemispherical engine (known as the "hemi"), which made their cars much more powerful, causing other manufacturers to blow their horns in protest. France (the guy, not the country) banned the hemi, and in a fit, Chrysler peeled out. Well, more accurately, they *pulled* out . . . their money until NASCAR leaders reversed the ruling. Since the sport motored on happily without them, Chrysler returned two years later with an approved customized version.

The sport slammed into overdrive in the 1960s with the appearance of Richard Petty, who like Elvis, became known as "the King." What, are there only like three nicknames in the South? Although not known to wash down fistfuls of pills with fried 'nanner sandwiches, the King became the preeminent driver of the decade. His father was the same Petty who'd won the very first Daytona 500, and Richard would not only follow in Dad's tire tracks but would soon make the old man eat his dust as he tore into the pages of racing history. Famous as #43, Petty would win two hundred races in his thirty-four-year career, including seven NASCAR championships (a feat tied only by Dale Earnhardt), along with seven hundred top-ten placings.

Dale Earnhardt, who began his career in 1975, would also walk away with seven championships and might have won more had his journey not been cut short due to a fatal accident at the Daytona 500 in 2001. Earnhardt was a fierce competitor, once saying that *second* place was the *first* loser. Known on the track (but hopefully not in the bedroom) as "the Intimidator," Earnhardt was famous for his skills in drafting (no, we're not talking architecture), the ability to use the momentum and wind resistance of neighboring cars to conserve fuel and gain speed.

NASCAR really became a family affair with the Earnhardts (Ralph, Dale, and Dale Jr.), the Allisons (Bobby and son, Davey), and the Pettys (Lee, Kyle, Richard and Adam, although distant relative Tom decided to make music history instead by becoming the ugliest man in rock 'n' roll).

Throughout the 1970s, the sport continued its winning streak, with the Winston Cup gaining popularity and ABC's *Wide World of Sports* carrying it into living rooms and trailer parks across the nation. The 1976 Daytona 500 was one of the most exciting races in history. Coming around the last turn, fighting for the lead, Richard Petty and David Pearson collided and spun out. Petty's engine cut out and he rolled to a stop 100 yards from the flag, while Pearson limped past him and crawled the last stretch at 20 mph to win. The 1980s, '90s, and 2000s have been the best decades for the sport, with audiences and ad revenues putting the pedal to the metal. However, 2000 and 2001 also proved the most fatal with the deaths of Dale Earnhardt, Tony Roper, Adam Petty, and Kenny Irwin, causing NASCAR to revamp its safety standards, car specs, and track design.

Jeff Gordon, who's been racing practically since he could walk, is the latest driver in the pole position. He currently holds four Winston Cup Championships (now called the Nextel Cup since their sponsorship began in 2004 and to be called the Sprint Cup in 2007 because of evildoings in the business world) and seventy-two victories in the Nextel series, closing in on the all-time record of eighty-four, held by Darrell Waltrip.

Interesting Tidbit: The worst crash in auto racing history was the 1955 LeMans Disaster. On June 11, 1955, Pierre Levegh was racing a Mercedes in the world-famous LeMans 24-Hour and struck an Austin-Healey while traveling at 150 mph. He launched into the stands where his vehicle burst into flames, killing himself and eighty spectators.

Ways to Bring Up NASCAR in Conversation

☀ Slow down, Ryan. This isn't the Daytona 500.

☀ Sara drives like Richard Petty. Let's just hope she doesn't crash like Dale Earnhardt.

☀ Don't eat so fast. No one's gonna give you the Winston Cup for finishing early.

How Not to Strike Out While Talking Baseball: A Primer

When Are We Talking About: Right now

Why Are We Even Talking About This: If you live in America, or know an American, then you better know something about the sport that is considered the country's "national pastime."

What You Need to Know to Sound Smart: For all you evil and unpatriotic souls who find watching grown men (two teams of nine playing the field and batting—while another bunch of guys earn a salary for sitting on their butts in case they need to "sub in") spit and scratch themselves through a nine-inning no-hitter about as enticing as a root canal without Novocain, we've presented a collection of essential facts that will help you take a swing at a basic baseball conversation. Unfortunately, no matter how you pitch it, baseball talk is about numbers. Sports enthusiasts drool over those figures with feverish fervor. If you're not a baseball fan, there is *no* way you can learn everything in one sitting, but the highlights below will at least keep you from striking out during your conversations. So just try to pick up a few names and stats, but don't worry about memorizing everything. Even sports fans get them mixed up from time to time.

First, let's discuss the much heralded "batting average." This number is derived from how many times a batter hits safely to a base, versus his number of at-bats (but not counting walks). At first glance you might wonder why a .500 batting average is considered nigh-superhuman. A .500 average means getting a hit one out of every *two* times at bat (great for a ballplayer, bad for a surgeon), but if you factor in that batters are using an approximately two-and-a-half-inch-diameter piece of wood (the width of a hair dryer) to hit an approximately three-inch-diameter ball thrown at upwards of 90 or 100 mph by the pitcher, it's a miracle they hit it at all. (Actually, the real act of God is that they convince us to pay $17.50 for a hot dog, soda, and bag of peanuts!) According to *Sports Illustrated*, hitting a baseball is actually the most difficult achievement in any sport.

Let's examine the sheer difficulty in squarely connecting with the ball, which requires the batter to make his decision to swing in approximately $1/25^{th}$ of a second. Doing so either $1/100^{th}$ of a second too early or too late results in the ball going foul. Given these numbers, hitting the ball three out of ten times in the majors makes you a potential candidate for the Hall of Fame. Perhaps now you begin to understand the mind-boggling achievements of Detroit Tigers center fielder Ty Cobb, who leads baseball with a career average of .355 (and unfortunately a wife-hitting average that was even higher).

And that's just getting a *hit*. A home run (HR) means sending the ball across the length of the field (about 400 feet) through the air and over the back fence. You can now appreciate the athleticism of Hank Aaron (look, just pretend you can), who leads baseball with 755 career home runs, with a career .305 batting average. The immortal Babe Ruth (now come on, you *had* to have heard of him) comes in second with 714 HRs, and a .342 career average, with a .392 high! Ruth was also a phenomenal pitcher before his slugging career began, unheard of in a sport where most pitchers hit like your mom. Come on, admit it, she sucks. The American League cheats (there are two leagues, the other is the National League) and uses batting ringers, called designated hitters, so that when it's the pitcher's turn to bat he won't shame himself in front of his kids. ("No, *that's* Daddy . . . he's just gained a few pounds this week . . . and gone bald.") Barry Bonds ranks third in American home run history and is the most recent record setter with 703 HRs and counting, but if you say 700, you're in the ballpark. However, the player who holds the record for the most *hits* ever in Major League Baseball (MLB) is Pete Rose—who gambled away his chances for the Hall of Fame, literally—with 4,256 hits, stealing the record from Cobb's 4,189.

Among the greatest names in baseball, and still argued to be one of the greatest players of all time, was New York Yankee Joe DiMaggio. DiMaggio (known as "Joltin' Joe" for his speed, not for his time spent as the spokesman for Mr. Coffee) had the longest hitting streak, getting on base fifty-six games in a row in 1941 (his career batting average was .325, with a .381 high). Ted Williams's .406 batting average in 1941 made him the last man to hit over .400, but Nap Lajoie holds the all-time high of .426. On the pitching end of things, strikeouts are what's key. Originally called "struckout" (as in, what most guys do at a bar), it's abbreviated as "K" in the stat system established by the *New York Herald's* first baseball reporter, Henry Chadwick, in 1861. Nolan Ryan is top of the mound with 5,714 K (don't worry, he earned way more than that), effectively striking out one out of every four batters, a total of 383 in his best year. Even Charlie Buffinton with his unbeaten 417 strikeouts in a single season, 1884, only averaged one in six batters. However, a much-touted Brooklyn Dodgers pitcher, Sandy Koufax (a Jewish guy from Brooklyn, go figure), actually beats Ryan in his strikeout average (in 1965, he had 382 Ks and struck out one of every three batters), and is renowned for being an observant Jew who refused to pitch on Saturdays. Hours of thrilling conversation can be had speculating whether his numbers would have been better or worse if he had. Red Sox pitcher Cy Young won the most games (511) and is the player that the MLB pitching award has been named after.

The best team in baseball history was the 1903 Chicago Cubs, which won 116 games, though the Seattle Mariners recently tied this record in 2001 . . . finally giving the people of that depressingly rainy city a sunbeam of hope. The worst team ever was the 1962 New York Mets, who lost 120 games. The most World Series titles go to the New York Yankees with twenty-six, which proves that maybe money can't buy everything, but George Steinbrenner's money certainly comes damn close!

Also, fans will talk about baseball's four "Clubs," which are standards that virtually guarantee a player entry into the Hall of Fame: the 500 HR Club, the 3,000 Hits Club, the 300 Wins Club (refers to how many games the pitcher won), and the 3,000 Strikeouts Club. But when talking about clubs, pay close attention just in case one of those sports goofs has suddenly switched to golf!

Interesting Tidbit: In 1963, a pitcher for the San Francisco Giants, Gaylord Perry, supposedly said, "They'll put a man on the moon before I hit a home run." Just a couple hours after *Apollo II* descended to the moon's surface, Perry launched his own rocket, hitting a shot over the fence for his first career home run.

Ways to Bring Up Baseball in Conversation

☀ Just say, "See the game last night?" and you're in.

The Religion Conversation

*T*he first of the ten commandments of conversation is, "Thou shalt not discuss religion." Because of the strength of some people's convictions, the religion conversation can lead to some awkwardness, alienation, and occasionally, even violence. (Of course, if that's what you're after, then go right ahead and tell people that Jesus was a cross-dressing Hindu.) If the state of the world is any indication, we think it's safe to say that people can get sensitive about their faith and what others have to say about it. Church socials, Passover seders, and Amish barn raisings are great socializing opportunities. People at religious gatherings are generally in a generous and festive mood, but just because you're at an event organized by, or around, a particular religion, there's no need to only talk about religious subjects.

However, if you are going to debate devotion and bat around beliefs, it's probably best not to preach if you're a guest at a party primarily filled with people of a different faith from yours. Similar to issues of race, while people are more willing to discuss religion with members of their own faith, this hardly means they're inclined to be more tolerant of what they consider sacrilegious points of view. In short, when talking religion, feel out the conversational waters of the faithful using historic information, before baptizing the crowd with a reading from your book of convictions. If there's anything we can all take away from thousand of years of socializing, it's that, when it comes to religion, right and wrong are a matter of what book you're reading. To sum up, use sensitivity and tact when talking religion, or socially speaking, you'll soon find yourself in the dogma house.

God Rules at the Council of Nicaea

When Are We Talking About: 325 AD

Why Are We Even Talking About This: This council was the first worldwide conference of Christian bishops that codified the religion in the Nicene Creed, the foundation of modern Christianity.

What You Need to Know to Sound Smart: In one of the most significant moments in human history, one man changed the shape of the world. Now we're not talking about a certain legendary carpenter who had walked the earth three hundred years earlier and made David Blaine look like your uncle with his dumb "look my thumb comes off" trick, but Flavius Valerius Constantinus, known to his drinking buddies as Constantine the Great. It was a time of religious confusion. The once mighty Roman realm had been divided into Eastern and Western empires and was now claimed by no less than four would-be emperors. In the midst of political turmoil, a growing cult of yarmulke-tossers called Christians were sweeping the known world.

Constantine, an inveterate opportunist and part-time weatherman, saw which way the spiritual winds were blowing and quickly "converted" from worshipping sun gods to God's son in 312, just before a battle with the army of Emperor Maxentius at Milvian Bridge on the river Tiber. Striding toward his foe, the royal Con-man claimed a heavenly voice spoke to him. "By this sign shalt thou conquer," and also gave him that day's winning Super Ball numbers. He looked up to see a mystical glowing cross floating in the sky. Dropping his hash pipe and picking up his sword, Constantine embraced his enemies with the love of Christ, divinely disemboweling an untold number of them in the name of the Almighty. Through the Edict of Milan in 313 and the subsequent defeat of the traitorous, self-proclaimed Eastern Roman emperor Licinius in 324, Constantine became absolute ruler of the Holy Roman Empire, officially ending the persecution of Christians and banning crucifixion, forcing parents to find alternate weekend picnic locations to which to take the kids.

Jumping on the biblical bandwagon in 325 AD, Constantine, fearing civil war, gathered bishops from across the civilized lands to what is now Iznik, Turkey, to once and for all settle their "minor" differences. Records show that anywhere between 250 to 318 bishops actually gathered (depending on who did the counting and how much they'd been drinking) from as far away as Africa and Georgia—Eastern-bloc-Georgia, not Sleep-with-Your-Sister-Georgia. Travel and lodging were paid for by the Church authority, as was the All-the-Communion-Wafers-You-Can-Eat buffet. The meeting commenced on May 20 in the imperial palace with the first item on the agenda: trouble with the Arian church (not the Aryans, dude, the Arians).

Arius, and his Arian sect within the Church, believed that Jesus was a separate and lesser entity to the Almighty, apparently still not quite onboard with the whole one God thing. They wanted the Nicene Creed, which would establish the ground rules for the God game, to read that the Father and Son were "homoiousion," or "of similar substance," and a word that sounds kind of iffy right off the bat. Meanwhile everybody else preferred "homoousion," or "of the same substance," which doesn't sound all that different or better. The whole argument boiled down to one letter, *i* (or "iot"), and this hair of difference is where historians believe we get the term "one iota." Angry that the delegates refused to go karaoking with him the night before, Arius actually sang his argument to the gathering, but the assembled clergy tore up their copies of his defense and plugged their ears for fear he'd break into a medley from *Rent*. Although Church history shows he made one hell of a Rum-Tum-Tugger. Arius performed, America voted, and the *i*'s didn't have it. So when he refused to accept their decree, Arius found himself excommunicated along with the rest of his knucklehead crew.

The next victim was the Meletian Schism, which sounds like a Tom Clancy novel or something made up by your dentist. The Meletian church was headed by Meletius (good thing his name wasn't Lesbius) of Lycopolis, who, being the Oral Roberts of his day, refused to admit Christians back into the church who had recanted their faith under the Roman persecutions. Meletius called these flip-floppers "traditores" mostly because he was miffed about serving time in a Roman prison and running from lions while his so-called brothers cheered from the stands. Unwilling to turn the other cheek, Meletius declared that all the Alexandrian bishops were a bunch of pulpit posers, but was shut down like Mahmoud Ahmadinejael at a Hanukkah festival. Meletius kept his title but retained absolutely no real power, thus making him the patron saint of U.S. vice presidents.

The next item up for bids was the vote on approximately twenty new liturgical laws including the prohibition of self-castration (you should always let someone else in on the fun), that clerics were no longer allowed to keep young girls in their homes as servants (young boys, however, were still apparently fair game), and the forbidding of clerical usury (money lending) since they were supposed to collect money from the poor, not lend it out to them at profit. Just when it looked like things were going to wrap up early so everyone could hit the local Applebee's in time for happy hour, some joker in the back decided to pipe up about what day Easter was supposed to be on. The Eastern Church used the Jewish calendar to determine the date, which put it near a Jewish holiday, whereas the Roman and Alexandrian churches used a different calculation that kept it away from the Jewish observance, figuring that if both holidays landed on the same day the supermarket would be an absolute total zoo. After much discussion, it was agreed that the bishop of Alexandria would get to decide what day Easter happened on every year, mostly because he was the only one who gave everybody solid chocolate bunnies instead of those crappy hollow ones that crumble as soon as you bite the ears off.

The Nicene Creed was then completed and spell-checked for typos, lest anyone be confused about the new official ruling on Christianity (the trinity, virgin birth, life of Jesus, that church coffee must always taste like crap, etc.) and was signed by all but three of the attending bishops. The meeting officially ended on July 25, and man, were their butts sweaty from those leather chairs. Everyone went to a big party celebrating the twentieth anniversary of Constantine's rule, which was off-the-hizzy until the Centurians broke it up after the Gauls, who lived next door, complained about the loud music. Even though the First Council of Constantinople in 381 would call into question nearly every point agreed upon, the institution of Christianity had been established and the world would never be the same.

Interesting Tidbit: Some historians believe that, due to in-fighting, more Christians were killed by other Christians in the century that followed the Council of Nicaea than were slain under Roman persecution the century before.

Ways to Bring Up the Council of Nicaea in Conversation

☀ It's time for you to lay down the law like Constantine did at the Council of Nicaea.

☀ Hey Meletius, people are allowed to change their minds sometimes.

☀ There's walking evidence the bishops got it wrong by outlawing self-castration during the Council of Nicaea.

Martin Luther: Rebel Without a Collar

When Are We Talking About: 1483–1546

Why Are We Even Talking About This: Luther was an ex-Catholic priest who authored the Ninety-five Theses, the document that started the Protestant Reformation and initiated one of the bloodiest conflicts in Europe that continues to this day.

What You Need to Know to Sound Smart: Martin Luther was born on November 10, 1483, in Eisleben, Germany, the son of an abusive copper miner. Not one to be beaten, Luther overcame his financial adversity and bruised ego to study at the University of Erfurt, where he received his master's degree in 1505. Much to his father's horror (possibly because he had cosigned his son's student loans), Martin abandoned law, joined a local branch of Catholic monks called the Black Monastery (though it was populated entirely by white guys), and was ordained a priest in 1507. Two years later, at the University of Wittenberg, Luther earned a degree in theology and soon after was sent to Rome to represent his sect, where he was horrified by the corruption he witnessed among the Roman clergy (it made Larry Flynt look like Kathie Lee Gifford). After returning home to finish his theological doctorate in 1512, Martin was given the chair of biblical theology at Wittenberg, which turned out to be a teaching position, and not an actual piece of furniture, probably much to his dismay. Martin enjoyed his work, but the same might not be said for those who worked with him, since the young priest himself claimed the ability to blow out communion candles from across the cathedral with his gas.

While Luther had job security, it was his spiritual security that troubled him. Catholicism's "grace plus good works" (a spiritual 401k plan) meant that his deeds in life were measured against God's perfection, thus not guaranteeing him a place in heaven. While studying the New Testament, Luther became convinced that our souls were saved by "grace *through* faith" (a proverbial Get-Out-of-Hell-Free card), and not by our own actions. So he began questioning many of the Church's teachings, which he felt were unbiblical in nature. In 1517, Luther was outraged to learn that a priest named Joseph Tetzel was selling "indulgences" to local parishioners. These black-market holy pardons, sold with the catchy slogan "as soon as the coin in the coffer rings, the soul from purgatory springs," allowed the purchaser to be forgiven for sins of the past, present, and even future. Incredibly, "indulgences" could also be purchased for relatives, making them the perfect holiday gift. Martin zealously preached against this QVC version of salvation and catalogued his grievances in a list called the *Ninety-Five Theses*, which he reputedly nailed to the front door of the Castle Church in Wittenberg on October 31, 1517. Reviews from the papal hierarchy were less than glowing, and Luther was excommunicated in 1521.

In April of the same year, the Judas Priest was summoned by Emperor Charles V before the Diet of Worms (Dee-et of Verms), which was not the sixteenth-century version of Atkins, but an ad hoc religious review board. Luther was commanded to recant his teachings, but he refused to do so unless the assembled clergy could logically prove, using the Bible, that he was wrong. When no one was able to meet his challenge, Luther was released, though a royally pissed Emperor Charles issued the Edict of Worms, declaring Martin an outlaw and pardoning any citizen moved to maim or perhaps even kill the uppity priest. Luckily for Luther, Prince Frederick the Wise of Saxony took a shine to the spunky German and protected him at Wartburg Castle.

In 1521, again giving the Church the spiritual finger, Luther married Katharina von Bora, a former nun. No wonder Prince Frederick thought he was cool.

In 1524 the Peasant Revolt broke out, during which the lower classes raided Catholic churches, killing clergy and looting their goods. Luther published *Against the Murderous, Thieving Hordes of Peasants* (1525) as a reaction to this uprising and encouraged the princes to put down the violent uprising, which he did not support, advice they were only too happy to comply with.

Martin wrote furiously while at Wartburg, and his books *On Christian Liberty* (1519) and *On the Bondage of the Will* (1525) are classics of modern theology. His most famous work, *The Small Catechism* (1529), is a Protestant interpretation of the major tenets of Christianity, demystifying God and giving the common man a direct line to the Holy Spirit, thus avoiding the transubstantiation markup. In 1546, Luther was asked to return home to arbitrate a dispute between two whining young nobles and died there of heart failure on February 18.

Interesting Tidbit: In order to avoid the papal charge of harboring a heretic, Frederick the Wise had Luther "abducted by bandits" on his way back from Worms and taken to Wartburg Castle, where Luther grew his hair out and went by the regrettable alias of Junker Jorg.

How to Bring Up Martin Luther in Conversation

☀ Dude, they threw me out like Martin Luther at the Vatican.

☀ She's such a whiner. Her litany of problems makes the Ninety-Five Theses look like a Post-It.

☀ Whoa! What a smell! Is Martin Luther in the house?

Blood and Fire on the Mormon Trail

When Are We Talking About: 1839–1846

Why Are We Even Talking About This: The Church of Jesus Christ of Latter-Day Saints, better known as the Mormons, is one of the fastest-growing religions in the world today.

What You Need to Know to Sound Smart: The Church of Jesus Christ of Latter-Day Saints has been dubbed by some as the American Religion, for its family values (primarily to have as big a one as possible), puritanical morals, and the squeaky-clean looks of its congregants. Mormonism's mecca is the desert community of Salt Lake City, Utah, but the story of how the "saints" came marching in to rule that state's culture and politics is a far dirtier tale than one might expect from such a seemingly sanitary religion.

On September 22, 1827, the founder of the faith, Joseph Smith, supposedly dug up a set of golden plates as per instructions from the angel Moroni (a name easy to remember: just add an *i* to the word "moron") on a hillside near Palmyra, New York. Smith had been born two decades earlier in Sharon, Vermont, on December 23, 1805, the same day in 1972 that Terry Bradshaw threw the Immaculate Reception to Franco Harris. But in 1816, Smith's family, falling on hard times, moved to New York (not the city, but the farmland part no one ever goes to) to find a new start. Now back to the plates, which were bound together as a book of sorts, covered in strange symbols (Smith claimed they were "reformed Egyptian" . . . which makes about as much sense as "orthodox atheism"), and just happened to contain the truth of God. Luckily, his Italian angel had also given Smith a pair of magic glasses to help him translate the Egyptian writing. Unfortunately, after a few months of deciphering, the plates disappeared. But Moroni was an understanding angel, and around the same time the following year returned the plates to allow Smith to continue his work (perhaps bringing matching bowls to complete the set), but this time Moroni withheld the magic glasses, maybe deciding they really looked better on him.

Smith also had a magic "peep stone" (not what you think) that helped him find buried treasure and other lost articles (though apparently it didn't work on golden plates). Smith rented out his services to locals ("The peep stone wants to know where you were when you last saw your car keys"), but in March 1826 he found himself in court for fraud. During the proceedings of *The People of the State of New York v. Joseph Smith*, it became clear that the only thing Smith had discovered was a way to swindle gullible villagers out of their hard-earned cash. Though now out of the highly competitive psychic treasure-hunting game, peeping Joe's new faith-based business was about to ascend the ladder of spiritual success.

Nine months after he completed his translation, it hit the shelves as *The Book of Mormon*, and almost immediately began attracting converts. The book claimed that, after his death and resurrection, Jesus had actually come to North America, donned a coonskin cap, and converted a number of Natives, accounting for all the Christian Native American tribes the settlers found when they first arrived. He went on to say that all other forms of Christianity were pure insanities, and only through Smith's "True Church" could salvation be found (no peep stone required). According to this word-of-God-smith in 1829, John the Baptist, along with the apostles James, John, and Peter, appeared in New York (maybe to visit the Statue of Liberty) and ordained Smith and others into the priesthood.

As the spirit moved among the early members, Smith and Co. began to receive revelations that they jotted into a rule-book called the *Doctrine and Covenants* (1835), which also revealed that faithful LDS adherents might achieve godhood, apparently proving that the god of their belief doesn't mind competition. However, even *these* rules were far from written in commandment stone, since the Mormons believe personal revelation supercedes biblical authority. For instance, the current head of the LDS church, Gordon B. Hinckley, whose official title is President, Prophet, Seer, and Revelator (which looks sweet on his business cards), can actually trump the authority of any other source, including the Bible and *The Book of Mormon*. ("Today the Lord told me, everyone must eat more Count Chocula!") This helps to explain some of the more "convenient" revelations God has revealed to LDSers over the years, including the command to end plural marriage (1890) coincidentally just after the Supreme Court ruled church property would be confiscated by the government if it continued, or the 1978 message he sent to stop banning African Americans from the priesthood (though that one was kind of doing them a favor) exactly as civil rights laws were being enforced across the nation. But we digress . . .

Joseph Smith and his followers began to gather in New York, until in December 1830, God IMed Smith on his BlackBerry, telling him to get the flock out of state and head for Kirtland, Ohio, home of the Herb Society of America, but not the one Woody Harrelson belongs to. Shortly after the Mormons' arrival, the Almighty apparently realized just how close Kirtland was to Cleveland and told Joseph that Jackson County, Missouri, was the actual promised land. ("Sorry, oh chosen peeps. My bad.") The fact that right around the same time, in March 1832, Smith had been tarred and feathered by the citizens of Hiram, Ohio, had absolutely no bearing on this vision-revision-decision.

Latter-Day settlers began flooding into western Missouri to build their Zion ("Yup, this is definitely the place! I think") and broke ground in 1838 for a new temple in the city of Independence. The locals weren't thrilled that their new neighbors were buying up the local property, and they were even less excited about their antislavery (that is, so long as blacks didn't try to join them) ideals. Soon many skirmishes broke out between the two groups, culminating in the 1838 Mormon War, during which the church fired on a group of state troopers, bringing an unholy rain of fire down on these religious riflemen. State governor Lilburn Boggs ratified an Extermination Order that called for all Mormon households to be cleaned out of mice, rats, roaches . . . and what was the other thing . . . oh, yes, Mormons. Twenty-five hundred state troopers took Smith and other leaders into custody, and after spending a few months in Liberty Jail (think they used to laugh at *that* irony?), they were kicked out of the state.

In 1839, the saints settled in Commerce, Illinois ("Are you sure this is it, Lord? Not to complain, but . . ."), which they renamed Nauvoo, which Smith claimed meant "beautiful plantation" in Hebrew (but doesn't really). As the group settled down, a bustling town sprang up, and it looked as if they'd finally get to have some peace and quiet. That is until May 1842, when someone tried to give their ol' buddy Governor Boggs a lead baptism back in Missouri, shooting him four times. While his eventual recovery was seen as a miracle by his doctors, who had declared him dead several times ("The miracles are supposed to be for *us*, God!"), eyes fell on Smith's henchman Porter Rockwell as the main suspect (we have no idea why a renowned killer, whose nickname was "the Destroying Angel," would have been so falsely accused), but nothing was ever proven.

Since U.S. President Martin Van Buren had turned

down the church's request of payment for damages during the Missouri debacle, it was little surprise that the state legislature also nixed Smith's petition to have Nauvoo declared a separate territory. The passionate pilgrim came up with the perfect solution—become the U.S. president. ("It's just crazy enough to work!") Joseph announced his intention in February 1844 ("No wars, no taxes, just plenty of wives!"), but the campaign trail got suddenly bumpy when in June of that year, the *Nauvoo Expositor* exposed the practice of plural marriages among the LDS leadership.

Apparently, God had revealed to Smith that Mormon men could take as many wives as they wished (to which most men would have answered, "One's plenty, thanks!"), and he began working the local populace to see if there were any takers. One man, William Law, took offense to this, especially when Smith propositioned Law's wife for a little in-depth biblical study, and the ensuing arguments between the two men resulted in Law's excommunication. Law fired back lawfully from his printing press, and the city began to take sides, until on June 10 of that year when two hundred members of the Nauvoo Legion (the Mormon army) broke in and destroyed Law's offices. ("He was one man! But against all odds we were victorious!") When the Illinois governor demanded Smith and his associates turn themselves in, Smith fled, but a letter from his wife (telling him he forgot his wallet) convinced him to return. Although twelve LDS leaders were charged, ten posted bail and took off faster than the apostles at the arrest of Jesus, leaving their messiah to meet his fate. Fortunately for him, the wait was not that long, since on June 27, a mob of 125 men from the neighboring town of Warsaw stormed the jail. The whole thing was a setup, with the guards firing blanks into the crowd to appear to be doing their duty. Smith was shot three times as he tried to jump from a window, falling twenty feet to his death.

In August of that year, church elder Brigham Young (ancestor of football phenom Steve Young) was given the religion's reigns, and as violent attacks from the surrounding communities continued to grow, Young (now known as the Mormon Moses) Exodus-ed stage left. By the time Brigham died, he'd married somewhere between twenty-seven and fifty-seven women, although he never admitted it until 1851. Only his first marriage was legally binding (and since several of his brides were under eighteen, some joke his name *should* have been, Bring 'em Young), with the rest termed "celestial marriages," which kind of sounds like they had Chinese weddings. At any rate, Young and about six thousand followers left Nauvoo on February 4, 1846 ("Let my people go . . . to Mexico!"), and headed south of the border. Well, the border at that time, which would become U.S. territory in 1848 with the Treaty of Guadalupe Hidalgo, where America basically annexed the Southwest, which Mexicans have been exercising their right to return to ever since.

Through many trials and tribulations, the transient tribe finally entered the valley of what would become Salt Lake City on July 24, 1847, now celebrated as Pioneer Day in Utah, which is definitely a more affordable celebration than Mother's Day for many Mormon men.

Interesting Tidbit: On September 7, 1857, a contingent of Paiute Indians and Mormons disguised as braves attacked and robbed a wagon train on its way through the Utah territory from Arkansas, fearing the settlers might stay. After five days of fighting, the 140 surrounded pioneers were out of food, water, and ammunition. A Mormon claimed to have struck a deal with the Indians and offered to escort the besieged out. The pioneers laid down their weapons and, under LDS guard, marched thirty minutes away, where the entire group, women and children included, was then executed. Only seventeen children survived what is today known as the Mountain Meadows Massacre.

Ways to Bring Up the Mormon Trail in Conversation

☀ Steve's always dating like five women at a time. The guy thinks he's Brigham Young.

☀ Can we just settle on one place to eat? I feel like I'm on the Mormon Trail, here.

☀ That girl is so Nauvoo. What? It means "beautiful" in Hebrew . . . well, according to Joseph Smith.

Well, Hello, Dalai: The Invasion of Tibet

When Are We Talking About: October 7, 1950

Why Are We Even Talking About This: The Communist Chinese government invaded the sovereign nation of Tibet and systematically destroyed its ancient temples and killed its citizens while the international community stood by and did nothing.

What You Need to Know to Sound Smart: On October 7, 1950, somewhere between 40,000 and 80,000 members of the Communist Chinese People's Liberation Army stormed across the Yangtze River into the provinces of Kham and U-Tsang in eastern Tibet, looking to paint the town red.

The Chinese claimed that in January, Beijing had received an urgent message from the Panchen Lama, second in command in Tibet, just under Mister Tenzin "Don't Worry, Be Happy" Gyatso, the fourteenth and current Dalai Lama. The communication supposedly asked for their help in liberating the country—from whom, we have no idea. ("Hi, it's Tibet, please come free us from the tyranny of . . . the evil yaks.") Tibetan soldiers (both of them) were vastly outnumbered and outgunned, their defenses amounting to a Red Rider BB gun and a set of sharpened lawn darts. The nation's clay-based technology stood absolutely no chance against the sophisticated Chinese military. The world community, their hands full in Korea (which as we all know turned out

Kim Jong-*ill* for everybody), refused to get involved in yet another war with an Asian communist state. Well, okay maybe just *one* more, but then we're only going after the Middle East.

Chairman Mao Zedong (Tse Tung? Say-tun?) claimed his nation was heroically reunifying two countries that had once been a single nation and vehemently denied that he was the one who made the call using a fake Tibetan accent. You see, in the thirteenth century the Mongols (who weren't Chinese by the way, but had conquered them) controlled both countries as part of their empire, and by some leap of strange logic, Mao felt this entitled China to invade Tibet in the twentieth century. ("Anything you Khan do, I can do better, I can do anything better than Wu.") China claimed that "no country ever recognized Tibet," but there is much speculation that this was because Tibet was wearing sunglasses and constantly changing its hairstyle. China claimed that Tibet had no rights to self-sovereignty, even though the nation had been self-sufficient for ages, ran its own postal service (something Europe could learn from), managed its own military, levied taxes, maintained diplomatic relations with the surrounding countries, printed its own currency, and was the home of the Lama Burger. Chinese leadership described the incursion as a "peaceful liberation" (sure, nice and quiet, since all the Tibetans were dead), refusing to accept responsibility for the piles of bodies, claiming, "They were like that when we got here."

On May 23, 1951, Mao presented the Dalai Lama with a fourteen-point agreement wherein the Chinese promised not to interfere with the government, religion, or any other major facet of Tibetan life ("that is, beyond the interfering we've done so far"). Of course, that promise barely lasted past dinnertime, since on September 9, 1951, Chinese troops marched into the capital city of Lhasa, causing riots and instigating an indigenous guerrilla war campaign that culminated in the March 1959 Tibetan National Uprising, where masses of people flooded the streets to protest a suspected kidnapping plot against their leader. Despite pleas for peace to both sides from His Royal Orangeness, wide-scale fighting soon broke out with the Chinese butchering thousands of men, women, and children in the streets, especially targeting monks who were easier to get a bead on because of their colorful robes. Gyatso, along with 100,000 of his posse, fled to Dharamsala, India, where he continues to this day to claim to be the leader of Tibet, despite the fact that he can't set foot across the border or make any decision concerning the governance of his country.

In 1961, the iron fist of impotency known as the United Nations drafted Resolution 1723 (oooh, scary!), declaring the Tibetan people had the right to self-determination and asked kindly that, if it wasn't too much trouble, maybe the People's Republic of China might leave the Tibetans alone and go home . . . if they wanted to. China, of course, apologized profusely and withdrew all their troops . . . yeah, right after the Easter Bunny sprinkled fairy dust and turned us all into children again. Four years later, the UN reiterated its position with an identical resolution (that's it, baby, flex those political muscles!) threatening China with economic sanctions that would lower the standard of living of the Chinese citizens, which sounded great until the Chinese pointed out that their citizens already had nothing. ("What are you going to do, take away their mud?")

Whatever the causes or nonsolutions of the Tibetan problem, the results have become crystal clear: Tibetan exiles claim that 1.2 million of their countrymen have been killed since the occupation. Over half the forested areas in the country have been cleared; over six thousand ancient temples, monasteries, and shrines have been destroyed; and thousands of monks, nuns, and other political and religious figures have been imprisoned, tortured, or killed. An estimated 300,000 Chinese troops are stationed in Tibet (hey, they have a lot of guys, maybe we should get *them* to send some "peacekeepers" to the Middle East), operating three nuclear missile bases. All of these pesky numbers aside, in 1989 the Dalai Lama was awarded the Nobel Peace Prize, despite the fact that prior to the Chinese invasion, he and his other lama buddies owned nearly all of the workable farmland in the country, which was farmed by 700,000 poor, uneducated serfs, who were often beaten if they tried to leave their farms without permission. But he seems like a nice guy, and he's got that great book, so what the heck.

Interesting Tidbit: In 1995, the Chinese government kidnapped the Panchen Lama, the second most important religious figure in Tibet today. Answering the call of injustice, thousands of American college students responded by placing "Free Tibet" bumper stickers on the backs of their Saab convertibles, proudly displaying them in the parking lots of Starbucks across the nation. This grassroots political campaign has been internationally recognized as wildly ineffective.

Ways to Bring Up the Invasion of Tibet in Conversation

☼ Most of the people here weren't even invited. It's like the invasion of Tibet.

☼ I'm like the Dalai Lama of my friends, exiled, and no one will admit it.

☼ Someone should speak up before she ruins something beautiful, like the Chinese did in Tibet.

The Business
Conversation

*I*n today's money-hungry society, everyone likes to talk business, so there is no wrong time to have the business conversation. Even aloof, artsy-fartsy types secretly long to be business savvy. It not only makes you look smart, but it gives you the air of a person who has their finger on the pulse of the money-making world and, from New York to Nairobi, that's attractive to most people today. Business parties come in many shapes and sizes, from swanky corporate affairs to small company picnics. Dressing the part is a large part of business. Business folks aren't terribly comfortable with overly individualistic people. If you want to climb the corporate ladder, stay away from pastel-colored hair, facial tattoos, and spouses whose work attire requires a thong. A suit and tie is always spot-on for an evening soiree, while "business casual" (i.e., Abercrombie and the L.L. Bean 'logue-wear) usually includes khakis mixed with a sexually questionable pink or green polo shirt. Most people take comfort in being around herds of folks who look and act just like they do. The danger of the business conversation is that it can end up being about as appetizing as a plate of saltines in the Sahara. Keep the business conversation entertaining with humor and a continual stream of reference to large dollar amounts. Everyone, except for the handful of "spiritually advanced" (usually penniless) people, is fascinated by numbers with the suffix "-illions" attached to them.

Madame C. J. Walker Made It Straight, to the Top

When Are We Talking About: 1867–1919

Why Are We Even Talking About This: This African-American businesswoman and philanthropist became the first female American self-made millionaire.

What You Need to Know to Sound Smart: Sarah Breedlove, which sounds more like her cause of birth than her name, dawned in Delta, Louisiana, on December 23, 1867, into an impoverished household. Feel free to assume that with pretty much anyone born in Delta in the 1800s. When yellow fever claimed her folks, who were former slaves (feel free to assume that with pretty much any *black* someone born in Delta in the 1800s), within a year of each other, the eight-year-old Sarah and her sister, Louvenia, found themselves orphaned and forced to pick cotton to keep food in their mouths. When local crops failed in 1878, the two girls crossed the river to Vicksburg, Mizzip, finding work and shelter as maids in a white household.

At fourteen, Walker married Moses McWilliams to escape her sister's husband, who was abusing her, and in 1885, happiness came a knockin' with her daughter, Lelia. Her girl would later become A'Lelia Walker, who entertained writers of the Harlem Renaissance in her New York City home, called "the Dark Tower," not to be mistaken for the cool 1970s board game of the same name that Orson Welles did that commercial for. Unfortunately, the good times left just as quickly when, two years later, Moses was killed by a white mob (the most common variety of mob at the time), leaving Sarah far from the promised land. With nowhere to turn, Sarah joined her four brothers, who'd opened a barbershop in St. Louis (which sounds like the plot of a UPN sitcom. Oh, wait, it was), earning a living as a scrubwoman to pay for her daughter's education while taking night classes herself.

By 1904, Sarah, married and divorced again, found her stressful life was causing her to lose her hair in clumps. Frustrated and embarrassed, she enlisted the aid of Annie Malone, known in the area for her crazy homemade remedies (" 'Crazy Homemade Remedy Annie,' that's my name"). Taken by the effectiveness of Malone's concoctions, Sarah decided to work for the modern-day alchemist, and, in July 1905, moved to Denver as her sales rep, living with her widowed sister-in-law. By the way, is there a city this woman didn't have a relative in? Anyway, Sarah would later claim that around this time she was visited in her dreams by a large Black man who gave her the recipe for her *own* line of hair-care products.

Shortly after this nocturnal apparition, Sarah moved to Colorado where she met the large real thing—Charles Joseph Walker. The two married, and Sarah changed her name to C. J. Walker, apparently not realizing she was only required to take her husband's *last* name. She began her business selling Wonderful Hair Grower (a product that Richard Marx apparently lives on), which is essentially a cure for damaged hair consisting of petrolatum and a medicinal sulfur (wacky, but it worked). Walker would later design a hair grower and straightener, as well as more than a dozen other products for African-American hair. For the next three years, the Walkers worked tirelessly, going door-to-door throughout the South, selling samples of Sarah's vegetable shampoo (although it could be used on those not in a coma as well), impressing her African-American clients with the quality of her product as well as her winning personality.

In 1908, now in Pittsburgh, Sarah founded the Leila College for Walker Hair Culturists, training young African-American women to sell her product line (think Avon with attitude). In 1910, operations were moved to Indianapolis, which at the time was the crossroads for all major railroad lines. It was also a great place to give her husband his packing orders, though she kept his name because Breedlove sounded better for a *different* kind of product. Through her inexhaustible spirit, relentless drive, decency, and an unwavering faith in herself and God (her biggest shareholder), Sarah made "the Walker System" (which gave new luster to hair through the use of her shampoo and pomade, along with a special hot comb that she developed) into a major cosmetics corporation with more than three thousand employees. It would make her one of the wealthiest women in America.

Years later, fears of a race war fed by local newspapers (ahh, the press, faithfully putting terror into our hearts) escalated into the brutal East St. Louis Race Riot of 1917 in which hundreds of Blacks were cruelly murdered. Walker and like-minded liberals wanted to straighten out much more than President Woodrow Wilson's hair and, using her unprecedented prosperity, she fought for equal rights for Black veterans of World War I and worked side by side with the NAACP to make lynching a federal crime. (Those damn liberals! What will they want next? A seat on the bus?)

After a decade of tireless work, Walker, now with multiple beauty schools and an army of saleswomen called "Walker Agents" across the nation as well as in the Caribbean and South America, had become a household name, even among whites. From an orphan left with nothing but her wits and determination in a time and place where both her skin and gender were liabilities, Walker became a self-made millionaire, the first woman in America ever to do so.

In 1918, Sarah built a giant home called Villa Lewaro in Irvington-on-Hudson, New York, just down the block from the Rockefellers (who must have had a coronary when they saw her climb out of the moving van). Unfortunately, she didn't live long enough to enjoy the new digs since she died on May 25, 1919, at age fifty-two from kidney disease and hypertension. She left vast sums of her fortune to support black schools, orphanages, hospitals, and other nonprofits.

Interesting Tidbit: Marjorie Joyner, while working for Walker, improved a device to help women perm their hair (adding waves or curls), called a Permanent Wave Machine in 1928. Amazingly, Joyner assigned the patent to the Walker Company, whom she continued to work for, surely an indication of her respect for and gratitude to its founder.

Ways to Bring Up Madame C. J. Walker in Conversation

☀ That girl beat the odds Madame C. J. Walker–style.

☀ Mary works so hard she makes Madame C. J. Walker look like a slacker.

☀ Now let's get one thing straighter than a Madame C. J. Walker hairdo.

Charles Ponzi's Scheme Didn't Make Much Cents

When Are We Talking About: 1882–1949

Why Are We Even Talking About This: While many people have forgotten this charismatic grifter, his name lives on in the pyramidal investment scam known as the Ponzi scheme.

What You Need to Know to Sound Smart: The truth about Charles Ponzi is difficult to nail down, due to the man's penchant for screwing with the truth. Though he was born Carlo Ponzi sometime in 1882 in Parma, Italy (famed for its cured ham and incurable liars), little is known of his childhood. Full of big ideas, the five-foot-two Ponzi, who sometimes went by Ponei or Bianchi, claimed that he'd been university educated, though others said his only diploma came from the school of hard knocks, since he earned a living as an unsuccessful petty thief. Ponzi emigrated to the United States in 1903 and found a country full of opportunity for a drifter grifter such as himself. Having blown through his small inheritance meant for his education while playing cards on his trip over, Carlo decided somehow, one day, he was going to get rich or die trying. Actually that was 50 Cent, but doesn't everybody always get those guys mixed up? Ponzi learned to read and write (so obviously, he did *not* attend public school) and got a job as a waiter but was fired for helping the customers with their tipping by taking his share from their change. By the way, all you Europeans totally *know* tips are not included in the United States, so stop playing innocent.

Charles wandered about until 1907, when no-buck Chuck found himself in Montreal, Canada, in the days before the city was blighted by the Expos baseball franchise. Working as a teller at a bank that was in dire financial straits, Ponzi figured a way to buy out the bankrupt company, of course while he was taking a smoking break when there were like a hundred people waiting in line, as international banking regulations clearly stipulate. Ponzi planned on forging checks from a wealthy old customer to finance his high-risk investment, but when the authorities caught on, he was withdrawn from society and deposited in a different kind of Canadian institution for a little cold, hard time.

Released in 1911, instead of turning over a new maple leaf, Ponzi jumped right back into a life of crime, making

some scratch as a Canadian coyote, smuggling Italian immigrants into the United States. This borderline plan failed to
go the distance and got Shorty another two years, this time in
Atlanta, because we all know Georgia straddles the Canadian
border.

Returning from "up the river," Charles headed to Boston,
where he met a gorgeous young Italian named Rose Gnecco.
The two wed in 1918. Ponzi wanted nothing more than to
spoil his new wife with furs, cars, and breast implants, which
unfortunately wouldn't be invented until 1963.

In August 1919, Chuckles stumbled upon a million-
dollar idea. While corresponding with a Spanish businessman,
he received a "postal reply coupon," a certificate that could be
traded for postage in Europe. With some quick math, Ponzi
figured he could purchase inflated foreign monies, use them to
buy the coupons (Now is it coo-pon or cue-pon? What's the
deal?), and trade them in for dollars, thus making a profit, albeit a tiny one of about four cents apiece.

Starting in December of that same year, he charismati-
cally convinced wealthy associates to fund his project, promising a 50 percent return on their investments in forty-five
days or 100 percent return in three months. As word of
mouth began to spread about these many happy returns, fru-
gal folks from all over flocked to Ponzi's facockta offices in
Boston's financial district. Soon, money was pouring in so
quickly (in one day Ponzi actually took in two million dollars,
in *cash*) that, not only did Charles hire multiple assistants,
but he was forced to store the money in anything big and
empty he could find: cans, boxes, political campaign promises. He opened branches all over the Northeast, and everything was running smooth as his silk ties. The only problem
was, Charles had slightly miscalculated his profit margin (as
in, there wasn't one), and Ponzi soon found himself using Peter's money to pay Paul and praying to Jesus no one would

find out. In other words, the returns he gave his old clients actually came from the investment money of his new ones. In no time Ponzi's perpetual motion machine began grinding to a halt.

By the end of July, the *Boston Post* began questioning Chuck's bucks, and an analyst for *Barron's* examining his business scheme concluded that it could never generate this kind of revenue, or any revenue, to be more specific. Ponzi was called before an investigating commission. The day he arrived a crowd had gathered to greet him with one supporter yelling he was the greatest Italian of all time. Ponzi humbly countered that Columbus and Marconi were greater, since the former discovered the New World and the latter, the wireless, though technically it was the Vikings and Tesla, but that's another story. His supporter screamed back, "But you discovered *money*!," and the idiotic crowd cheered him on.

However, Ponzi's business was already losing steam, and without new clients to feed his financial furnace, the money train soon derailed. After paying out as many investors as possible, sorry Charlie found himself with five million dollars in unpaid debts, and so served four years, but since it was a white-collar time, he didn't have to shiv anyone. When he got out, Ponzi found himself facing new charges, and after posting bail, he bailed for Florida (that haven for criminals and the criminally beautiful), where he was arrested for yet another scam, this one promising 200 percent returns on the clients' money. Free again in 1934, Ponzi was at last booted back to the boot from whence he came, leaving Rose behind in the United States to divorce him.

By 1939, Charles was in Brazil helping run LATI airlines for Italy, but he got shut down when the Brazilian government realized the Axis was using the planes to smuggle information and head wax to Mussolini. (What top secret info did Brazil have? Where to hide your car keys while at a nude beach?) The pauper Ponzi went belly up in Rio on January 19, 1949, dying of complications from a stroke. While few remember the man, his name lives on as the term used to describe the thousands of pyramid, or get-rich-quick, schemes pulled every year.

Interesting Tidbit: A new biography reveals that this unconscionable con man may have had a heart after all. It claims that, in his youth, Charles donated some of his own skin to a woman dying of burns, a procedure that caused him a great deal of pain. Hopefully, it was equal to that suffered by the poor people whose money he stole.

Ways to Bring Up Charles Ponzi in Conversation

☼ Invest in that company? Are you kidding? I'd sooner give my money to Charles Ponzi.

☼ These are happy days? You must be referring to the Ponzi kind, not the Fonzi kind?

☼ Don't tell me you're taking financial advice from Nate? That guy got his degree from the Ponzi School of Business.

Up the Love Canal Without a Paddle

When Are We Talking About: 1955–

Why Are We Even Talking About This: Love Canal is one of the worst displays of corporate and government negligence in American history, leading to the poisoning of an entire community.

What You Need to Know to Sound Smart: Once upon a time there was a kindly land developer (just go with it, it's a fairy tale) by the name of William T. Love. At the end of the nineteenth century, he had a grand idea to build a fairy-tale community south of Niagara Falls, free from evil, pollution-belching smokestacks. He envisioned gloriously clean hydroelectric power harnessed from a benevolent canal dug from a nearby crystal-clear river. Sadly, the dastardly Bank Man refused to give the big-hearted Mr. Love his magic seed money, and the fabled community vanished into thin air. Only the lonely canal remained as a memory of the dream and a harbinger of the nightmare to come. In time, this sleeping beauty would be soiled by the city of Niagara and the U.S. military, used as a receptacle for discarded garbage, pesticides, and defunct munitions.

In 1942, in the Age of Chlorofluorocarbons, the canal was purchased by the Hooker Chemicals and Plastics Corporation, who for the next eleven years used the area as a dumpsite for 22,000 tons of discarded chemical weapons and drums filled with stuff from the lower right side of the periodic table of elements. In 1953, Hooker decided that the landfill was full and sealed the entire area in a thick layer of clay.

Around the same time, Niagara City was looking for areas to expand its borders and an abandoned waste disposal site containing millions of pounds of 248 different toxic elements seemed like the perfect location for its vision of Tomorrowland. The geniuses in the city planner's office decided they would buy the property from the jolly chemical giant. Astoundingly, this Hooker had a heart of gold and strongly suggested alternative locations better suited for human habitation, such as the inside of a nuclear reactor or the passing lane on the Autobahn. Convinced the Hooker crew was hiding buried treasure beneath their enchanted clay, the city threw down the gauntlet of litigation and, knowing full well the folly (and cash money) of courtly jousting, Hooker Chemicals surrendered the land under protest, agreeing to receive only a single dollar in payment for the spoiled spoils.

Construction began immediately, and by 1955 the Ninety-ninth Street Elementary School ("Go Isotopes!") was open for business. Show-and-tell was always a big hit, with kids presenting new eyes and limbs to the class as well as body parts that had recently fallen off family members. A thriving suburb would soon follow, but over the years, many members of the community complained of continual illness, leaking chemicals, and a disgusting smell that, due to their upstate location, could not be blamed on Jersey City. By the late 1970s, locals had little love for the canal as independent researchers found an alarming rate of birth defects, miscarriages, and cancer clusters among them. The area around the Ninety-ninth Street School (later known as Professor Xavier's School for Gifted Youngsters) was fenced off and evacuated.

On August 7, 1978, in response to the findings of state agencies, President Jimmy Carter declared a state of emergency, ordered cleanup measures, and then had some cookies and took a nap. Despite the fact that EPA reports showed the presence of chromosomal damage among residents, the Occidental Corporation (Hooker's new sugar daddy), as well as local government officials, vehemently denied any connection between the presence of tons of lethal industrial agents and the rash of mutations, perhaps even pointing out just how cool it is to be like the X-Men.

Despite years of petitions and complaints, it wasn't until locals started dropping like pants off a porn star that these squeaky wheels finally got their grease. Eight hundred families were at last relocated and reimbursed for the cost of their homes, which were now worth about the same as a week-old issue of *TV Guide*. Now that the residents of Niagara had them over a barrel, the Occidental Corporation agreed to chip in $230 million toward cleanup efforts. The case set a precedent in environmental regulation and helped encourage the development of Superfund, an EPA project designed to hold industry and private parties responsible for the cost of pollution cleanup, which, thanks to government bureaucracy, is largely ineffective.

Interesting Tidbit: A thriving community center and fun-filled playground have been erected mere feet from the edge of the contaminated area. Luckily, the chemical fumes and deadly radiation are held back by a special impenetrable protective barrier, known the world over as a chain-link fence.

Ways to Bring Up Love Canal in Conversation
☼ Nice perfume. What's it called, Eau de Love Canal?
☼ Eww! This bottled water tastes like it was imported from Love Canal.
☼ Oh my God, you like that neighborhood? I'd sooner live in Love Canal.

Three Steps Back in China's Great Leap Forward
When Are We Talking About: 1958–1960

Why Are We Even Talking About This: Mao's great leap forward was one of the most devastating economic reform plans ever forced on a country. The changes Mao made to the Chinese economic system resulted in horrifying famines and the deaths of somewhere between 10 to 40 million Chinese citizens.

What You Need to Know to Sound Smart: In 1949, Mao Zedong became leader of the People's Republic of China, thanks to the support of the uneducated gullible masses who backed his land redistribution policies, which Commie-sense dictated, since it promised to take from the rich and give to the poor. Nearly a decade later, after a rather nasty falling out with Soviet leader Nikita Khrushchev (maybe from an argument over whose fat face looked more like the moon), Mao realized that if China was going to be technologically and economically competitive with the rest of the world, he could no longer count on his Russian allies. Unfortunately for the people of China, a titanic disaster lay ahead, and Mao's vision of China's Great Leap Forward to the future was just the tip of the iceberg.

In 1958, deciding the modern symbol for industrialization was steel (not knowing it was really the George Foreman Grill), Mao called for sweeping reforms across the country, commanding millions of farmers to convert their plowshares to steel. Gathering the farmers into 23,500 communes, each containing 5,000 families, Mao repossessed the land that he had given them during the Revolution the decade before, reverting it all to state property. Each commune was instructed to build a backyard blast furnace (right next to the swing set) and begin steel production immediately, which of course was a cakewalk for semiliterate farmers who had absolutely *no* clue about ore or smelting, let alone making steel.

On the farming front, Mao followed the theories of Trofim Lysenko. You're going to love this guy. Trofim was the Soviet "scientist" in charge of agricultural experiments under Joseph Stalin, whose pseudoscience plunged the Soviets into a famine (1931–33) that resulted in the death of 5 million peasants, which to his credit, is actually less than the *usual* body count for Soviet blundering. Among Lysenko's hairbrained farming schemes was "close planting," the idea that sprouts of the same type will not compete, no matter how close you pack them. Get it? Just like all our happy comrades living seven families to a house. Another idea, "deep plowing" involved planting seeds three to four feet deep in the ground. Needless to say, farmers were dismayed when their densely packed seeds could only be harvested by gravediggers. That is, if only they could smelt some steel shovels to dig them out.

When the crops failed, Mao claimed sparrows were the real villains (and don't even get him started on blue jays), believing that they stole a large portion of the grain in the fields before it could be harvested. FACT: Sparrows are renowned burrowers and are often referred to as "the moles of the sky" in Mandarin. Mao called for the extermination of these birds ("Bring me the head of Robin Red-Breast!") and hundreds of thousands of them were killed within the year, which helped a little with the starvation problem by leading to the opening of sweet-and-sour Sparrow Shacks everywhere. With those evil, vicious, sparrows finally out of the way, the insect population soared through the roof . . . and the windows, and the walls. Those few regions that had crops, where farmers were smart enough to ignore their leader's farming tips, were picked clean by the bugs.

Expecting his reforms would soon result in a massive influx of both grain and steel, Mao imposed absurd quotas on the farming collectives. Rather than speak up, the local Communist overseers kao-tao'd to Mao and, terrified of the consequences of failing, demanded their peasants reach the required numbers at all costs. With the only existing steel in the country being wasted on useless objects like cooking pots and farming tools (which, since there were no crops to harvest or eat, weren't really needed), these implements were quickly collected and thrown into the neighborhood furnaces and turned into slag, a smelting industry term meaning "useless crap." Now, not only was there no new steel, the old junk was pretty much gone too ("Son, remember that bike we promised you for Christmas . . ."). Consequently, in those miraculous places where crops had actually grown ("What's this? You have crops! You obviously did not pack your seeds deep and tight enough!") they could not be harvested and so rotted where they grew. The first year alone, grain output in China dropped by 40 million tons.

Fearing for their lives, the overseers reported huge production increases ("Come on, who's going to notice we don't have 675 tons of steel and 150 tons of grain?") that resulted (now this gets pathetically comedic) in the people being taxed on these inflated amounts . . . leaving them with even less grain than they already did *not* have. When Chairman Chucklehead decided to tour the countryside to see how well things were moving along, his underlings constructed an elaborate plan to deceive their fat, fearless leader. Using trains (those hadn't been melted down . . . at least not yet), authorities shipped a pile of steel I-beams ahead of Mao, unloading them into the middle of whatever village he went to next. That Papa Ooh-Mao-Mao never questioned how his emaciated, uneducated farmers wielding stone-age tools (those who were wealthy enough to afford stone-age tools) were able to forge steel I-beams is the true testament to his genius. At the barren farm communities, officials actually planted mature crops into the dead fields, burying them just below the topsoil, and kept their tours brief lest Mao should notice nearby trees that had been painted brown to hide the fact that starving villagers had eaten the bark off of them.

What the chairman didn't see were those villages of the damned where folks had taken to digging up the recently dead to eat for dinner. ("Leftovers again?") The famine was so awful that in some of the most truly horrible cases, families traded children so that they would not be forced to kill and eat their own kin, and keep in mind, this was just fifty years ago! Pleased as a Peking duck that things were going so splendidly, Mao continued exporting rice and grain to other countries (though we're not sure where the heck he was getting it from) and even allowing those crops stored previously in silos to sit and rot, believing there was still plenty to go around. It wasn't until peasants began revolting and breaking into the grain banks that the chairman finally realized what a horrible situation he had created. Death tolls from starvation are estimated between 10 and 40 million, depending on who was doing the counting and how many of their family members would be shot if they counted too high.

As a result of the widespread chaos, Mao stepped down as leader of the People's Republic, though he never apologized or admitted any wrongdoing (Now's not the time to point fingers . . .), retaining his position as the chairman of the Chinese Communist Party until his death on September 9, 1976.

Interesting Tidbit: While demanding never-ending work from his people, Mao was actually one of the laziest leaders of all time. He would often spend the whole day in bed surrounded by concubines with whom he generously shared his syphilis.

Ways to Bring Up China's Great Leap Forward in Conversation

☀ Trade my stocks for *those*? That's dumber than Mao's steel production plan during China's Great Leap Forward.

☀ When's our food getting here? I feel like a villager during the Great Leap Forward.

☀ It's a little crowded in here. I feel like a Trofim Lysenko agricultural experiment.

Blowing Bubbles at Three Mile Island

When Are We Talking About: March 28, 1979

Why Are We Even Talking About This: The partial meltdown at Three Mile Island threatened to become one of the greatest disasters in U.S., if not world, history and raised national awareness about the dangers of nuclear power.

What You Need to Know to Sound Smart: At 4 a.m. on March 28, 1979, the workers at the Three Mile Island nuclear power plant in Pennsylvania looked away from their Employee Atari Night-Driver Tournament long enough to notice something "funny" going on in the reactor. Not funny "ha-ha," more funny peculiar. Several new lights were flashing on their Bat-computer that weren't supposed to be flashing. You know, the ones labeled "Danger," "Meltdown," and "Kiss Your Butt Good-bye." So much for tonight's screening of that bootleg VHS of *Close Encounters* on their brand-new VTR.

In the early 1960s, Metropolitan Edison, an offshoot of that PCB-proliferating company known as General Electric (whose morbidly ironic slogan was "We bring good things to life"), decided that the best way to create a lot of poison (and a little power) would be to construct a nuclear power plant. Of all the possible locations surveyed, the company judiciously chose Three Mile Island, a tiny swatch of land smack in the middle of the Susquehanna River, not ten miles south of the Pennsylvania state capital of Harrisburg, population 250,000, to ensure they'd be in the delivery range of Pizza Hut. Construction began in 1968 on the first of two separately operated reactors, cleverly nicknamed 1 and 2.

By 1974, TMI 1 began generating power, though TMI 2 wouldn't spark up until four years later. Of the twin reactors, TMI 1 has been controversy-free and continues to be productive to this day, while TMI 2 (the Mary-Kate Olsen of the pair) has had all kinds of trouble. After being up and running for a mere three months, things went horribly wrong when the pumps running the main cooling system on reactor 2 took a number 2, or more precisely, an unscheduled break. Apparently they were union pumps. This caused an automatic shutdown of the turbines and, in turn, of the reactor itself, which was a real drag since the thirty-day warranty had just expired the week before. As a result, pressure inside the system began to build dangerously (like your grandfather after too much broccoli casserole), but luckily, a safety valve opened, releasing the pressure (whewww!). Except one thing, the valve apparently malfunctioned and wouldn't close again, causing a significant pressure drop, and inspiring Jimmy Cliff's hit reggae tune. As if things weren't bad enough already, the backup water-cooling system, apparently feeling neglected, quit working, and the water wouldn't come out until given the attention it felt it deserved. Though this second problem was soon rectified, returning the cooling fluid into the system, an erroneous computer reading informed the operators that everything was back in shape (which was about as accurate as those "how to keep your man happy" tips in *Cosmo*), and the coolant was prematurely shut off. The poor, sick little nuclear reactor, lacking the ice water to keep its temperature down, started burping huge bubbles of radioactive hydrogen gas into the environment.

A little over two hours after the "incident," an employee shift change sent Homer Simpson home, and the "new guy," after checking with tech support in New Delhi, confirmed his suspicions that irradiating the atmosphere wasn't scheduled until *next* Monday, and shut the valve down (double wheewww!). All was quiet on the emission front until 7 a.m., when an emergency was suddenly declared and all nonessential employees (i.e., those who could run fast enough) were evacuated off the island. Harrisburgians blissfully microwaved their dinners, unaware that a bike ride away plant workers were struggling to keep TMI 2 from doing the job for them. Just before 2 p.m., control room workers heard a deep thud, which, since they worked in what was essentially the largest explosive device in the Western Hemisphere, was a small cause for concern. It was actually the hydrogen trapped inside the containment unit exploding. In the greatest miracle since the burning bush and John Tesh's recording career, due to a lack of oxygen, the minor explosion caused almost no damage. To repeat: There was an explosion inside a nuclear reactor that somehow didn't wipe out that part of the continent. At this point a decent portion of the core had gone into meltdown, kind of like your dad after you smashed the family car, and started leaking into the containment building. Fifteen hours after the nuclear bake-off began, with the reactor threatening to collapse like a chocolate soufflé, workers averted this recipe for disaster by reactivating the primary cooling pumps and the overcooked core was at last chilled to room temperature.

Two days later, on March 30, Pennsylvania governor and Harrisburg resident Richard Thornburgh was alerted to the situation and immediately sprang into action by quickly updating his résumé and sending it out to any friends who might be hiring. He also publicly called for the evacuation of children and pregnant women and suggested that anyone concerned with becoming a Kingsford briquette join them, while reminding his female constituents that plutonium *is* nature's greatest exfoliant. One hundred and forty thousand citizens voluntarily left the area and made their way to nearby Motel 6s where they lounged by the pool and enjoyed the wonderful breakfast buffet, though it does make one wonder what the other 110,000 were thinking. ("A nuclear explosion? Is that supposed to scare me or somethin'?")

Over the next two days, the unsung heroic operators periodically vented the building pressure, averting Pennsylvania's destruction by shrinking the expanding trouble-bubble. On March 31, President Jimmy Carter and his wife, Rosalynn, toured the facility ("And to your left is where Phil's face melted right off!") after which he was given a "Junior Reactor Specialist" sticker to put on the corkboard in his room. As it turned out, peanut farming was Carter's second career, with his less well-known profession being nuclear engineering . . . so, he already had the sticker and asked for a balloon instead.

While specialists have concluded that radiation released on that fateful day will result in only one death over the next thirty years (though it unfortunately will *not* be Rush Limbaugh), the accident was far more costly from a financial perspective. The removal of the 100 tons of hazardous waste (picture a truck loaded with 333,000 Kid Rocks) cost the country $975 million, good money that could have been better used paying for personal escorts for congressmen. Babcock and Wilcox Company (the two cocksmen who really screwed the country), which painstakingly designed and built the over-reactor, switched to selling steam generators after fifty-one orders for new plants were canceled following the incident, making their product as popular as Morton Thiokol's space shuttle O-rings during the late 1980s.

As the facts came out about how close Pennsylvania had come to being the nation's number one hot spot, American enthusiasm for atomic energy sagged considerably. Of the 129 reactors that were scheduled to be built in the United States, only fifty-three ever actually were. Furthermore, not a single additional nuclear power plant has been approved outside of *SimCity* since.

TMI 2 remains unused to this day and is available for bar mitzvahs and weddings. ("Just look at the bride, she's simply glowing.")

Interesting Tidbit: As luck would have it, the partial meltdown at Three Mile Island occurred just twelve days after the release of the film *The China Syndrome*, which featured Jane Fonda as a reporter digging up safety violations at a nuclear power plant. It just goes to show what lengths those greedy movie studios will go to in order to promote their films.

Ways to Bring Up Three Mile Island in Conversation

☀ Whew! That was some serious chili. I'm beginning to feel like Three Mile Island.

☀ I like that Arthur's so bubbly, but sometimes he can be a little too much like Three Mile Island.

☀ I need some water before I go into meltdown like TMI 2.

☀ **12** ☀

The Film and Performing Arts Conversation

*T*his is probably the easiest of the conversations to use to get things moving and to hold one's own in, since the bulk of it will have to do with current movies and TV shows (and occasionally plays or musicals) that everyone has seen. Still, should you find yourself at a party filled with film buffs or professionals, it does pay to have a more in-depth conversational vocabulary to impress, beyond the man-on-the-street review of *Weekend at Bernie's*. What's awesome about this conversation is that it's primarily opinion-driven, built on rumors, gossip, and hearsay, and seldom backed up with any real information. But be warned . . . this conversation can often turn ugly since many of these folks like to spend their time discussing who's dumping or divorcing whom in Hollywood or the the flaws and foibles of those untouchable stars they secretly despise for having bigger houses, better cars, and a personal assistant who picks up their dry cleaning.

Konstantin Stanislavski Had a System for Acting

When Are We Talking About: 1863–1938

Why Are We Even Talking About This: This artistic revolutionary cofounded the Moscow Art Theatre, whose work has influenced modern acting and the careers of performers from Brando to Pacino.

What You Need to Know to Sound Smart: Konstantin Sergeyevich Alexeyev first stepped through the curtain on January 5, 1863, in Moscow, Russia, into a wealthy family. It was a time of difficult transition during the worldwide Industrial Revolution. Russian workers were moving out of the oppressive fields to enjoy the glorious freedom of the factory assembly line. Fortunately for Konstantin, punching a clock would never be a necessity, since his family was stinking rich from years of silver and gold thread manufacturing, because if there's one thing everyone needed in post-feudal Russia, it was sparkly string. Unlike most families at the time who were preoccupied with what dirt-covered outfit they wanted to toil in that day, Stanislavski's family spent their free time starting an acting troupe called the Alexeyev Circle (hopefully, not making their kids sing that goofy "So Long, Farewell" song from *The Sound of Music*). It was in this creative milieu that Konstantin grew up working his artistic chops. By the age of twenty-five, he had adopted the name Stanislavski, either to distance himself from his blue-blood reputation or in an effort to protect the family name in case he forgot his lines or farted on stage or something.

In 1888, Stan the Man created the Society of Art and Literature, a group that met in the Maly Theatre, whose members probably wore black turtlenecks and a lot of facial hair . . . even the girls. Here, while the young director was playing around with plays, he became dissatisfied with the whole scene, finding many of the traditional theatrical practices, such as being melodramatic, rolling their *R*'s, wearing poet shirts, etc., inauthentic. Ten years later, working with Vladimir Nemirovich-Danchenko, Konstanin founded the now legendary New Moscow Arts Theatre, the first real acting studio in his country's history. The theater's goal was to get rid of the prevailing overly indicated acting style, such as fake sobbing or put-on angry tirades disconnected from any real emotion (to see a little, just watch *Days of Our Lives*). Stanislavski's "system" focused on getting his performers to *not* appear like actors on a stage, but like real people in real situations. He used techniques such as the "magic if" to make actors visualize what they would do if they were put into the same position as the character (like what you would do if you were an ogre whose best friend was a talking donkey). Another of the Russian's tricks for the kids was called "emotional recall," which had actors think back to a time in their lives when they went through a circumstance similar to that of the character and then recall the event in every detail, which left many sobbing onstage while mumbling something about a big truck and a cat named Snowball. Under Stanislavski, in each scene the actor had to know the character's "objective" (what they want in that particular section of the drama) and what "obstacle" blocks their path to success.

The theater's first production, in 1898, was *Tsar Fyodor Ioannovich*, written by Aleksey Tolstoy (cousin of Leo) and was only produced when Stanislavski felt he could ensure a quality show after a record seventy rehearsals. That same year, he directed Anton Chekhov's *The Seagull* (1898), the perfect choice to showcase his new teachings, since the play was written with the modern theories of psychological realism in mind (the original concept that characters should talk and react like real people instead of, well, Victorian people). Stanislavski believed that theater should not be only for entertainment, but that artists should speak to their audiences about social and political questions through the action on stage.

During the aborted revolution of 1905, Stanislavski continued to direct thought-provoking, socially relevant works. After the more successful October Revolution of 1917, when the Bolsheviks ran about the country crying, "Kill all the smart guys with nice clothes!," Stanislavski would have been toast were it not for the fact that he was protected by none other than Lenin himself (not John, the British rock martyr, but Vlad, the Russian's top Marxist . . . besides the first guy spelled his name Lennon). With the Red Brigade running the show in Russia, Stanislavki's troupe toured the United States, influencing an entire generation of theater dorks and film geeks. Among this theater god's apostles are such famous acting teachers as Sandi Meisner (as in, "I study with Meisner." "You study with Meisner?" "I study with Meisner." "You study with Meisner."), Stella Adler, Richard Boleslavski, and Lee Strasberg.

Near the end of his life and career, Konstanin began to forgo his own system for a new belief that emotional context was best revealed to the audience through physical movement. Imagine Blanche DuBois break dancing to express her fear of Stanley. Though Stanislavski is often associated with the founding of Method acting, many experts believe he would have disagreed with the Method acting system and the classroom techniques used at Strasberg's Group Theatre.

Stanislavski's books—*An Actor Prepares, Building a Character, Creating a Role,* and *My Life in Art*—are all considered classics and form the canon of acting training in many schools around the world.

On August 7, 1938, Stanislavski bowed out of the theater game, dying of apparently natural causes in Moscow, Russia. *Interesting Tidbit:* An actress once came up to Stanislavski and told him that she had been taking copious notes on his lectures for quite a long time, and she was curious what she should do with them. Her teacher's puzzling answer was, "Burn them."

Ways to Bring Up Konstanin Stanislavski in Conversation

☼ Let's play a Stanislavski theater game, using the "magic if" with the idea that you come home with me.

☼ Either you stop causing such a scene, or I'm calling Stanislavski!

☼ You're so melodramatic. Stanislavski would never have approved.

Cecile B. DeMille Was Ready for His Close-up

When Are We Talking About: 1881–1959

Why Are We Even Talking About This: DeMille was a director, producer, writer, and actor, who some call "the founder of Hollywood." He created classic films such as *The Squaw Man* (1914), *The Greatest Show on Earth* (1953), and *The Ten Commandments* (1956).

What You Need to Know to Sound Smart: Cecil B. DeMille was born in Ashfield, Massachusetts, on August 12, 1881, and raised by strict religious parents who would influence his future as a filmmaker but not his future as a philanderer. Though he began his career as a Broadway actor, DeMille was drawn to the then questionable world of film, based at the time in Brooklyn, New York. With the help of Jesse L. Lasky and Lasky's brother-in-law, glove salesman Samuel Goldfish (who wisely changed his name to Goldwyn), DeMille formed the Jesse L. Lasky Feature Play Company in 1913, which would eventually evolve into Paramount Studios.

DeMille's first film, *The Squaw Man* (1914), was slated to shoot in Flagstaff, Arizona, but unprecedented biblical rains forced them further west to a podunk town called Los Angeles. Credited as the first director to work full-time in the city, De Mille loved L.A. The radiant sun, the glittering coast, and the cultural bankruptcy made the City of Angels the perfect place for the entertainment capital of the world. With *The Squaw Man*'s critical and financial success De-Mille flourished as a director, even transitioning to "talkies," unlike most of his silent film contemporaries who believed their trite, ham-acted, cue-card snore-a-thons would outlast the amusing new fad.

DeMille's real fame came through his innovative filmmaking using color tinting in *Joan the Woman* (1916) and his effective recording of sound on set by muffling the camera for *Dynamite* in 1929, as well as his star-making power. DeMille launched the careers of Gary Cooper, Gloria Swanson, Charlton Heston, and many more. DeMille was also a renowned tyrannical, self-centered taskmaster, once informing his staff, "You are here to please me. Nothing else on earth matters." He became infamous for humiliating actors, like what they did to the cast of the film *Cutthroat Island*.

Though married for sixty years, the man who once said, "Give me any two pages of the Bible and I'll give you a picture," apparently missed that sixth commandment: "Thou shalt not repeatedly hump thy coworker in the employee lounge." DeMille had two long-term affairs, one with actress Jeannie Macpherson and the other with Julia Faye, who he directed in *The Northwest Mounted Police* and who, apparently, was Cecil's mount of choice.

Mr. Hollywood was awarded the Oscar for Best Picture

in 1952 for *The Greatest Show on Earth*, where he demon-strated his brilliance as a filmmaker, transforming circus life into an attractive, exciting world, as opposed to the syphilitic, dung-filled horror show we know it to be today.

DeMille's magnum opus, a remake of his earlier epic *The Ten Commandments* (1956), cost more than any other film of its time, a whopping $1.5 million.

Beyond his cinematic accomplishments, DeMille helped found the Directors Guild of America, was nominated for California Senate, and built Mercury Aviation, the country's first full-time passenger airline.

DeMille died on January 21, 1959, in Hollywood, Cali-fornia, when his heart burst into glorious Technicolor.

Interesting Tidbit: A stickler for realism, DeMille once had an actor fire real bullets through a door with other actors standing behind it but warned the actor to be *very* careful . . . because they only had two doors.

Ways to Bring Up Cecil B. DeMille in Conversation

☀ I'm ready for my cocktail, Mr. DeMille.

☀ Jeez, it's coming down cats and dogs. What, is somebody shooting a sequel to *The Squaw Man*?

☀ That guy's got a Cecil B. DeMille outlook on sex. We're all here just to please him!

The Eighth Samurai: Akira Kurosawa

When Are We Talking About: 1910–1998

Why Are We Even Talking About This: Among the most famous and influential movie directors of all time, Kurosawa is the filmmaker who brought us such cinema classics as *Rashomon* and *The Seven Samurai*.

What You Need to Know to Sound Smart: Akira Kurosawa was born in Tokyo, Japan, on March 23, 1910. His father was a military man, descended from the samurai class, and his mother was from a merchant family. She was forty when she had her son, which, in 1910, was the age of most grandmothers. It was Papasan's frequent family outings to the movies that would inspire his sons' passion for cinema, though Akira initially dreamt of becoming a painter. After failing the entrance exam to the cool art school in Japan, he was accepted at the Tokyo Academy of Fine Arts (think CUNY versus SUNY), where he finally committed to a film career, sparing himself from a life of poverty and acrylic-paint-stained fingernails. Kurosawa briefly flirted with Communism, joining some freak-o art league, but wisely realized he wanted to own a car and a TV before he died and so left.

Akira's big brother, Heigo, worked as a *benshi,* a film narrator for silent foreign films, translating to audiences in the dark, offering color commentary. ("So Charlie Chaplin says, 'Blast off, you hose head!' which angers big bad man who looks like my girlfriend's mother, who I think is misunderstood.") Heigo's future ended up on the cutting room floor with the advent of talking pictures. Depressed and out of work, he made an edit of his own, committing suicide when Akira was only nineteen. His brother's death would deeply change the way the young painter saw the world around him, and Kurosawa soon began pursuing a career in film.

In 1936, Akira found work as an assistant director to Kajiro Yamamoto in Japan's burgeoning film market. Fact: The AD's job is difficult and thankless, and about as much fun as being circumcised by an epileptic mohel. Kurosawa worked on several films, learning the celluloid ropes before his directorial debut with *Sanshiro Sugata* (1943), a *jidai geki* (historical movie) set in Japan in the mid-1880s. The film follows the development of judo and the troubled relationship with its bastard cousin jujitsu and was very popular with stocky men who break things with their foreheads. *The Most Beautiful*

(1944) starred the lovely Yoko (no relation to "Ono") Yaguchi, and Kurosawa, agreeing with the title of his project, married the actress shortly after the film's release. In 1945, Akira directed the much-awaited *Sanshiro Sugata 2* (because there were so many unanswered questions from the first installment, like "will the hero use a judo chop or a judo kick?"). Most of these early films were not-so-thinly-veiled propaganda pieces, made under the watchful jaundiced eye of the World War II–era Japanese government.

By 1950, Kurosawa had directed ten films and was a giant in the world of Japanese cinema (literally, since he stood over six feet tall, which, in Japan, made him an NBA contender), but it was *Rashomon* that won Kurosawa the Golden Lion at the Venice Film Festival (Venice, Italy, a city of art and culture, as opposed to Venice, California, a city of graffiti and annoying street performers), elevating him to international fame. *Rashomon* followed the investigation of a murdered samurai, told several times over through the different perspectives of each character in the movie (even the dead guy) and to be honest is kind of a snooze because by the third guy, you're like, "I get it. It's *Groundhog Day* in Japanese." Kurosawa demonstrated not only his storytelling skills but also his innovative vision. Kurosawa was the first director ever to shoot directly into the sun, which by the way if you mention this to film buffs, they'll be very excited and probably start yammering something about Orson Welles and *Citizen Kane*.

Three films later, Kurosawa-san scored another hit with *The Seven Samurai* (1954, the first film on which he'd work with his number one leading man, Toshiro Mifune), which this time landed him a Silver Lion ("All I need is the Jade one, and my collection will be complete") and a mess of other accolades. *Samurai* is a sword-fighting action flick. Kurosawa was actually captain of the kendo team in junior high—while we're learning dodgeball and finger painting, Japanese kids are learning how to seriously whoop butt. It tells the story of a helpless village threatened by bandits who scrape together enough money to hire a team of seven trained samurai warriors to defend them (the villagers not the bandits). *Samurai* would become the template for a dozen modern knockoffs such as *The Magnificent Seven, The Dirty Dozen,* and *Gymkata.* The film clearly shows the influences of American filmmaker John Ford, with whom Kurosawa was obsessed. After meeting the legendary Western director (of westerns), Kurosawa even began dressing like him while on set.

Kurosawa based many of his later films on literary classics. *Hakuchi* (1951) was derived from the plot of Dostoyevsky's *The Idiot,* and Shakespeare's *Macbeth* was the inspiration for *Throne of Blood* (1957). *Yojimbo* (1961) is essentially an East meets "Western" following a *ronin* (masterless samurai, like Stuart Copeland without Sting) who plays two warring gangs against each other and saves the town they've enslaved.

Kurosawa was notoriously intense and obsessed with little other than moviemaking, like PETA and the whole leather thing . . . come on, it's obvious God made those creatures to be our car seats. He believed that it was the director's job to personally oversee every aspect of production from the storyboards (which he drew himself) to the final edit, as opposed to the guy who helmed *Battlefield Earth* who it seems phoned in his direction while vacationing in Cabo. Kurosawa's unorthodox technique of shooting simultaneously with three camera units kept his actors off balance and gave him extraordinary performances as well as ample choices in the editing room, a style few modern directors can afford, aside from the shogun of Hollywood, Steven Spielberg, who is said to watch *Seven Samurai* before going out to shoot any movie.

In 1970, Kurosawa was hired to shoot the Japanese portion of *Tora! Tora! Tora!*, but his contract was tora-ed up after clashes with movie execs over his shooting choices. ("What's with all this artsy staring at the clouds crap? We want planes and guys blowing up!") The 1970s continued to prove difficult for the aging auteur, who found funding harder to find than fresh sushi on Sunday. His first color film, *Dodesukaden* (1970), about a group of people living on a filthy waste heap, did very poorly at the box office, especially in Gary, Indiana, where locals felt they deserved residuals for inspiring the story. Ashamed by his failure (shame and honor is huge in Japan), Kurosawa tried to follow in his brother's wrist-steps, slashing his in a fit of depression (along with his throat).

Luckily, the filmmaker did not use a Ginsu knife and so survived the ordeal to direct *Kagemusha* (1980), a modified prince and pauper tale about a guy who's the spitting image of the emperor and takes over the job (think Kevin Kline in *Dave* but with katanas and kimonos). The film, which was executive produced by Hollywood small fries George Lucas and Francis Ford Coppola, won the Palme d 'Or at the Cannes Film Festival. *Ran* (1985) was a Japanese *King Lear*, renowned for its breathtaking epic battle scenes with thousands of extras running around in period costume (thank God they don't have those pesky unions over there or that ridiculous minimum wage thing).

In 1990, Kurosawa received an honorary Academy Award though his last three films, including his portmanteau movie *Dreams* (1990), would receive less notice from critics and audiences. Though he always wanted to drop dead on the set, Kurosawa died of a stroke at age eighty-eight in his home in Setagaya, Tokyo, on September 6, 1998.

Interesting Tidbit: George Lucas credits much of the inspiration for his movie *Star Wars* to the Kurosawa classics,

especially *The Hidden Fortress* (1958), including two comedic characters who became R2D2 and C3PO.

Ways to Bring Up Kurosawa in Conversation

☀ I appreciate the offer, but I can take care of it myself.
But if I need you and the *Seven Samurai* I'll be sure to
holler.

☀ Nice cowboy boots . . . now all you need's a ten-gallon
hat and you can look like Akira Kurosawa.

☀ I take the *Rashomon* approach to an argument. I like to
get all points of view.

Bob, Bob, Bob, Fosse, Fosse, Fosse

When Are We Talking About: 1927–1987

Why Are We Even Talking About This: This jazz dance
choreographer-cum-film director completely retooled the
Broadway musical, bringing a sexual energy to stage and
screen that had never been seen before. He is considered to
be one of the greatest choreographers to ever grace the stage
with his work.

What You Need to Know to Sound Smart: Robert Louis
Fosse brought a raw sexuality to theater and dance (you
know, the way Janet Reno did for the White House) that
changed the face of modern choreography. Plié-ing onto the
world's stage on June 23, 1927, in Chicago, Illinois, Fosse
was born to Vaudevillians who indoctrinated their boy into
the world of musical theater during the opening number of
his life. Despite knowing the lyrics to "Day by Day" and "The
Music of the Night" by the time he reached puberty, Fosse
somehow managed to grow up a heterosexual. Yet his folks
must have been disappointed since, to further test little Rob-
bie's manhood, they enrolled him in the Frederick Weaver

Ballet School. ("Are you sure you're not gay, son? We don't mind if you are. In fact, we'd kind of like it.")

By thirteen, Fosse was touring and dancing with his pal Charles Grass as the Riff Brothers. (Performing thirteen-year-old boys? What are we in Thailand?). Two years later, he choreographed his first routine while emceeing at a local dance joint back when dinner theater was good, which was . . . when? The risqué piece featured four females ("See? I told you, Mom and Dad. Now stop trying to set me up with your hairdresser!") with only a couple of billowy ostrich feathers covering their general-talia. The overt sexuality of this dance, which would become a common thread in both Fosse's work and personal life (naked women, not ostriches), aroused more than a little attention. The after-hours life of the nightclub scene also had a lasting impact on Fosse, its ambiance and visuals heavily influencing nearly everything he created.

Fosse, the only guy who could make the name "Bob" sound sexy, graduated from high school in 1945, and like any red-blooded American ballet dancer, joined the Navy . . . not to beat a dead horse, but seriously, the guy *was* straight. Bob got to the war just as Japan took its final bow and missed all the fighting. Not wanting to let his cute little white bellbottoms go to waste, Fosse formed a group to entertain the troops, with fun numbers like *We Got the Bomb, So Let's Dance!* and *Watch This, So You Can Forget What Your Wife Did While You Were Gone!*, which he both directed and choreographed. But *There Ain't Nothin' Like a Dame* if you're stuck on a boat full of guys in the South Pacific, so Fosse returned to the States with a new focus on how he wanted to spend the rest of his life—drinking and screwing, and, oh, yeah, also doing something in the theater.

Bob took his first wife, Mary Ann Niles, for a spin in

1949, dancing with her at a variety of venues (nightclubs, stage, and TV) before trading her in for a new model three years later. Fosse soon found his Broadway rhythm in the musical *Dance Me a Song* (1950), and later became the lead in the tour of another show, *Pal Joey*. His star still on the rise, Fosse signed as a contract player with MGM and moved to Hollywood, where thousands of young actors, having trained their entire lives, go . . . to become professional waiters. Wedding bells were ringing for Bob and his gal in Tinseltown in 1951, when he married his second wife, Joan McCracken ("Heh-heh. He said 'My crack in!'"), also a dancer.

Everything was coming up roses for Bob, who worked steadily in the Studio system, including a role in the movie version of *Kiss Me Kate* (1953). In this he won the attention of Broadway legend, writer-director George Abbot, who hired the horny hoofer to choreograph his next musical, *The Pajama Game*. Fosse micromanaged his slinky dancers painstakingly through their erotic gyrations, which, coupled with slow-motion movement and body isolation, turned the wholesome "bring the kiddies" world of musical theater on its tin ear ("I don't think we're in *Oklahoma* anymore, Toto"), and earned him his first Tony—not a gay partner, the award.

Flush with success, Abbot and Fosse collaborated again on *Damn Yankees* (1955), a lighthearted romp about America's two favorite pastimes, baseball and selling your soul to the devil to be rich and famous (which sounds a lot like the autobiography of Sean Young . . . anyone remember her?). While choreographing his players, Bob took another swing at romance with his next future ex-wife, Gwen Verdon, later known as the "definitive Fosse dancer." Verdon, who made Karen Carpenter look "meaty," was known for her complete muscular control and unbeatable stamina. (And she was also a pretty good dancer . . . we're here all night. Try the veal.) Fosse and

Verdon were inseparable (for now), working together on *New Girl in Town* (1957) and *Redhead* (1960), marrying as soon as he divorced Joan. Everyone, follow the bouncing Bob!

For his next projects, Fosse began directing *and* choreographing, a feat that might have proved too much for one man, but *not* one man supplementing his boundless energy with a regimen of strict exercise and mounds of uppers. *Sweet Charity* (1966), a musical based on a film by Federico Fellini, was another smash hit that he then turned into a film three years later (now let's get this straight, a movie based on a musical based on a movie?). It brought an edginess that redefined cinematic musicals (no more ladies in bathing caps doing synchronized swimming). *Pippin* (1972), starring Ben Vereen (who you *know* just had to have made all African Americans proud by dancing in blackface at Reagan's inauguration), would earn both Bob and Ben matching Tonys.

Fosse directed a small movie that same year called *Cabaret,* starring a young ingénue, Liza Minnelli (pre–Norma Desmond days), which told the dark and steamy story of a lounge singer in Weimar Germany right before the Nazis took power. The movie was a mild success, winning a paltry eight (yes, eight) Academy Awards. Yet Fosse, not quite done high-kicking butt, in 1973, finished the year by directing *L Is for Liza* (man those must have *really* been some good drugs!), a television special featuring waaaaay more Liza Minnelli than anyone remembered asking for, which earned him an Emmy Award. This television honor completed Fosse's "hat trick" (hockey reference, not the bowler hat flipping thingy) and made him the first person ever to win all three major entertainment honors and the less coveted, "Jonesing Award," for best morning shakes. With nowhere to go but down, Fosse's next film, *Lenny,* starring Dustin Hoffman—yeah, definitely, definitely, Hoffman—as the tragic Lenny Bruce, a foul-mouthed comedian who slept around and used a ton of drugs, was a flop (hmm, maybe happy-go-uppy Bob just couldn't relate to the material).

In 1975 Bob nearly choreographed his own finale, suffering a heart attack while directing the stage version of *Chicago,* a smash hit that ran for over two years on Broadway, and was forced to curtail his extravagant lifestyle (only popping and humping on days ending with the letter *y*). Verdon, who starred in all of Fosse's shows, finally had enough of "dancing with the devil," and that same year, exited their relationship, stage right.

In 1979, just when fans and critics thought the showman couldn't go on, Fosse stripped himself naked with his movie *All That Jazz,* about a Broadway choreographer (played brilliantly by Roy Scheider, whose agent would one day misguidedly convince him to do *Sea Quest*) who drinks too much, sleeps with anything on two legs, and abuses frightening amounts of drugs. Still flying high in 1983, the song and dance man directed *Star 80* (starring Mariel Hemingway), which depicted the tragic murder of Playboy Playmate Dorothy Stratten at the hands of her psycho actor husband (sounds like Eric Roberts), played by Eric Roberts.

Fosse's last Broadway production was *Big Deal,* a musical based on an Italian movie. It should have been titled *No Big Deal* since it closed, a financial failure, after only sixty-two performances. Bob shuffled off, shuffled off, shuffled off this mortal coil on September 23, 1987, when his heart finally stopped a tap-tapping while walking with his estranged wife (no not her, not her either . . . it was Verdon) in Washington, D.C.

Interesting Tidbit: Fosse died just minutes before the curtain was raised on his Broadway comeback, a revival of the show that started it all, *Sweet Charity.*

Ways to Bring Up Bob Fosse in Conversation

☀ Hey, now! Those are some sexy moves. Been taking dance lessons from Bob Fosse?

☀ Rachel's a bit of a pill. I don't even think Bob Fosse would take much of her.

☀ I like to jazz things up around the office . . . I'm like the Bob Fosse of the financial sector.

☀ **13** ☀

The Literature Conversation

Most people who are in, or have been to, school *should* have read at least one book (though a few somehow manage to get through without doing so). Yet due to the very nature of our memorize-and-regurgitate–based educational system, most of us have blissfully washed away (either through time or too many Jell-O shots) any recollection of the details contained in the myriad pages we scanned for essential tidbits, while fighting to keep our eyes open the night before a pop quiz. Cut to: Your life, a few years later, when all of a sudden the titles of books and names of authors you thought you no longer needed are raising their ugly head in social settings, demanding you know the difference between *The Great Gatsby, Great Expectations,* and *The Great Space Coaster.* The literature conversation is the proof of the truly well-rounded and educated person. Though the written word may have lost its prestige in popular society, it has not diminished in its impact or importance to our exploration into the human experience.

More important than the tales themselves are their moral/social commentary (like Kafka's *Metamorphosis* and Ellison's *Invisible Man*), or their exposition of the inner workings of the mind (Dostoyevsky's *Crime and Punishment* and Camus's *The Stranger*). Therefore, sounding smart in the literary conversation involves more than knowing the narrative and the names of the key characters; it is the ability to relate the story to the present world (whether current events or a friend's personal problems), and more importantly, the present conversation, either as a problem-solving parable or a parallel illustration of "what can happen when." For example, when dealing with a friend who's been lying about their age to their lover, you might draw attention to the fate of Tennessee Williams's Blanche DuBois, pointing out the pitfalls of pretending rather than having a relationship based on honesty.

The ability to quote from literary sources is a fantastic party trick, and while you may have seemed like a brown-nosing dweeb in grade school, now you'll be the envy of lesser brains who wish they could remember something more meaningful than the Mentos jingle. Ever been in a room when someone quoted Chekhov? Well, maybe you were and didn't know it. You know it's that moment where everyone nods and smiles ooohing and aaahing, but inside, you're desperately either wishing you'd said that or wondering what the hell it meant.

Dante Alighieri's Life Was a Living Hell
When Are We Talking About: 1265–1321
Why Are We Even Talking About This: Italian poet and author of the *Divine Comedy*, recognized as one of the great-

est writers in the history of civilization, ranked with Homer, Shakespeare, and Anne Rice.

What You Need to Know to Sound Smart: Abandon all hope ye who would follow in the footsteps of Dante Alighieri. Dante was born May 12, 1265 (the same day that in 1937, devil's advocate George Carlin would be born), in Florence, Italy, then a collection of squabbling city-states. Dante was an heir to a decadent noble family that, though once famous, like the cast of *Beverly Hills 90210*, had no cash to back it up (*also* like the cast of *Beverly Hills 90210*). But, *che peccato*, Mama died when little Dante was only *sette* years old, while Papa (pronounced *Paaah-pa*), a money-lender and notary, would also die before our *bono* boy was full grown. Dante studied theology (particularly St. Thomas Aquinas) and philosophy among the Franciscan monks who ran the Stilnovo Poetical School. Perhaps the most significant person in Dante's life was nine-year-old Beatrice Portinari, and though they never "knew" one another (come on man, they were nine. What are we in Provo?), she would always be his first and only true love.

At eighteen, Dante gained a small inheritance and two years later, in 1285, married Gemma Di Manetto Donati, to whom he had been betrothed since age twelve. ("You may now kiss the bride . . . and then help her with her homework.") While Gemma popped out four kids (two of each), Dante studied at the University of Bologna (1287), did a stint fighting with the Florentine Guelph League cavalry, and then began to pursue politics (since the cavalry had made him comfortable around simple animals that were full of crap).

In 1290, tragedy struck Dante's soul when Beatrice died at age twenty-four. ("Nooo! Nooo! Why couldn't it have been my wife! Sorry, honey.") Though Beatrice was married to another man, Dante was heartbroken and turned to philosophical study for solace, writing odes to her memory such as *Vita Nuova* (The New Life, 1293), which idealizes women (well, really her), praising the power of love (well, really his love for her). Though cheesier than a quattro fromagi pizza, the poem is significant for its innovative stylistic break with traditional love poems of that time (think the lyrics of Coldplay versus Ricky Martin), but the poet's passions were about to plunge him into a storm of turmoil.

When Florence radically reformed its constitution under the Ordinances of Justice (1293), it became a democratic city-state where nobles were forbidden from holding governmental positions and could be subject to criminal prosecution for abusing commoners. Hey, that sounds cool. Maybe we should try that Democracy thing here in America. Dante had worked his way up to *priore* (part of a ruling council) when his Guelph political party split into two battling factions in 1300. Neri (black) Guelphs were pro-nobility (boooo!), while Dante and his Bianchi (white) Guelphs were for the people (yaaaay!) opposing the imperialist, antidemocratic Pope Boniface VIII (boooo!) who wanted to restore the Florentine aristocracy (yaaaay . . . we mean boooo!). Unfortunately, the Black Guelphs defeated the White Guelphs (why do politics in the Middle Ages always sound like an excerpt from the *Chronicles of Narnia*?) and Dante, who refused to pay the fine levied on him by his enemies, was sentenced to death by immolation. ("How much was that fine again? Let me check my other pants.") Dante fled Florence, never to return to his native city, or his wife, again (which she probably didn't mind all that much).

Dante roamed around Italy a bit, even visiting Paris (which, by the way, isn't in Italy), publishing various works. In *De Vulgari Eloquentia* (1304–7), Dante examined the origin of language, and the poet decided Italian was better than Latin for love poetry (though not more romantic than the seductive clicking of Tagalog) and therefore, all books should be written in it. That way more people could have access to them, and Dante could make more cash. Around the same period, Dante published *Il Convivio* (The Banquet, 1306–8), which was to be fifteen *canzone*, or odes (though he only finished fourteen of them), that examined poetic syntax, style, and structure, while whining about how his first book was so misunderstood. ("Okay you didn't get the last one, but this new one on syntax is hilarious.") The trilogy *De Monarchia* (On Monarchy, 1309–13) was a long argument about Dante's political views that blasted the pope and flattered Luxembourgian (Luxemburger? Luxemburgite?) Emperor Henry VII, whom he hoped would restore order to Italy. Once again on the losing team, his book was burned by the pope.

Turning from politics, Dante chose a less volatile subject for his next, most famous work . . . religion. Called the *Comedia* (Comedy), which is defined in traditional dramatic terminology as any work with a happy ending (but not the massage kind), and later renamed *The Divine Comedy*, this epic poem, organized into one hundred *cantos* (chapters), tracked Dante on the ultimate spirtual surfin' safari through hell, purgatory, and heaven (Inferno, Purgatorio, and Paradiso, respectively). Beginning in 1307, Dante wouldn't complete the work for another ten years, until just before his death. In the story, our poetic protagonist begins lost in the woods and is rescued by the spirit of the ancient Italian poet Virgil (who wrote the *Aeneid*, an epic poem about the events that led to the founding of Rome). Oddly enough, Virgil has been sent by none other than Beatrice to guide Dante to meet her for "happy hour" in heaven. Inferno (Part I) is everyone's favorite part of the work (because that's where all the really cool people are). In the Inferno we're treated to one grisly scene after another as Dante descends hell's nine levels (inside a giant underground funnel), each level being reserved for particular types of sinners: gluttons, thieves, cannibals, traitors, heretics, and people who drive slowly in the left lane. The sins get worse the lower we go, culminating in a visit with Lucifer at the bottom, who sits frozen in ice (like a brimstone snowcone) at the very center of the earth. Interestingly, Dante placed famed poet and politician Brunetto Latini, who had men... ..d the poet, on the seventh level among the sodomites. Is there something you're trying to tell us, big D?

Emerging on the other side of the earth, Virgil and Dante stop for some Chinese food before beginning Part II, their climb up Mount Purgatory (and not a Tenzing Norgay in sight). Throughout the journey, Dante is a simpering whiner who Virgil must constantly coerce to go on with the reward of seeing his Beatrice when it's all over. Sure enough, as promised, guess who's waiting at heaven's doorstep? Virgil has to clam up once at the pearly gates, because he's not allowed inside since he's a pig-burning, idol-worshipping pagan. Kind of hard on the poor Roman, considering Christ wouldn't turn his first Evian into Manishevitz until Virgil had been dead for about fifty years.

Beatrice, being such an angel, guides Dante the rest of the way, taking him through the whirling planetary spheres that circle the earth. Despite the claim that this book has a happy ending, hanging with martyrs, righteous judges, theologians, and other early bird–special types is far from what we would call a party. Soon Beatrice makes us believe a man can fly when she takes Dante's hand and ascends with him up to the heavens. Our gal even garners Dante a glimpse of the One and Only, his big bad self (a seemingly undeserved reward for our hero, who has up until now in the story been pretty much a spineless whining git).

Critics have debated Dante's intentions and messages in the Inferno, but the author wrote that he hoped to uplift people from the misery of earthly life and fill them with divine joy . . . unless they were going to hell. Dante believed that it is the choices we make (free will) that dictate our fates in this life and the next.

In 1317, Dante settled in Ravenna where he was joined by his children. After returning from a diplomatic mission to Venice, he became sick and died on September 14, 1321, and was buried there in the church of San Francesco ("I left my heaaaaaart in San Francesco . . .").

Interesting Tidbit: Exiled even in death, Dante's remains were moved several times. The first time was not long after his passing, when the Catholic Church declared him a heretic. Franciscan monks hid Dante's remains in 1519, when Pope Leo X decided to deliver them to Florence, planning to construct a glorious tomb, but they were shuffled around again in 1677. Dante's remains were finally discovered in 1865 by accident by construction workers.

Ways to Bring Up Dante Alighieri in Conversation

☀ Man! I spent last night in Dante's forgotten ring of hell, dinner at the in-laws'.

☀ History repeats itself again and again. It's amazing today's political parties are no different from the White and Black Guelphs back when Dante Alighieri was alive.

☀ He's totally smitten. She's the Beatrice to his Dante.

Anton Chekhov Was Not Onboard the *Enterprise*

When Are We Talking About: 1860–1904

Why Are We Even Talking About This: Considered one of the greatest playwrights in history and the father of modern drama, Chekhov's works *Uncle Vanya*, *Three Sisters*, and *The Cherry Orchard* are renowned theatrical classics.

What You Need to Know to Sound Smart: If drama is defined as opposing forces in conflict, what better place to father a theatrical revolution than Mother Russia? Anton Pavlovich Chekhov's first act opened on January 29, 1860, in Taganrog, Russia, a coastal town along the Black Sea, where he was born into a lower-middle-class family. Chekhov's devout papa, Pavel, worked as a grocer and used the traditional Russian governing techniques of intimidation and oppression to raise his children. In contrast, his mother, Yevgeniya, was soft-spoken and a wonderful storyteller who taught her son to read and write, as opposed to his old man, who taught him to weep and duck. Grandpa had been a serf who had bought his family's freedom, but he had been *this close* to buying a 63-inch DLP plasma TV instead. The struggle between classes would become a recurring theme in Chekhov's works, with the rich fighting for meaning amid their boredom and the poor fighting not to die in front of the kids.

In school, Chekhov was an average student (see, there's hope for us all) and a prankster with a passion for words, reputedly making up nicknames for his teachers (Mr. Bigbeardski, Mrs. Vodkalov, etc.). Excelling in creative writing, Chekhov created his own short farces, taking part in school plays and watching community theater featuring actors on loan from the Renaissance Faire. Chekhov is rumored to have written his first play, *Fatherless*, while still a boy, but he later destroyed the manuscript, perhaps afraid his old man would be pissed about the part where the father character gets "blowed up" with a stinger missile.

In 1875, Chekhov's life got a little better when Dad moved to Moscow for work and to avoid debtor's prison, leaving the boy with his adoring mother. This Oedipal bliss was tragically undone by a local bureaucrat who blinded Chekhov's mom with friendship and swindled the family out of their home (later inspiring the plot of his play, *The Cherry Orchard*). At age sixteen, Anton was left alone in his village to finish schooling, and his mother, now homeless and no longer burdened with housework, joined her husband in Moscow, which for the young boy meant one thing . . . *party!* Well, actually tutoring, that is, if he wanted to eat. Times were tough, and with the nearest Del Taco three villages away, Anton was occasionally forced to sell off household items to keep afloat, though his papa's rubber toilet doughnut didn't bring in nearly as much as he had hoped. Receiving a scholarship to study medicine in 1879, Chekhov reunited with his folks in the big city, and this early medical training would heavily influence his literary career in terms of his depth of character and his analytical intensity.

To help keep peas kulesh on the table, Chekhov wrote scathingly satirical articles for the slew of popular sociopolitical comic magazines, such as *Streekoza* (Dragonfly) and *Mildly Amusing Yet Inoffensive Anecdotes About Our Beloved Czar Quarterly*. To protect his identity from backlash for fear the government might take away the family shoe, Chekhov wrote under numerous pseudonyms given to him by his schoolteacher such as "Antosha Chekhonte," and "A Man Without a Spleen" (which, if you're Russian, is soooo hilarious, trust us). In 1882, Chekhov met Nicolas Leykin, publisher of *Oskolki* (*Fragments*), the top 'zine of the weekly comic rag heap. Their mandate for two-page comedy pieces forced Sir Spleenless to hone his craft, shaping the bare-bones, subtext-rich style that would become the hallmark of his work. Finally getting his degree, Chekhov began practicing medicine but had trouble earning a living since his patients died of boredom while reading his work. (Note: Most of us can agree Chekhov's stuff can be drier than stale saltines, but it's not smart to say it out loud.)

In the mid-'80s (1880s folks, he wasn't listening to Banarama), Chekhov began publishing more serious works under his real name in respectable journals like the *New Times*, based in St. Petersburg. However, because this paper was owned by ultraconservative anti-Semitic Alexei Suvorin, Chekhov's material was received with largely upturned noses from his audience of liberal intelligentsia, a few of whom *might* have also been Jewish. That same year Chekhov completed his first and only novel, *Shooting Party* (1884), and he contracted his first and only deadly disease, tuberculosis. Though Anton tried to deny his sickness for two years ("No! I did not cough up that lung on the floor! My dear, when I cough up a lung you'll know it!"), he would battle it for the rest of his short life. Chekhov had a brief "engagement" to his sister's friend, Dunya Efros, in January 1886, but his only real interest was the women he brought to life on the page, saving him a fortune on dinners and movies. By 1887, Chekhov had gained some notoriety with a collection of short stories, *Motley Tales,* and over the next two years, he began focusing on the inner workings of the characters' minds rather than the exterior plot elements of the world around them, effectively transforming the literary world. Despite his success, Chekhov remained broke, mostly because he was forced to pay the debts of his two deadbeat brothers.

Chekhov's first play was commissioned by a producer looking for a farce (again with the farces), but *Ivanov* (1887), about the suicide of a young man in debt whose wife is dying of tuberculosis (stop, my sides are killing me), amazingly had few laughs and received a hissing ovation from the crowd. While his next few one-act comedies fared fairly better, it was his short story anthologies that established Chekhov as a serious writer, even garnering him the coveted Pushkin Prize for *The Steppe*, a meandering plotless story about a boy trekking across a wasteland with his uncle and a priest, which, several Hollywood rewrites later, would become the script for *Con Air*. Yet Chekhov remained unhappy, partly because he was terribly self-critical but mostly because of the blinding migraines, bloody coughs, heart palpitations, and dizzy spells from his TB. Socially, he was easily bored by others . . . oh, and like he was *sooooo* interesting. Anton found the theatrical productions annoying (even the ones he wrote) and the press even more so. Well, we can't fault him for that.

The Seagull (1895), which would someday become one of Chekhov's signature plays, was first performed in St. Petersburg in 1896, but stank like bad Beluga, primarily due to lousy acting. So Chekhov split during the second act, vowing never to write another play. Two years later, Vladimir Nemirovich-Danchenko, cofounder of the New Moscow Arts Theatre along with acting legend Konstanin Stanislavsky, convinced Chekhov to let them restage his play with their new style. Chekhov barely survived two lung hemorrhages over the next year to "see" his play transformed into an overwhelming success in 1898. The audience was reputed to have erupted into applause after the end of just the first act, maybe believing they could finally go home. Unfortunately, the author was actually convalescing at his recently purchased estate in Yalta and so could not hear the adulation.

That same year, Stanislavsky and Co. produced Chekhov's *Uncle Vanya,* which was originally written in 1889 as *The Wood Demon* but had flopped after three performances. This play was about a man whose life is ruined by the financial ineptitude of his family members and should have been titled *My Mooching Moron Brothers.* Though busy churning out copious amounts of new fiction, Chekhov found time to marry Olga Leonardovna, an actress from the Moscow company, in 1901. However, wedded bliss it was not-ski since the couple was often separated, with her acting in Moscow and him hacking up organs in Crimea. In contrast, Chekhov's marriage with the Moscow Arts Theatre couldn't have been better.

The Three Sisters (1901), curiously about three sisters (no, really?) who dream of ditching their family to go live in the big city, and *The Cherry Orchard* (1904), about a once-wealthy family forced to sell the beloved family cherry orchard in order to eat ("Sell the cherry orchard? Oh, Crimea river!"), were both enormous successes. These new dramas were the first in history to use psychological realism, where characters behave the way people do in real life rather than soap operaesque melodrama. Chekhov's plays are essentially character pieces with little by way of plot or dramatic emotional moments, and despite the lack of car chases or nude scenes are somehow considered masterpieces of modern literature.

Yet even with rave reviews, the puking playwright was unhappy with Stanislavsky's style (i.e., good) of emphasizing the play's tragic elements (as if there were any others to choose from), since Chekhov thought of his plays as comedies (which leads one to wonder if he ever read them), satirizing the difficulties and miseries of life in Russia. Frostbite, starvation, and deadly disease . . . this guy knew funny. Chekhov wanted to hold up a mirror showing us how routine and dreary our lives are (gee thanks, and that's why we all go to the theater) to inspire us to strive for something more. He empathized with the plight of the common peasant and used his works to voice their concerns while lounging seaside at his villa where he spent his declining years.

Chekhov faced his final curtain on July 14, 1904, at age forty-four when TB took him while at a spa in Badenweiler, Germany, a ringing endorsement for the place's healing waters. After Chekhov's death, his body was shipped back to Moscow in a refrigerated train car stuffed into a box marked "oysters."

Interesting Tidbit: Chekhov was once quoted, "If you, in the first act, hung a pistol on the wall, then in the following one it should be fired." This philosophy of dramatic structure where any threat (physical or metaphoric) revealed early in the play _must_ be carried out during the course of the drama has been dubbed "Chekhov's Gun," and is now a part of literary vernacular.

Ways to Bring Up Anton Chekhov in Conversation

☀ That Yvonne has as much character as a Chekhov play, but is far more exciting to watch.

☀ Ya gotta chickity Chekhov yourself before you wreck yourself by getting too serious about things.

☀ Is this story going anywhere? I feel like I'm reading Chekhov.

What's Bugging Franz Kafka?

When Are We Talking About: 1883–1924

Why Are We Even Talking About This: Kafka's works are recognized by scholars as some of the finest fiction symbolizing modern man's grotesque alienation in an unintelligible, hostile, or indifferent world.

What You Need to Know to Sound Smart: So depressing he should have been German, Kafka was born on July 3, 1883, in Bohemia, part of present-day Austria, then part of the Austro-Hungarian Empire (and close enough to Germany in our opinion). The eldest child and only son of four, Kafka (whose name is Czech for "jackdaw," a type of bird that, unlike Franz, often travels with a mate) grew up in the city of Prague under the shadow of his domineering father, Hermann, a relationship that would become the central focus of both his art and life. Franz attended German schools and received a PhD in law from the University of Prague in 1906, which he never really used. After graduating, he went to work for an insurance company by day (which explains his never-ending bouts with depression), and spent late nights filling page after page of his private journals with accounts of his interminable impotence and consequent overwhelming frustration with his "condition." The limp literary legend never married, though he apparently wanted to, and was unable to free himself from dependence on his father (the impotence thing probably didn't help any either).

While most of Kafka's earliest writings were destroyed

by the author in fits of understandable self-loathing, he reluctantly published several pieces, including a collection of short stories called *Meditation* (1913). His other work of that year, *The Judgment* (1913), was about a son driven to suicide by his relationship with his father and, well, they do say write what you know. These were followed by his most famous work, *The Metamorphosis* (1915), about a man who wakes up to find he has been transformed into a giant insect and, what's worse, no one really seems to notice or care. Like the rest of Kafka's books, *The Metamorphosis* is an allegory for modern society's dehumanization of man.

In 1917, Franz contracted tuberculosis, which combined with his headaches, insomnia, boils, and constipation, made him quite the catch. Kafka was often self-conscious about his looks (why, we have absolutely *no* idea) and so tried to counter his hellacious health problems by maintaining a vegan diet supplemented by chugging gallons of unpasteurized milk, whose phlegm-manufacturing quality must have done wonders for his TB.

Franz published other works, *The Penal Colony* (go ahead, you can giggle) (1919) and *A Country Doctor* (1919), as well as several other small pieces. In 1923, Kafka made a last-ditch effort to cut away his daddy's apron strings by moving to Berlin, where he attempted to establish normal "relations" with Dora Dymant, a young Jewish woman who encouraged Franz to read the Talmud, after which Kafka must have remarked, "that Job guy . . . so lucky." Of course, Franz would soon be forced to break up with the girl because of his health. ("It's not you. It's me. I have a headache, I can't sleep . . . or use the can . . . and well, I got these boils . . .")

Shortly before his death, Franz published *A Hunger Artist* (1924), a very personally significant title, since his tuberculosis made his throat so sore that swallowing was now painfully impossible. On June 3, 1924, still a young man,

Kafka starved to death in a hospital in Vienna, Austria. Kafka's real fame did not come until after his passing. Despite the wretched writer's last wishes that his works be burned, close friend Max Brod published Kafka's novels, *The Trial* (1925), *The Castle* (1926), and *Amerika* (1927), more cheerful bedtime stories about anxiety, alienation, hopelessness, and the futility of life.

Interesting Tidbit: Sexually, Kafka apparently waffled between an aversion to intercourse, which he romantically referred to as "the punishment for being together," and an attraction to prostitutes, both of which put a considerable damper on any hopes for a long-term relationship.

Ways to Bring Up Franz Kafka in Conversation

☀ That guy keeps bugging me. Maybe he's been reading Kafka's *Metamorphosis*.

☀ I've got to work on my game. Franz Kafka was smoother with women.

☀ I've been breaking out like crazy lately. I think I'm beginning to know how Franz Kafka felt.

Vladimir Nabokov Wrote Children's Books

When Are We Talking About: 1899–1977

Why Are We Even Talking About This: Nabokov is the Russian-born author of the now legendary novel *Lolita*, about a middle-aged man who falls in love with a twelve-year-old girl.

What You Need to Know to Sound Smart: Vladimir Vladimirovich Nabokov was born April 23, 1899, in St. Petersburg, the eldest of five children, to a cultured, liberal, aristocratic, yet loving and supportive family, who must've had a few skeletons in the closet, because you wouldn't see Peter Brady writing a book with a pedophilic hero (Greg, maybe). Nabokov's father was a lawyer and politician, and outspoken against anti-Semitism, making him really popular with the Russian pogrom-program subscribers who happened to be his neighbors. His mother inspired Vladimir's creativity, ensuring he received lessons in painting and sketching. The family lived on a large estate fifty miles south of the city, where Nabokinder learned to read and write Russian, English, and French by age five. He inhaled everything in the family library he Nabo-could: Tolstoy, Chekhov, Poe . . . which might explain why he was soooo serious. Nabokov also liked nothing more than to wander the local area, honing his lepidopterist skills (which sounds like someone who does bad things to kids, but it actually means he studied butterflies), with Vlad the Impaler pinning butterflies into what would become a massive collection of framed mats. Nabokov would help discover several previously unknown genera. His collection is on view at the Cantonal Museum of Zoology of Lausanne where it now bores Swiss schoolchildren year-round.

By the age of twelve, attending the elite Tenishev School in St. Petersburg, Nabokov was aloof and precocious, arriving for class in the family Rolls. In 1915, the rich just got richer as the young man inherited two million dollars and vast land holdings from his Uncle Ruka and self-published a book of poems, probably about how hot his girlfriend was or how his parents *totally* didn't understand him. But Nabokov's silver spoon was soon melted down to make bullets, as the Russian Revolution robbed his family of their wealth and beloved Russian culture. ("*You* work the land and *we* live off the fruits of your toils . . . how could you take away our traditions?!") Initially Nabokov found work with the provisional government, but when his father was arrested by the Bolsheviks in 1919 for wearing an outfit that wasn't gray or black, the family fled to England, where Nabokov studied ichthyology at Trinity College, Cambridge, but he later switched majors when he discovered all the hot twelve-year-olds were enrolled in other classes.

Well served by his elite education, Nabokov cruised through his studies, spending most of his time playing sports, socializing, and translating into Russian *Alice in Wonderland*, written by Lewis Carroll, another man you wouldn't want baby-sitting your daughter. The family moved to Berlin, where Nabokov's father was shot and killed in 1922 while debating at a political rally, heroically leaping in front of a bullet meant for his opponent (now *that's* a noble noble). In 1923, Nabokov graduated with honors in French and Russian literature and worked in Berlin for the next decade as a tutor ("Let me help your daughter score . . . high on her next exam!"), translator, and a writer of short fiction and poetry, even creating the first Russian crossword puzzle. ("What's a seven-letter word for dirty old man? Starts with N.") Working on his craft in what spare time he had, Nabokov wrote about love and death and so naturally gained a following in the cheery Russian community. Ever the old-fashioned aristocrat, Nabby (may we call you Nabby?) refused to type, writing everything by hand. He also refused to kiss Lenin's red butt, so his books were banned in Russia. On April 15, 1925, Nabokov married Véra Slonim, a Jewish woman, though life was difficult for the young couple as they struggled to pay the bills. ("Wait, I thought you Jews *all* had money?")

Nabokov's first novel, *Mashenka* (*Mary*), was written in Russian in 1926 and is about a young Russian immigrant forced by the Communists to flee his country. The character lives in a seedy boarding house in Berlin and dreams about a girl (who may or may not be twelve) who he will never have. Where *does* this guy come up with this stuff? That was followed four years later by *Zashchita Luzhina* (*The Defense*), the story of Aleksandr Luzhin, a master chess player who finds himself caught between two realities: his life and his role as a pawn on a chessboard. While these early works were well received, sales were hardly Clancy-rific since Nabokov's readership was primarily Russian émigrés living in Berlin and Paris. ("I particularly like the part where the Russian immigrant wins the lotto.") It is interesting to note that many of his critics accused Nabokov of a lack of Russian-ness, apparently because some of his characters were occasionally optimistic. When the Nazis seized power in 1937, Vladimir immediately realized he and his Semitic wife would likely end up in matching Nabokoffins and so moved to Paris, because the Nazis would *never* be able to get them *there*.

His 1938 work, *Invitation to a Beheading,* was a fantasy where the remaining days of the central character are equal to the length of his pencil (uh-huh). Then in 1939 Nabokov published an early version of what would become his most famous novel as a story called *The Enchanter*, about a middle-aged man who marries a sick widow so he can spend time with her twelve-year-old daughter with whom he's fallen in love. Besides developing his pedostyle, Vladimir also composed his first novel in English, *The Real Life of Sebastian Knight*, though it wouldn't be published until 1941. He hung out with James Joyce and composer Sergei Rachmaninov until the Nazis became all the rage on the Champs-Elysées, and so still wanting no part of "la vie en Reich," he said adieu to gay Paris and hello New York F——kin' City (that's not a Russian word by the way).

During the 1940s, Nabokov found work classifying butterflies ("Is there a lepidopterist in the house?") for the Museum of Natural History at Harvard while teaching creative writing during summer sessions at Stanford. Eventually, he ended up at Wellesley (because none of the all-girl elementary schools were taking applications) and Cornell, teaching Russian literature while also publishing stories in *The New Yorker* and *The At-*

lantic. Nabokov's second novel written in English was *Bend Sinister* (1947), whose title refers to a stripe on a coat-of-arms, indicating that the bearer is a bastard. This novel is renowned for it's eloquence and literary style. What makes this book so remarkable is that though English was the Slavic scribe's second language, he was writing better than 98 percent of those of us who already talk good English. Continuing his passionate obsession with small, beautiful, fragile creatures (we're talking butterflies), Nabokov took a position at the Museum of Comparative Zoology at Harvard until 1948. Over the next ten years, Vladimir merrily traversed some 150,000 miles across the globe in search of butterflies (and someone funded this), driven everywhere by his wife because he refused to learn to drive.

The book you've all been waiting for, *Lolita*, was initially published in 1955, winning Nabokov critical acclaim for his literary skills, while its pedophilic subject matter shocked readers. The book was banned in Paris (What? In *Paris*? That *can't* be right) and was not available in the United States until 1958. The story follows the pinings of Humbert Humbert, a European expatriate with an idiotic name and a disgusting obsession for a twelve-year-old girl who, surprisingly, is *not* named Lolita, but rather, Dolores Haze, info that is *key* to sounding smart. Lolita is actually the name of a girl Humpervert loved as a boy and keeps a diary about, whom our "hero" creepily refers to as the "fire of my loins" in the opening pages. At one point in the story a writer and pornographer named Clare Quilty (the only guy who could make this pedo-tagonist look sympathetic) steals Dolores away from Humbert. In his jealousy, Humbert murders the man and dies in prison while poor Dolores dies giving birth to a stillborn daughter (and this is a Russian comedy!). The success of *Lolita* catapulted Nabokov into literary stardom, allowing him to quit teaching.

His next work, *Pnin* (1957), is about a Russian literature

professor and his experiences working and living at an American university. Look for his follow-up tale about a guy who puts on his socks and eats breakfast. This riveting piece was followed by the literary experiment *Pale Fire* (1962), about Charles Kinbote, an exiled king who explores a poem written by his neighbor (cousin's uncle's best friend's butcher) and was *not* adapted to the big screen for reasons that should seem fairly obvious.

During this time, Vlady-Daddy and his wife moved to Switzerland to join their son, Dmitri, who was pursuing a career in opera. Busy translating Russian literary works into English (Gee thanks, now we *don't* have a good excuse not to read Pushkin), it would be another ten years before Nabokov published *Ada* (1969), a sci-fi love story set on the world Antiterra, which was a mix of Russia and America (think modern-day Coney Island, better known as Little Odessa). *Transparent Things* (1972) and *Look at the Harlequins!* (1975) were Nabokov's last novels, and incorporated yet more of his life experiences into a narrative about a young writer who has issues he should keep to himself.

Nabokov died in Montreux, Switzerland, of a lung ailment (i.e., a really bad Nabo-cough . . . sorry!) on July 2, 1977.

Interesting Tidbit: Nabokov reported in his book, *Strong Opinions*, that he was a synaesthete, which again sounds dirty, but actually refers to a neurological disorder that he shared with his wife, where the subject's senses get mixed and so they taste things they touch, smell words, and see sounds. Wow, like he wasn't creepy enough.

Ways to Bring Up Vladimir Nabokov in Conversation

☼ Back off Humbert Humbert. She's only sixteen!

☼ Michael creeps me out like a Nabokov novel.

☼ So you got fired. You can always become a lepidopterist like Nabokov.

Tennessee Williams Always Depended on the Kindness of Strangers

When Are We Talking About: 1911–1983

Why Are We Even Talking About This: Williams is among the most famous playwrights of the twentieth century and the productions of this prolific two-time Pulitzer Prize winner's plays revolutionized the modern American drama.

What You Need to Know to Sound Smart: Thomas Lanier Williams was born March 26, 1911, in Columbus, Mississippi, to Cornelius and Edwina Williams. His old man was a *real* role model: a shoe salesman who made Al Bundy look like Mike Brady, and who bolstered his boy's confidence by affectionately referring to him as "Miss Nancy." When not contracting gonorrhea at sex parties, his dad was having his ear chewed off in bar fights and replaced with cartilage from his ribs, making amusing anecdotes for the third graders on Bring Your Dad to School Day. Van Gogh Williams (as we like to call him) also had the unfortunate middle name of Coffin, and indeed, young Tom often wished his father was dead. Edwina, on the other hand, came from southern aristocracy and compensated for her husband's cruelty by smothering her boy with love. Meanwhile Tennessee's more athletic and outgoing brother, Dakin, got what little attention his father had to offer. Williams's sister, Rose, whom he adored and who would influence a great majority of the female characters of his plays, was rumored to have a few screws loose (about a Home Depot's worth, to be exact) and was committed after insanely alleging her model father had attempted to rape her. Whether or not she was truly schizophrenic (as diagnosed) has never been determined, and if she wasn't, it was nothing a few high-voltage shots to the melon couldn't induce. Regardless, in the late 1930s, a parent-approved botched lobotomy relegated Rose to the produce section of the food chain for the rest of her eighty-seven years, a deed Williams never forgave his parents for.

Much of Williams's youth was spent in the home of his maternal grandfather, an Episcopal minister. In 1918, the family, broke as a joke, moved to St. Louis, where Thomas's effeminate demeanor made him the object of derision among his classmates and his southern drawl earned him the nickname "Tennessee," which, much like the rubber bands endlessly fired at his head from the back of the classroom, stuck.

At sixteen, Williams sold his first piece, *Can a Good Wife Be a Good Sport?* (originally titled, *Please Put the Chair Down, Dear . . . I Didn't Mean to Burn the Meatloaf*) to *The Smart Set* magazine and shortly after sold a sci-fi story to *Weird Tales*. But it was while attending the University of Missouri that Williams's life changed. In 1929, while watching a production of Henrik Ibsen's *Ghosts*, the stage door to his passion for theater was officially opened. Sadly, writing was forced to take a backseat to eating, when failing family finances forced Williams to drop out of school and into a job at the factory of the International Shoe Company, which also employed his heel of a dad. Who knew the endless hours of mindless drudgery would someday pay off? (All nine-to-fivers take heart.) Not only did the job inspire the play that would launch Williams to fame (see below), but it also earned him enough money to finish his schooling at the University of Iowa in 1938. Williams's first play, *Cairo, Shanghai, Bombay,* produced in Memphis in 1937, whetted his appetite for success.

Williams moved to Chicago, full of hope for his future, but found it was more famine than feast, because everyone knows midwesterners don't really appreciate plays about Arabs, Asians, and Indians the way southerners do. He then moved to New Orleans ("N'awlins" to natives) and officially changed his name. In New Orleans Tennessee began attracting attention in literary circles and in gay bars after hours. The young writer won a Group Theatre Award for *American Blues* as well as a $1,000 grant from the Authors League of

America in 1939. Though his play *Battle of Angels* (1940) belly flopped in Boston, four years later *The Glass Menagerie* was a Broadway smash, winning the New York Drama Critics' Circle Award for Best Play, as opposed to their Award for Best Snooty Remark at a Premiere with a Glass of White Wine in One Hand. If you were doing bong hits while the rest of teen America was reading this play in high school, it centers on a sensitive young man desperately trying to pry his way out from under the controlling hand of his domineering mother while working at a shoe factory, and may as well have been titled *Hi, I'm Tennessee Williams!*

In 1947, Williams met Frank Merlo in New Orleans, a man who would become his guy Friday. Merlo was the best thing that happened to Williams, stabilizing Tennessee's terribly erratic and wildly erotic personal life, where most nights found the promiscuous playwright choking down cheap booze and cheaper men.

Pulitzer Prizes for his plays *A Streetcar Named Desire* in 1948 and *Cat on a Hot Tin Roof* in 1955 catapulted Williams into the stratosphere of superstardom, elevating him to the divine circle of the greatest playwrights in history. *Streetcar* tells the tale of the savage and brutal Stanley Kowalski and his relationship with his sister-in-law, Blanche DuBois, a southern "lady and school teacher" (who at once bears a striking resemblance to both Williams and his sister, Rose), who has come for an extended visit. Blanche and Stanley are like oil and water, and when she tries to turn his wife against him, he tears away her veneer of gentility, unveiling her dark secret of sleeping with students. Stanley ultimately rapes Blanche as part of his celebration for the birth of his son. *Streetcar* has become an American theater staple, with audiences across the nation treated to high school performances starring scrawny Stanleys screeching *"Stella!"* in their pubescent voices. *Cat on a Hot Tin Roof* follows the downward slide of a wealthy southern family whose ambiguously gay son, Brick, struggles to deal with a loveless marriage as well as the questionable death of his lifelong "companion," which might have alarmed Merlo, given Tennessee's tendency to write from life.

Williams's other legendary plays include *The Rose Tattoo* (1951), *Orpheus Descending* (1957), *Sweet Bird of Youth* (1959), and *The Night of the Iguana* (1961), which unlike a lot of "important works" really *are* great reads. Many of Tennessee's dramas were eventually turned into successful films, expanding his influence beyond the stage to the cinema and the world.

In 1961, Williams lost Merlo to cancer, destroying Tennessee's spirit, wracking him with guilt over the abuse he had subjected his devoted lover to (philandering, belittling, and forcing him to watch the movie *Beaches*), and sending Williams spiraling ever further into a world of alcohol abuse, prescription drug addiction, and promiscuous sex. Despite a concerted attempt to break his addiction, Williams was only able to fight off his depression demons with a shield of booze, while unsteadily continuing to wield his pen. Though he wrote nearly every day for the rest of his life, his later plays were dark and strange (don't let anyone talk you into believing *Camino Real* isn't real crap), and never garnered much positive attention from critics or the public at large. Amazing for a man who was half in the bag three-quarters of the time, Williams was one of the most prolific writers of the twentieth century, producing twenty-five full-length plays, dozens of screenplays, hundreds of poems, sixty short stories, two novels, and an autobiography.

The great tragedian's streetcar fatally crashed on February 25, 1983, after Williams, while downing a handful of pills, accidentally swallowed the bottle cap with them, choking to death at his residence in the Hotel Elysee in New York City.

Interesting Tidbit: In addition to playing the lead in both the film and stage versions of Williams's *A Streetcar Named Desire*, Marlon Brando also played the lead in *The Fugitive Kind*, the film version of Williams's play *Orpheus Descending*, despite the fact that the playwright originally wanted Elvis Presley to play the role.

Ways to Bring Up Tennessee Williams in Conversation

☼ That Fran is flirtier than Blanche DuBois, and she likes her guys young too.

☼ I'm worried about Geoff. He's sober about as often as Tennessee Williams.

☼ You think your dad's tough? You should have met the guy who raised Tennessee Williams.

The Music
Conversation

One of the safest and easiest discussions to initiate and carry on is the music conversation. First, there's almost no one who doesn't like music, and second, there's almost always music playing at a party. While music is very personal to people, there are only a handful of fanatics who actually become enraged when certain Mariah Carey songs are played. Even hardcore music lovers, such as jazz snobs or antimelodic punk rockers, are easy to talk to. The worst thing you can say to a music fanatic is that you don't care (the second worst is that you like country).

It's pretty basic stuff. Either you both like drum and bass or one likes trip-hop and the other loves klezmer music. So the information listed in this chapter is more about the origins of different types of music or the background of influential music makers. That way, when you talk about it, you're just sharing info about how all this great music we all love, in one form or another, came into being.

Atmospheres at music parties will vary as much as the sounds of the tunes themselves. Classical music lovers dress up: Dinner jackets, or at least button-down shirts, are the norm. Ladies are casually elegant, or at the very least, not wearing Juicy sweatpants. They enjoy their merlots, pinots, and Gruyère. Classical music lovers are often well read, interested in literature, arts, and dance (ballet more often than krunking). Jazz and blues lovers still seem to be stuck somewhere between the 1930s and the 1970s. Stylishly urban, they are generally a socially aware, though occasionally pseudo-intellectual bunch. If you're unfamiliar with jazz, you'll find it's thrilling live and a little annoying as background music. Jazz lovers are passionate, love smoky, dimly lit rooms, and listen to music with their eyes closed. Rock and roll fans come in all shapes and sizes. Classic rockers love their long hair, neorabbinical beards, and vintage concert shirts, while among Deadheads the tie-dye never dies. Conversation among rockers usually orients around how f——d up the world is and the need to change it in one way or another . . . after we all sober up. Though these rules fall apart among Christian rockers, who tend to dress and act a lot like your accountant. For alternative rockers, dress varies from rockabilly to shabby-chic, expensive labels custom designed to look like you're the fourth person wearing them. Alternative rockers love to talk about the cause of the minute but tend to be more interested in looking hip, being cool, and hooking up. (You say unfair? We say, Hoobastank.) If you're partying with the house, trance, or club crowd, there might not be that much conversation. This party loves to dance in trendy, hipster wear, which often looks like a cross between *Logan's Run* and Urban Outfitters, so bring your best boogie shoes. Interestingly, because the club crew tends to be skewed younger than other groups, they enjoy heated political, socially relevant, or modern art movement conversations. On the negative, clubsters are somewhat obsessed with their nightlife, and their velvet rope world breeds a cosmic club caste system and "in crowd" snobbery that may be hard to initially penetrate. (Plus they might O.D. in front of you.)

Richard Wagner Wrote Rings Around Other Composers

When Are We Talking About: 1813–1883

Why Are We Even Talking About This: This German composer was famous for his Ring Cycle operas, and was a massive racist who, believe it or not, looked a lot like a white Redd Foxx.

What You Need to Know to Sound Smart: Wilhelm Richard Wagner sounded his first note in Leipzig, Germany, May 22, 1813. His mother was Johanna Rosine, that much we know, but it appears she'd been making sweet music with someone other than her husband, Carl Friedrich Wagner, a clerk for the police department. Many suspect "close friend," playwright, actor, and poet Ludwig Geyer was actually Wagner's father. Pencil pusher or guy who wrote red-hot poetry? You make the call. However, a paternity suit was soon moot anyway, since Carl was good enough to die of typhus six months later, avoiding any of those "just tell me the truth" conversations we all dread. Johanna and Ludwig married within the year (again, you make the call), and Richard was forced to keep this "Geyer" name for the next fourteen years.

In 1820 Ricky G was enrolled in a private school outside of Dresden where he learned to play the piano and developed aspirations of being a playwright, just like his dad . . .

we think. The following year, through the tragedy of papa number two dying, little Richard continued to pursue music and theater, heavily influenced by the bigwigs of the German Romantic movement, Carl Maria von Weber, Louis Spohr, and Heinrich Marschner (which sounds like a law firm, but isn't), who all resided in Dresden. In 1826, when Wagner's mother got a role at the Prague theater, she took her daughters with her, but left the boy behind alone to finish school. Richard distracted himself from the heart-wrenching pain of abandonment by writing *Leubald und Adelaide*, a charming play about a young man who goes on a killing rampage after the death of his father, which must've made his roommate a little nervous.

In 1827, the family moved to Leipzig, and this time generously brought Richard with them because there was room in the backseat. Here Wagner's music began taking leaps forward. At the Thomasschule he studied with a composer named Christian Weinlig, who thought so much of the boy's abilities that he refused to be paid for his instruction. ("Oh no, I couldn't take a penny . . . and if you have any laundry you need me to do, or mopping, perhaps . . .") By 1832, Wagner had conducted his first overture, proving extraordinarily skilled at waving a tiny stick in the air in front of highly trained musicians. Right, like that's something any of us haven't done with a pair of chopsticks. The budding composer soon began working on his first opera, *Die Hochzeit* (*The Wedding*), later shot as a made-for-cable movie called *Die Hochzeit, Die!*, starring Dolf Lundgren (who by the way is a Fulbright Scholar, has an IQ of 160 and speaks five languages. Who knew?).

In January of the following year, his real/half brother Karl, a singer in Wurzburg (where they have the wurz singers), got Wagner a job at his theater, where Wagner wrote his first finished opera, *Die Feen* (*The Fairies*) (1834). In July, Wagner was offered the post of music director for a theater groupe (pretentious spelling may vary) in Magdeburg that was well on its way to bankruptcy. Tricky Dick initially refused, that was until he set eyes on Christine "Minna" Planer, a lovely actress (with a daughter who she passed off as her younger sister) who tugged at the heart-strings of the composer, causing him to rethink his position (or positions, as the case may be) about scoring. By 1836 however Wagner was at the helm of this sinking partnership and the company premiered his *Das Liebesverbot* (*The Love Ban*), a thrown-together production with some performers actually making it up as they went along (and keep in mind, this is opera, not *SNL*). It would be the company's final curtain. Minna joined a theater in Königsberg, lobbying for Wagner to be their conductor. He thanked her with the gift of marriage (the gift that keeps on taking) on November 24, 1836. The marriage didn't exactly start off on a high note as Minna ran off with a military officer, though she eventually came crawling back to Wagner. In March 1839, Wagner was given his pink slip, and the unhappy couple headed for gay Paris in the middle of the night, the perfect romantic getaway to dodge his creditors. However, since it wasn't the 1940s, Parisians were not receptive to this German invader, and Wagner struggled along, writing articles for music newspapers and arranging the works of other composers.

It was during this period that he wrote *Der Fliegende Holländer* (*The Flying Dutchman*, 1843), based on either a Nordic legend or a chain of bad seafood restaurants. In the summer of 1841, Wagner learned that an opera entitled *Rienzi* (1840) that he had written was being produced at a theater in Dresden and he was excited since nobody bombs in *that* city. The show was a huge success, and as if someone had waved a magic conductor's wand, Wagner was suddenly enjoying a whole new arrangement, this one involving fame and a lucrative job as a court music director in the city. Wagner began working on librettos (which sounds like a female's sex drive, but refers to a dramatic musical text) such as *Lohengrin* (1848), featuring the Bridal March song that half the world has boogied down the aisle to.

Unfortunately, in 1849 a revolution sprang up against the repressive Saxon king, Frederick Augustus II, who'd disbanded the parliament after refusing a constitution presented to him. Unable to ignore the drums of battle, Wagner put down his baton and picked up a bayonet, well not really, but he did harbor leftist agitators and purchased them a few grenades. When the May Uprisings were put down, Richard decided to conduct his business elsewhere and headed for Zurich, though the mutinous maestro's life now became a classic soap opera. Richard was unemployed again and stricken by a painful skin condition that made writing difficult, while Minna battled bouts of depression. Wagner worked on several essays. *Das Kunstwerk der Zukunft* (*The Artwork of the Future*, 1849) expounded his *Gesamtkunstwerk* ("total artwork") theory—i.e., opera is awesome because it synthesizes all the other arts (dance, singing, acting . . . sleeping) into one. In *Oper und Drama* (take a wild guess . . . , 1851) he discussed the need for social change through art and gave the world a sample of that change with *Das Judenthum in der Musik* (*Jewishness in Music*), a well-orchestrated attack on Jewish composers whom he subtly referred to as "freaks of nature" and "worms feeding on the body of art." Wagner soon began *Das Rheingold* (*The Rhine Gold*, 1854), the first opera for his famous four-part *Der Ring des Nibelungen* (*Ring Cycle*) spanning fifteen hours (FYI, BYO Pillow).

In 1954 Wagner became inspired by the philosophies of Arthur Schopenhauer, deciding that *music* was the most important thing in opera (not drama, as he used to believe, or horned helmets). In 1852, the King of Kettledrums found his heart pounding for Mathilde von Wesendonck, a poet, whom he dreamed of showing his horn section. Her *husband*, a successful silk merchant, who was a big fan of our covetous conductor, even allowed Wagner and Minna to stay in a cottage on his property. Over the next few years, Wagner began mis-conducting himself in an affair with Mathilde that, strangely, she kept her husband routinely updated on, which is weird, but you know those swingin' Swiss. Wagner's new musical muse inspired him to begin *Tristan und Isolde* (1859), the Arthurian love story of Tristan the knight and his love, a married woman named Mathilde (we mean, Isolde). In 1858, things came to a crescendo when Wagner's wife, Minna, found a letter meant for Mathilde and went absolutely bonkers. ("How dare you cheat on me, after I cheated on you!") When her shrill screams were no longer music to his ears, Wagner went solo, heading for Venice but ending up in Paris, where he worked on a production of his *Tannhäuser* (1845). However, the premiere was a disaster when the Jockey Club (rich theater snobs) booed the production off the stage for Wagner's refusal to put a ballet in the second act, the opera equivalent of drunken rednecks screaming, "Play Freebird!" from the back row of a Skynyrd concert. Friendless, wifeless, and penniless, a disconcerted Wagner settled in Prussia where he began *Die Meistersinger von Nürnberg* (*The Mastersinger of Nuremberg*, 1867).

In 1863 Wagner published a portion of the Ring and in the foreword shamelessly placed a personals ad for a rich German to sweep him off the street. Amazingly, eighteen-year-old Ludwig II, who had recently ascended to the Bavarian throne, answered his call, inviting Wagner to court for casual drinks and whatever. Suddenly royally flush, Wagner rolled the dice by premiering *Tristan und Isolde* and received raves. He also began making amorous overtures to Cosima von Bülow, wife of Hans von Bülow (distant relative of Claus "Take My Wife Please" von Bulow), a big fan of Richard's, who might not have been as excited had he known the guy was shtuping his wife. Cosima had an illegitimate daughter, who they adorably named Isolde (we know *we* feel queasy) and the ensuing scandal exiled them both from court, though their patron graciously financed snazzy digs back in Switzerland. In August 1870 the couple was married.

Wagner took another spin with the Ring Cycle, working on the second opera, *Die Walküre* (*The Valkyries*, 1856), containing the famous tune "The Ride of the Valkyrie" (you know, the ditty Robert Duvall plays while blowing up hapless Vietnamese in *Apocalypse Now?*). Big Rich then decided he needed a new theater constructed for its premiere. He chose the town of Bayreuth, Bavaria, for the location and began touring the country raising the money (think Cochella unplugged). The Festspielhaus opened its doors in August 1876. Though a critical success, the show bombed financially, leaving Wagner with nothing but his wand in his hands and forcing him to launch a comeback tour to pay his bills.

Wagner, now suffering from severe chest pains, began the creation of his final work, *Parsifal* (1882). During one of the opera's final performances, Wagner snuck into the pit during intermission and conducted the end of the show himself. After the celebration, Richard and his family vacationed in Venice, where the fat lady must have started singing because he died of a heart attack on February 13, 1883.

Interesting Tidbit: Because of his outspoken anti-Semitic beliefs, Wagner's music was embraced by the Nazi regime as a tool for propaganda. His Teutonic tunes were often played at rallies for Hitler, who described Wagner as the "one legitimate predecessor to national socialism."

Ways to Bring Up Richard Wagner in Conversation

☼ Dude! Maybe it's time to get a little Richard Wagner and compose yourself.

☼ Oh my God. Renee's married life is an ongoing saga, like some updated version of Wagner's Ring Cycle.

☼ Stop telling me what to play. I'm not part of the orchestra, and you're not Richard Wagner.

Night and Day, Cole Porter's the One

When Are We Talking About: 1891–1964

Why Are We Even Talking About This: Porter is among the most famous and prolific songwriters in music history. His lively tunes and witty lyrics have become part of our modern vocabulary and continue to be standards for singers around the world.

What You Need to Know to Sound Smart: Cole Porter hummed his first few bars after the doctor gave him a loving spank (the first of many men to do so) on June 9, 1891, in Peru, Indiana, renowned as the "Circus Capital of the World." ("Visit the Circus City Museum and Gift Shop, won't you? Please? For the love of God, somebody please visit us!") His parents were Sam Porter (a schlubby drugstore clerk) and Kate Cole, daughter of James Omar (or J.O. to his coon-hunting buddies), a shoemaker who had transformed himself into possibly the wealthiest man in the state. Keep in mind, though, that it *is* Indiana. The Porters were completely subsidized by Grandpa J, despite the fact that he disapproved of Sam, although we're *sure* he just kept that to himself.

By age six, Cole was already studying piano and showing an aptitude for music, practicing two hours a day after having rejected the violin's squeaky, high-pitched sound. Cole's smothery mother spoiled her son rotten and was the driving force in his life. She used her father's power and influence to turn her little dipper into a local star. Cole-hearted Kate even had his principal alter Porter's school records to make him appear brighter. Don't scoff, a lot of powerful people have used their influence to get their otherwise "Bush-league" children ahead. She also financed regional music concerts featuring her precious prodigy as the main attraction. In 1901, Porter wrote his first song, an ode to his mother (No kidding? You don't say?) called "The Song of the Birds," which she subsequently published and distributed to family and friends, who probably thought the song was "for the birds." In 1905 Porter ruled Worcester Academy, a prep school in Massachusetts. His effervescent carefree charm won him numerous friends, and Cole was named valedictorian. More significant was his friendship with music teacher Dr. Abercrombie, whom Porter claimed as his greatest influence, citing his mentor's philosophy that the lyrics and melody should become as one, kinda like a martini and cigarettes.

Later, at Yale in 1913, Porter accepted that men, not women, tickled his ivories, though he would never publicly say so. Most of the musicals he wrote were for the Yale Dramatic Association or his brothers in Delta Kappa Epsilon and focused on heterosexual exploits, which makes perfect sense since frat guys are known to be sooo accepting of gays. Cole wrote and performed with the various singing and performing school clubs, which, for Porter, meant touring alumni parties and hobnobbing with America's society elite. He even wrote fight songs for the football team that are still sung today by Yale players, and by the time he'd graduated, Porter had composed six full shows and more than three hundred songs for his alma mater.

After receiving his diploma he took a stab at Harvard Law School but hated it because . . . it was law school. Despite Porter's eventual enormous financial success, Grandpa would never forgive Cole for secretly switching majors and studying music.

However, in the beginning everything wasn't coming up roses for Porter as his Broadway debut, *See America First* (1916), was a fiasco lasting only fifteen performances, about the same number as *Carrie: The Musical*. Yet despite this minor setback, living at the Yale Club on Fifth Avenue, Porter remained undaunted as he traipsed his way through the society scene. During World War I, Cole hung out in gay Paris, adopting the city as his home away from home. Cole threw wild parties full of bisexual orgies and drug use, while doing a song and dance number on the American press, painting himself as a war hero in service of the Foreign Legion.

Back in the States by 1919, and unenthusiastically giving law another trial for the sake of Grandpa (who financed Porter), Cole had a new gal-pal around town, Linda Thomas, a wealthy socialite divorcée. The two were the perfect couple; Cole needed Linda to mask his sexual orientation and raise his respectability, since she certainly wasn't raising anything else, and Linda needed Cole to keep her from falling into spinster status. The two became beard and groom, marrying on December 19, 1919. The bridal gown was a beautiful chiffon number with a twelve-foot train, but at the last minute Porter decided to wear a tux instead. In the 1920s, the newlyweds partied their way across Europe, with Linda enjoying a sailor in every port and Cole enjoying a Porter in every sailor, while our lusty lad continued to hone his musical craft at the Schola Cantorum in Paris in 1923.

The following year, Cole had his first Broadway hit, with the very un-Porteresque *Greenwich Village Follies of 1924*. This was followed by two more smashing successes, *Revue des Ambassadeurs* (1927) featuring the song "Let's Misbehave" and *Paris* with, "Let's Do It, Let's Fall in Love." Porter's lyrics were smart, witty, sexy, romantic, tender, sophisticated, and playful. But keep in mind, in the 1920s, two of the top ten hits were "O-Hi-O (O-My-O!)" and "Yes! We Have No

Bananas." Porter's show tunes quickly became radio classics performed by every major singer of the time, Billie Holiday, Ella Fitzgerald, and later, Frank Sinatra, though we're waiting for Bad Religion to do "Don't Fence Me In."

In 1929, Porter's first duet with Hollywood, *Battle of Paris*, fell flat. However, in the 1930s and '40s, as the golden age of the musicals dawned, Porter became Tinseltown's "tune fairy," and the silver screen sang with his lyrics in *Silk Stockings* and *Born to Dance*. Furthermore, with a strong gay (albeit closeted) community in Hollywood, Cole found a new playground filled with jungle Jims. Needless to say, this caused some troubles with his wife, since wives never seem to understand their man's need to hang out with the boys . . . His increasingly public antics sent rumors flying, damaging both of their reputations.

Meanwhile, as of the 1930s, Porter had quickly become a theater sensation, with the hit song "What Is This Thing Called Love," from his *Wake Up and Dream* (1929), produced in London, and "You Do Something to Me" from *Fifty Million Frenchmen*. *The New Yorkers* (1930) featured "Love for Sale" (which could have doubled as a very public personal ad for Cole), while *The Gay Divorcee* in 1932 (which sounds like a Porter autobiography, considering his marital problems, but isn't) featured the eternal classic "Night and Day." In 1934, Porter's shooting star lit up the sky with the worldwide smash success *Anything Goes,* starring Ethel Merman, then young and thin . . . and alive, featuring the songs "Anything Goes," "You're the Tops," and "I Get a Kick Out of You." But the toast of Broadway wasn't done buttering up his audiences, releasing *Jubilee* (1935), featuring "Just One of Those Things" and "Begin the Beguine"; *Red Hot and Blue* (1936), with the de-legendary song "De Lovely"; and *Born to Dance* (1936), which summed up romance with "I've Got You Under My Skin."

Tragically, the same year that *Rosalie* (1937) debuted, Porter's happy-go-lucky life was crushed along with his legs (and spirit) in a horseback riding accident from which, despite more than thirty operations, he would never fully recover. Porter was a notoriously narcissistic man who was superficially obsessed with appearance, and was devastated since much of his creativity was tied to his virility. Though enduring relentless penetrating pain, Porter courageously never showed even a wince to the outside world, his charming smile masking it all. After he got back in action by 1939, with smash shows like *You Never Know* and the film *Broadway Melody,* the 1940s were a mixed bag for Cole, who many thought had passed his prime by the middle of the decade. Then, in 1948, Porter rubbed his talent in the world's face with the chart-busting *Kiss Me, Kate,* a musical based on Shakespeare's *Taming of the Shrew.* An alleged biopic called *Night and Day* (1945) starred Cary Grant in an almost humorously heroic and heterosexual charade that was supposed to pass for Porter's life. While Cole continued to write into the 1950s with *Can-Can* (1953), *Silk Stockings* (1955), and *High Society* (1955), by 1958 he was done. Four years after Linda's death, Porter, unable to endure the agony any longer, had his right leg amputated. He had waited to do so until after her passing, as she had requested . . . nice.

His joie de vivre drained, Porter went into seclusion, living with only a registered nurse to take care of him. The world lost one of the greatest musical composers ever to draw a g-clef when Porter's heart stopped a beat-beat-beating like a tom-tom on October 15, 1964, at age seventy-three in a nursing home in Hollywood. By the time his last note had sounded, Porter had composed more than fourteen hundred songs.

Interesting Tidbit: Cole Porter was buried in a plot between his wife and, oddly enough, his father.

Ways to Bring Up Cole Porter in Conversation

- ☀ Are you kidding? There were more straight guys at Cole Porter's bachelor party.
- ☀ You must be related to Cole Porter, because you have a way with words that's music to my ears.
- ☀ That guy has a way with the ladies. He's smoother than the lyrics of a Cole Porter tune.

The Devil in Mr. Johnson

When Are We Talking About: 1911–1938

Why Are We Even Talking About This: Though few recordings of his music were made, this singer, songwriter, and guitarist, known by many as the "King of the Delta Blues," continues to help shape and influence modern music even today.

What You Need to Know to Sound Smart: The history of Robert Johnson is as difficult to pin down as one of his turnback bass beats. Depending on which falsified record you believe, Johnson was born anywhere from 1909 to 1911, but Johnson himself claimed May 8, 1911, to be the day the doctor taught him his first lesson in the blues. He was born on a backwater southern plantation in Hazlehurst, Mississippi, to Julia Dobbs and Noah Johnson. His mama soon hit the road as a migrant plantation worker, landing in Memphis at the home of Charles Spencer, whom she'd previously been "involved with." Moving in with Spencer and his current girlfriend and *their* children, Robert settled in nicely, that is until Mom hit the road again, this time leaving him behind. ("You looked so happy I didn't want to disturb you by staying.") Unfortunately, young Johnson was more than a little "spirited" (and you really have to wonder what would make the boy act out) and, at seven, was sent to Robinsonville, Mississippi, back to the loving arms of his mother (he recognized her by the shape of her back), now living with Robert's newest dad, Willie "Dusty" Willis. It wasn't until he learned his *real* father's name that he began going by Johnson, sometimes introducing himself as a relative of famed blues guitarist Lonnie Johnson.

Robert loved music from boyhood, playing the harmonica, the only instrument he could afford, while sitting in with house bands at local dances, strumming away on their guitars during breaks. Legendary blues guitarist Son House, former preacher, and ex-con for murder, remembered Johnson's early attempts at harmonizing as a "racket, you've never heard." Undeterred, Johnson, now growing into a handsome young man, continued to practice his skills with both the guitar and the ladies, though finally settled down in February 1929 by marrying sixteen-year-old Virginia Travis (practically an old maid in Mississippi). Virginia was soon pregnant, and Robert earned money playing and doing occasional farm work. Sadly, Johnson was given yet more grist for his blues mill when in April of the following year both bride and baby died during childbirth. The call of the road was the balm for his soul, and Johnson, knowing all too well his fingers were made for picking strings, not cotton, set out to find his real father, a search that led him back to Hazlehurst. The traveling bluesman developed a rhythm, supporting himself without actually working by wooing the ugliest, loneliest girls in town, who were often all too eager to take care of a stud like him. Once in Hazlehurst, Johnson met and married Calletta Craft, an older woman with three children of her own in 1931. Calletta served him breakfast in bed while he worked on his craft.

Johnson spent his time with local blues man Ike Zinnerman, who practiced guitar in the local cemetery at night and who is commonly considered among the founding fathers of the genre. The two men would jam for hours on end, and Ike taught Johnson what would become his trademark, alternating bass finger-picking method, enabling Robert to appear as if he was playing both lead and bass with the same guitar (like when you try to sing like the whole chorus of "Bohemian Rhapsody" by yourself, but better). In fact, many listeners wondered where the other player was hiding. Johnson took to practicing in the woods by himself, keeping a tiny journal handy for lyrics that popped into his head. ("My woman left me. My mama left me. I left my woman . . . what else?") When Johnson had picked Zinnerman's strings clean of knowledge, his wanderlust got the best of him again, and he headed out. While on the road, however, Johnson practiced another long-standing blues tradition and abandoned his family in Clarksdale, Mississippi (just like his mama taught him).

Johnson strutted into his old stomping grounds in Robinsonville, and for a crowd that included old Son House, he poured his heart into a mournful banquet of nothing but the blues, so stirring those present that rumors soon spread (supposedly by Son) that Johnson had sold his soul to the devil for the ability to play like a god (yeah, that was the most likely explanation). Johnson, according to the tale, was told if he really wanted to learn to play the guitar, he should take his instrument to the crossroads near Dockery's farm at the stroke of midnight. At the appointed time, the Devil (or Karl Rove, whichever name you prefer) stepped from the shadows and tuned Johnson's guitar to the key of sin and then returned it to the youth. From that time forward Robert would be possessed with hands that were less than idle but were certainly the devil's plaything.

Johnson took his infernal act to the booming metropolis of Helena, Arkansas (believe it or not, the musical center of the Delta), shacking up in a shack with a woman named Stella and her son, Robert, whom Johnson took a shine to, teaching the boy tricks of the guitar trade. With his woeful blues whine, Johnson was soon playing every town along the Mississippi/Arkansas Delta, disappearing for months at a time. He was notoriously protective of his style, and if he thought a musician in the audience was watching his finger movements too closely he'd walk out in the middle of the set, never to return. Through his travels his repertoire grew, and Johnson began playing everything from blues to gospel and ballads to polka (much to his shame).

Musically, Johnson had incredible instincts and could play a tune proficiently only a few days after he had *heard* it. As his fame grew, so did his thirst for liquor, parties and, of course . . . women, causing townsmen, who feared Johnson would put his instrument where it didn't belong, to guard their ladies more closely whenever he passed through. Though he earned a good living, Robert became discontented with the endless stream of bars and supper clubs, wanting to share his gift with the entire world.

Johnson met Ernie Oertle of the American Record Company, and in a studio in San Antonio, Texas, he recorded his most famous tune, "Terraplane Blues," as well as many other classics such as "Hell Hound on My Trail," which sold fairly well for Vocalion Records and brought even larger crowds to his shows. Upon returning home, Roberts took an impromptu tour with fellow musicians Johnnie Shines and Calvin Frazier, playing all over the South and East to packed houses before returning to Helena as a legend of the musical world.

After a "pick-stop" in Robinsonville to see his kin, the gallivanting guitarist headed to Greenwood, Mississippi, where on Saturday nights he played at the Three Points, a local juke joint (while on all the other nights he played with the club owner's wife). Details are sketchy regarding the night in question, but reliable sources (drunk or half-asleep people) agree that during his show he was handed a bottle of whisky laced with strychnine by his new lover's jealous husband, who it seems was less than thrilled about the musician's latest "hit." A short time later, Johnson began complaining of stomach pains and was taken to a nearby home where he barely clung to life for the next two weeks. Amazingly, the bleary-eyed blues master made a full recovery only to contract pneumonia and die three days later on August 16, 1938.

Though he only recorded twenty-nine songs (or forty-two, if you include alternate versions), the spirit of his music can be heard all over the airwaves in the sounds of Muddy Waters, Eric Clapton, Elvis Presley, and Jimmy Page, who all claimed Robert Johnson as a significant influence on their careers.

Interesting Tidbit: The space reserved for cause of death on Johnson's death certificate simply read "no doctor."

Ways to Bring Up Robert Johnson in Conversation

- ☀ Hey buddy, you're drunk, and your idea of sweet music don't sound nothin' like Robert Johnson.
- ☀ Pete's had it so rough. Robert Johnson could write a song about his life.
- ☀ That girl's almost ugly enough for Robert Johnson.

Play That Funky Music, Motown!

When Are We Talking About: 1960s–

Why Are We Even Talking About This: Motown Records discovered and produced some of the most famous singers of all time and defined a whole new genre of music.

What You Need to Know to Sound Smart: Berry Gordy Jr. first got his groove on November 28, 1929, in Detroit, Michigan, though sadly, he was too young to move elsewhere. What began as a tiny fur-trading colony had become a booming in-dustrial mecca renowned for its steel and automobile produc-tion . . . and little else. Gordy would bring cultural cachet to this urban wasteland turning the city itself into a musical Oz (but with far better tunes than "The Lollypop League"). The Berrys lived in a neighborhood (light on the "neighbor," heavy on the "hood") dubbed Paradise Valley, though Pair of Dice Valley would have been more apt, since it seemed like every-one who lived in the squalid slum had crapped out in life. Berry's father and mother had come from Milledgeville, Georgia, as part of the Great Migration of the early 1920s, when southern African Americans fled the fields to the indus-trial cities of the North in search of better jobs and treatment, seldom finding much of either. Interestingly, Berry's great-grandmother had been a slave, while his grandfather was a slave owner, which must have made dinnertime conversation a little tense. Gordy's folks were hardworking (Dad was a plasterer and Mom sold insurance), God-fearing folk, who tried to instill basic religious principles in their eight chil-dren, as well as knowledge of the correct spackling com-pound to use in a bathroom and how to get the best rates on automobile coverage.

Gordy, however, initially missed this message, since the Superfreak dropped out of Northeastern High his junior year to try his fists at boxing before being drafted in 1951. Re-turning home from the Korean War, Gordy decided it takes two and married Thelma Coleman, opening a jazz record store called 3-D Record Mart, while also pursuing his true passion, antique furniture . . . just kidding, it was songwrit-ing. A year later the first of Berry's three children was born. Though musically untrained, Gordy possessed an intuitive sense of song structure and sound, and knew what America most wanted. Gordy cried the tears of a clown less than two years later when his record store went belly-up, and everyone heard it through the grapevine that he was now working the assembly line at Ford Motor company making a paltry $85 a week, which left him anything but dancing in the street. Berry continued to write and enter contests, giving his songs to whomever would listen ("Wait a minute Mr. Postman. Mr. Postman look and see . . . I've got this song for you to read. Mr. Po-wo-wo-wo-stman!")

Gordy's first taste of success came from a ditty he wrote in 1957, with his sister and a friend, called "Reet Petite," which was recorded by Jackie Wilson and earned Berry about $1,000 in residuals. Gordy wrote four more songs for Wilson, including the hit "Lonely Teardrops." As his reputation grew, so did his ear for talent, and he discovered William "Smokey" Robinson at a high school talent show in 1957. That same year, Gordy got into producing, working with the Miracles, and began his relationship with the Holland Brothers, future songwriting legends Eddie and Brian. It was the success of these early tunes that enabled Gordy to reach out for his dream of owning his own label.

In 1959, though he and Thelma wondered where did our love go and divorced, Berry was also able to establish Jobete Publishing Company (from his three kids' names—Hazel Joy, Berry, and Terry—condensed into one). In January 1959, Gordy formed Tamla Records with money borrowed from his family ("This better not be like that record store!"). He produced songs for Marv Johnson, including "You Got What It Takes," which had what it took to became a top ten hit. On December 14, 1959, Berry opened a second label named after his hometown's nickname Motor City, calling it Motown Records (the other choice of Unemployed-Ex-Auto-Workers-Drinking-Themselves-to-Death-Town Records just didn't have the right ring) and releasing his first single, "Bad

Girl" by Smokey Robinson and the Miracles, not the Donna Summer disco song.

Though in the early 1960s Gordy began working with Barrett Strong (today one of Motown's most famous), it was Mary Wells with her classics "Bye, Bye Baby" (1960) and "My Guy" (1964) who would become Motown's first "star." The Marvelettes' "Please, Mr. Postman" (1961) was Motown's first number one on the pop charts, and Smokey and the Miracles' "Shop Around" (1960), its first million-copy-selling single. But the true beginning of the "Motown sound" was in 1963 when the Hollands teamed up with newcomer Lamont Dozier (a songwriting team that would become immortal), to write and produce "Come and Get These Memories" (1963) performed by Martha and the Vandellas. The Primettes, who Berry met as teens but refused to work with before they finished high school, were now signed, sealed, and delivered as the Supremes, led by the stunning Diana Ross. The group became *the* most successful female band of all time, and Diana became one of the biggest loons of all time. Their hits, such as "Baby Love" (1964), "Stop! In the Name of Love" (1965), and "You Can't Hurry Love" (1966) made them the third largest sellers (with the Beatles and Elvis holding the number one and two spots) in music history. In 1971, during a few late-night "jam sessions," Gordy taught Ross the old adage "the darker the Berry . . ." and before anyone could say what's goin' on, they produced a surprise single . . . a daughter, little Rhonda Ross Kendrick (who would become a soap-opera star).

During his run, Gordy discovered young talent all over the city, including Marvin Gaye, the Temptations (originally called the Distants), the Four Tops, and an eleven-year-old sightless singing sensation Steveland Morris (aka the swaying superstar, Stevie Wonder) whose album, *Twelve-Year-Old*

Genius, was Motown's first number-one pop album. Since few of his singers played instruments ("Hey, the Monkees get away with it!"), Gordy assembled a house band composed of the top jazz and blues musicians in Detroit, calling them the Funk Brothers, getting them to play on pop albums by offering recording deals on his newest label, Workshop Jazz (1962). Under Gordy's guidance, his musical arrangers crossed R&B with soul and gospel, "popifying" their jazz and blues with a rock and roll backbeat to open its appeal to the masses. Berry even tweaked the studio mix so it would sound better while being played over car speakers. By 1964, Gordy understood how sweet it is to be loved by you and your money, moving his offices from 1719 Gladstone Street into his two-story house at 2648 West Grand Boulevard, where he also built a recording studio, and painted "Hitsville, U.S.A." over the door.

By the mid-1960s, 75 percent of Motown releases placed somewhere on the R&B charts, an unheard-of percentage in any market, which is as difficult as batting .400 or finding the perfect bra. Soon, new groups like Gladys Knight and the Pips and the Isley Brothers (both signed in 1966), as well as an up-and-coming family of superstar singers known as the Partridge Family (okay, okay, we're kidding, actually it was the Jackson 5 . . . but who doesn't jam to "I Think I Love You"), were flocking to the label. Gordy was record executive, songwriter, producer, business manager, and image-maker all rolled into one. All Motown clients took dance and etiquette classes to polish their personalities and performances. ("Ever see the band *Kiss*? Do everything they *don't* do.") By the end of the 1960s, Berry was burying the competition with more hits on the radio than any of the corporate (white) labels and had defined an entirely new genre of music that would bear the name of his label. However, even as

Gordy was movin' on up, he ran into trouble when Holland-Dozier-Holland clashed with him over money and left the company, creating the Hot Wax label, though nothing they would later write matched what they did at Motown.

In 1971, though several acts had jumped ship to bigger labels, Motown set sail with "What's Going On," written, produced, and performed by Marvin Gaye. Though Gordy was initially reticent about the album's strong social commentary (on the Vietnam War, the Equal Rights Movement, the fact that *Hee Haw* had been canceled . . .), it was ironically these very themes, backed by Marvin's soulful sound, that touched the nation and sold over one million copies. In 1972 Motown relocated its headquarters to L.A., and though they continued to do fairly good business, many felt that by leaving Detroit, Gordy had lost touch with his roots, signaling the end of an era. Despite success with new groups like the Commodores (led by Lionel "Dancin' on the Ceiling" Richie), Motown would never match the number of hits it enjoyed from 1960 to 1972, signing Pat Boone in 1974 (truly producing the tracks of our tears) but losing the Jacksons to Epic in 1975 (who had promised the family all new faces). Gaye, Wonder, Richie, and newly signed Rick James (bitch!) helped Motown make it through the night into the late 1970s with hit after hit, scoring number ones and Grammies like nobody's business.

By the 1980s the music industry had become the territory of multinationals, and Gordy quickly found his small-town ways could not contend with the megalabels. Toward the end of the decade, Berry sold his baby love to MCA and Boston Ventures for somewhere in the neighborhood of $60 million, a considerably nicer neighborhood than the one he started in, while retaining control of his vast publishing catalog. By the time he was done, Gordy had made over $350 million in less than two decades, not bad for a kid from the wrong side of the music tracks.

Interesting Tidbit: Motown's history isn't all glamour. Mary Wells died of throat cancer, penniless at age forty-two. A twenty-five-year-old, Tammi Terrell, collapsed and died of a brain tumor onstage in the arms of Marvin Gaye, who was, in turn, shot by his father, a cross-dressing pastor. Saddest of all was the fate of Jackie Wilson, with whom Gordy got his start. Shot by a fan in New York in 1961, he lost his sixteen-year-old son in 1970, and suffered a heart attack in 1975 that left him in a coma. When at last he died, Wilson was buried in an unmarked grave.

Ways to Bring Up the History of Motown in Conversation

☀ You've got great taste in music. Berry Gordy would've hired you in a pinch.

☀ If you stay with your dreams you never know what can happen. Look what Berry Gordy did with Motown.

☀ Luke made more money last year than Motown Records made in the 1960s.

Two Turntables and a Microphone: The History of Rap

When Are We Talking About: 1970s–

Why Are We Even Talking About This: Rap music now comprises one of the largest portions of CD sales in the world and has influenced music, TV, film, fashion, and culture for the last three decades.

What You Need to Know to Sound Smart: What we call rap today was originally termed hip-hop. Despite the attempt to differentiate the two terms, with rap being singing rhymes and hip-hop being the overall culture of the music (including dance), they are often used interchangeably. The 1970s were a dark time in American culture when polyester jump-suited cheeseballs roamed the dance floor, brandishing metallic medallions that gleamed from their bestial hairy chests, moving to a cacophony of whistles, synthesizers, and drum machines known as . . . (you may want to remove the children from the room) disco! Fortunately for modern music, a star shone brightly in the East, where, in the fabled borough of the Bronx, New York, a new movement was brewing. In the streets, struggling Black working-class kids who, thankfully, didn't have the bread to loaf around in the expensive Manhattan clubs, threw their own parties in their tiny tenements (though still called "house parties") or right out in the street. The disc jockeys (or DJs) were local kids who schlepped their entire record collections to the gatherings, even sometimes bringing their stereo sets (then the size of a Buick) to spin their favorite songs.

Versions of the story differ, but most agree that Kool DJ Herc (Clive Campbell), who had moved with his family from Kingston, Jamaica, to the Bronx in 1967, was among the originators of rap. Herc initially had trouble finding audiences interested in his reggae-influenced "dubs" (lyrics chanted over reggae instrumentals), but gradually found a niche as he altered his play list to more popular genres of funk, soul, disco, and R&B (James Brown, the Jackson Five, Sly and the Family Stone). To annoy his neighbors and extend the length of his instrumentals, Herc played two identical records simultaneously and used a mixing box to switch between them, thus extending the song indefinitely, the length of play of your average Cher song. Soon, Herc was DJing parties all over the borough, using his cross-fader to create "breaks" in the beat and a unique dance experience never heard before by anyone, especially your average New Yorker, who considered Tony Bennett to be ethnic music.

Herc's urban musical stylings quickly gained a cult following (as in underground cult, not chant-with-a-tambourine cult) who dubbed themselves "B-boys" (Bronx boys or Break Beat boys) and began cultivating a new dance (further frustrating Caucasians, who still had that whole rhythm issue to contend with) to go with their music, called break dancing. Like the precision with which the DJs would mix beats, these dancers commanded their bodies to perform stunts like urban ballerinas and would "battle" in the streets in the middle of a circle of onlookers, showing off their astounding new moves, an experience familiar to New Yorkers who often battled muggers before a crowd of onlookers. In direct rebellion against the increasingly soulless music of the disco craze, Herc and his devotees embraced their street culture, and his sound not only revolutionized music and dance, but pervaded fashion, hairstyle, art (especially graffiti), and even inspired a language all its own that would eventually weave its way into mainstream vernacular (word!).

Herc's main rival at the time was DJ Pete Jones, a disco jam-master and, therefore, the villain of our story, who spun to the mostly white crowds who were "dancing" (and if you've ever seen the Electric Slide at a wedding you'll understand why we use the quotes) in the hot Manhattan clubs.

Just for the record, a DJ and an MC are two different things. Originally, the DJ was the featured act at a party or show, while the MC (emcee) just revved up the crowd, kind of like a cheerleader, or perhaps, Chris Tucker back when he was funny. Originally, MCs would make "shout-outs" to the crowd in a call-and-response technique, but soon their rhymes became more elaborate. Have we already lost our white readers? Please try to stay with the group.

MCs competed with one another for recognition and bragged or boasted about the DJs they were "representin'," and by the next decade, it would be the MCs whom people came to see. In fact, as Herc's own mixing grew more complex, he focused on the music, turning the MC duties over to two friends, Clark Kent and Coke La Rock, who effectively formed the first rap group, Herc and the Herculoids (no relation to the cool cartoon with Gleep and Gloop). The first true rapper was DJ Hollywood, an MC who took his madness one step further by mixing simple rhyming chants to disco music and incorporating even more call-and-response from the crowd. Gaining a following at the Bronx hotspot Club 371, by the mid-1970s, Hollywood was the number one MC in the city, playing for thousands in packed clubs, which flagrantly violated local fire codes. His rhymes, such as "throw your hands in the air," can still be heard to this day as they are often shamefully imitated by drunk white people at corporate Christmas parties. Herc and Hollywood were adversaries, with their musical tastes dividing them and their fans into two distinct groups: B-boys (good) and disco (evil).

As Herc's beat began to fade, a new player named Joseph Saddler stepped up to the turntables. Saddler, who went by the moniker Grand Master Flash (as opposed to Tara Reid, the Flash Master), was a true innovator, bringing the battling worlds together as he combined Herc's street-level beats with Hollywood's MC chants, his amazing speed on the turntables, and the new innovations of scratching and cutting. Scratching (actually scratching the record with the needle to produce music) was discovered by Grand Wizard Theodore (sort of an odd title for a Black man to choose) when his mom banged on his door, telling him to turn his music down and he, stopping the record with his hand, created a new sound. While cutting (reversing the album as it played) one record and mixing it with another playing simultaneously, the DJ created entirely *new* instrumentals over which emerging rappers could chant their rhymes.

By the late 1970s Saddler had teamed up with Melvin Glover (Melle Mel), Nathaniel Glover (Kidd Creole), Eddie Morris (Mr. Ness), Guy Williams (Rahiem), and Keith Wiggins (Cowboy) to form one of the most famous hip-hop groups of all time, Grand Master Flash and the Furious Five. Their song "The Message" (1982) was the first to use rap as social commentary about the bleakness of the urban world. In 1979, the first rap record, *King Tim III*, by the Fatback Band, was released. In the following year, the Sugar Hill Gang's *Rapper's Delight*, sampling Chic's hit "Good Times," was the first song to break the top forty, changing the music world forever. Songs such as 1983's "White Lines" (a song surprisingly *not* about crowds at Hootie and the Blowfish concerts), by Grandmaster Flash, opened the country up to the world of inner-city drug problems, ironic since Cowboy would die in 1989 from his addiction to crack cocaine.

Afrika Bambaataa (born with the whitest name on the planet, Kevin Donovan) was an ex-gang leader of the Black Spades (among the largest gangs in the city in the 1970s) who having recently returned from a life-altering Africa trip, stopped busting caps and started busting rhymes, while founding the Zulu Nation, an organization devoted to peace, harmony, and picked-out afros. Bambaataa was influenced by white electronic groups such as Germany's Kraftwerk and is credited with bringing a techno sound to rap music. He is often called the Grandfather of Rap (and Grandfather of Soiled Trousers for anyone who's seen his picture), and was reputed to haul his twenty-five crates of records to every show he played.

But it was three boys from middle-class households in Queens, New York, who would put rap on the map. Run (Joseph Simmons, whose brother is now entertainment overlord, Russel Simmons), DMC (Darryl McDaniels), and Jam Master Jay (Jason Mizell) became Run DMC. They were educated rappers, who were able to take A.P. Bio without sacrificing their street cred. Their complex and meaningful lyrics catapulted them into the mainstream and made them the first rap group to go platinum as well as star on MTV. They would later be the first musicians to cross rap and rock in their hit collaboration with industry legends Aerosmith on the song "Walk This Way."

Rap grew through the 1980s and 1990s and became a means of social commentary through the politically powerful rhymes of Chuck D and Flava Flav's group, Public Enemy, and the angry protests against social conditions and oppression from the uncensored NWA (you'll have to look up what that stands for yourselves . . .), featuring Ice Cube and the Elvis of Rap, Tupac Shakur. The Beastie Boys became the first famous *white* rap group (disproving the theory that white men can't . . . jump, jump), whose hit "You Got to Fight for Your Right, to Party," became the anthem for binge-drinking college kids everywhere.

Today, rap is a cross-cultural phenomenon with performers from every nation on the planet embracing this musical medium to spread whatever message is in their hearts, while others just long for the bling that success in the entertainment industry can bring.

Interesting Tidbit: There are those who argue T. Texas Tyler's single "Deck of Cards," released in 1948 as a "talking song," was the first rap song, and that rap has been a white music phenomenon. Those people are *wrong*. In the immortal words of Flava Flav, "Don't believe the hype."

Ways to Bring Up the History of Rap in Conversation

☀ The music here is kind of lame. Wish we had a guy like Kool DJ Herc.

☀ That guy is huuuuge! Makes Afrika Bambaataa look like Danny DeVito.

☀ That's an interesting story, but I'm gonna go Flava Flav on this one.

Appendix

WHO'S WHO AT THE PARTY

While it may seem obscenely inconsiderate of everyone's individuality to reduce our social world to a dozen simplistic categories, you'll find that, despite our best efforts, even the most maverick among us falls into one or more of them.

The Average Joe. As much as we are loathe to admit it, when it comes to the world of conversation, there's a little Average Joe (or Jane, if you like) in all of us. And that's perfectly okay. People like people with whom they share things in common (like being average). Average Joes make up the bulk of most partygoing crowds. The really great thing about Average Joes is that, chances are, they haven't read this book . . . which will make you appear to be very, very smart.

The Rebel. The Rebel loves controversy. Government corruption, the destruction of the environment, corporate greed, these are the meat and potatoes of any table-talk with a Rebel. Talking about fighting the power or the evils of "the system" will get the ball rolling, but be warned: Rebels are passionate and never bashful about yelling their opinions and showering you with fervent spittle.

The Zealot. Zealots believe that their (state, religion, company, ethnicity, sports team, or low-carb diet) is the *best!*

If you're not wholly supportive of their fanatical point of view, you may be in for a bumpy ride. Zealots have trouble accepting new ideas, and even when faced with irrefutable facts, will fall back on rationalizations to justify the philosophy they have built their lives on, even resorting to absurd platitudes ("support our troops," "fear the man," "look at my butt," etc.).

The Social Climber. Social climbers only talk to people who can help them get up the next rung on the ladder of success. If that's you, the Social Climber will laugh at your dumbest jokes, find your opinions on Turtle Wax fascinating, and always love your outfit. While not much good for conversation (since they're often craning their necks to see who *else* is in the room), social climbers are great for fetching you a fresh cocktail or holding your seat while you go to the bathroom . . . unless someone better comes along.

The Gossiper. Gossipers live by the credo If you don't have anything nice to say about someone, come sit next to me. The Gossiper's favorite topics are movie celebs, TV celebs, music celebs, fashion celebs, and Carson Daly. Of course, there's a little bit of the Gossiper in all of us, but be careful, gossiping gets around and if you're spreading rumors about friends, family, or your mailman, chances are they'll find out. Gossiping about dead people, however, is a much safer bet, since chances are Nietzsche won't be calling you in the middle of the night to vehemently deny he was secretly in love with his sister (especially since it was probably true!). As a conversational-jedi, you must trust your feelings and beware of the dark side.

The Self-Helper. Self-helpers are all about personal growth and love conversations about philosophy, psychology, introspection, self-discovery, and Oprah. As long as we're speaking in broad, sweeping generalizations, self-helpers usually have several cats, are avid readers, are willing to admit they can remember their past lives, know both their rising sign and their Chinese zodiac animal, have tried to quit smoking using hypnotherapy, think Tony Robbins is passé (but have a few of his tapes), and are often good with their hands, since many of them have massage licenses.

The Neurotic. Look, we all have problems. While some of us have spent years slumped on a couch hoping our analyst will solve them, others have spent years slumped over a pew, hoping their god will do the same. Neurotics are easy to start rolling, just ask them how they're doing and get comfy. Neurotics will be ever so grateful if you tell them that the thing in their neck *does* look like a tumor or that their car probably is getting towed right now.

The Uptight Guy/Gal. Whether it's about sex, money, or even expressing their emotions, Uptight folks are uncomfortable with anything that threatens their very safe, very controlled boundaries. If you need to impress an Uptight-ite (and we're very sorry if you do), try to avoid off-color remarks, bathroom humor, sexual inferences, or pretty much anything worth talking about. Interestingly, Uptight people are usually hiding a deep secret, some burning desire within them that their mind has rebelled against, thus resulting in the puckered personality you see before you.

The Expert. After reading this book, you'll have essential information on a myriad of subjects, certainly much more than the average partygoer. Still, parties tend to be like a big game of King of the Mountain, and there's always someone younger, and stronger, ready to push you off the top. Enter the Expert. Now remember, we never said you had to be smarter than everyone else. It's not about winning, it's just about *sounding* smart. As long as you can hold your own with the Expert, you're doing just fine. As soon as you find yourself running out of material, simply steer the conversation to another topic (usually, the farther from the one you're on, the better). Most Experts are masters of only one or two subjects, and usually, both are in related fields (e.g., a baseball expert will also know a ton of football info, but probably doesn't know squat about Albert Camus . . . and you do).

The Devil's Advocate. While some Devil's Advocates are truly in search of thought-provoking "what ifs," others simply get their jollies being a jerk. Good-natured Devil's Advocates just want to hear your ideas on an alternative scenario and are truly interested in what you're talking about. They're willing to go beyond "the facts" into the realm of "let's pretend." This is a great conversation, because now we're talking personal feelings, and you might get the chance to see someone cry. However, someone taking a contrary point of view while being sarcastic, bombastic, or smug, is just plain trouble, and chances are, is just trying to make you look bad, so our suggestion is . . . head for the buffet.

The Skeptic. Worse than the consummate Devil's Advocate, there's no pleasing Skeptics, since they are invariably unhappy. Yes, it's true, deep, deep, deep down. Don't get into a head-to-head with a Skeptic. Their whole deal is catching you in a mistake and discrediting you. No matter how smart you are, you can't know everything, and history has proven time and time again that today's facts are tomorrow's fiction. Just ask all the guys who were afraid to sail off the edge of the world.

Acknowledgments

The authors would like to acknowledge:

The O'Quinns, Lenons, Benschs, and Wietings for their friendship and enthusiasm.

The Sweivens, Escalas, Macibobas, Shoustals, McGriffs, Migoyas, and Bellinis for their relentless encouragement.

Doc Larson, for telling Chris, "You can write, kid!"

A.T., Big Matt, Carley, Dave-O, Johnny Mo, Manu, McCafferty, and Mello for believing in me year after year . . . after year . . .

Our agent Nikki for taking a chance.

Elle for playing the name game over pasta.

Nicole Woolsey for typos and telling us to make it funny.

Jenna and all our pals at Susina for keeping the coffee coming.

Beth H for getting us rolling.

Alison at RH for her undying excitement and for making our vision 20/20.

Pete Larson for hooking a brother up.

Mike Nelson for being cooler than cool.

Scott Sandow for his strategic Web support.

All of those teachers who were probably paid far too little for their efforts to make us smart.

About the Authors

© Lucia Sullivan

David Matalon Had His Way with Words

When Are We Talking About: Right now . . . wait, we mean now . . . no . . . *now!*

Why Are We Even Talking About This: With a thick head of hair that shows no sign of receding, he is our greatest hope in the ongoing battle against androgenetic alopecia.

What You Need to Know to Sound Smart: Born to a business-minded father and a dancer mother and raised on the streets of Brooklyn where speech was often reduced to a number of primal grunts, it seemed unlikely that David would grow up knowing how to "tawk so good," let alone read. However, summers spent traveling with his family transformed the monosyllabic Matalon into a loquacious lad as he learned there was more to life than watching re-runs of *Happy Days*. Matalon (whose last name rhymes with "battle on," "tattle on," and "paddle fun") penned his first screenplay at age fifteen and was later accepted to NYU's il-lustrious film school after a brief stint in Vermont, where his shaved bleach-blond flat-top went over oh-so big with the cow-tipping, overall-wearing gen-pop. Comfortably back among the freaks and geeks of New York's Greenwich Vil-lage, Matalon spent the next four years in a haze of club-filled nights while running through the streets with a shopping cart full of film gear, and amazingly graduated in only four years before going . . . to look for a job. Over the ensuing century, David worked various odd jobs in the fi-nancial sector, the food business, as a teacher, a life coach, an exotic dancer for bar mitzvahs, and finally a writer. David has written for both television (well, cable) and film (didn't you see *Nutgobblers III*?), and has recently begun directing feature films in Hollywood. Throughout his life, David has attended many social engagements and has charmed his way into the hearts of people all over the world. David cur-rently lives in Los Angeles and New York, making him bi-coastal (woo-woo!).

Interesting Tidbit: Though a capable athlete, David is the worst basketball player on the planet despite years of drug therapy.

© Lucia Sullivan

He Who Laughs Last Is Chris Woolsey

When Are We Talking About: 1972–

Why Are We Even Talking About This: This writer, co-median, and all-around student of pop culture is a pretty great guy and will sometimes lend you money in a pinch.

What You Need to Know to Sound Smart: Chris was born in Indianapolis, Indiana, on May 15, 1972, the same day Alabama governor and presidential hopeful George Wallace was shot during a campaign speech. Though authorities were never able to make a solid connection between the two events, they have nonetheless kept a watchful eye on the young man ever since. According to family members, Chris began to acquire way too much arcane knowledge at an early age and never missed an opportunity to let others know it. While he spent his formative years in the Midwest, he made parole and fled to California where he attended the University of Sacramento and earned degrees in theater and environmental studies. Much to his parents' elation, Chris wisely opted to avoid a legal career in order to pursue a secure future in the entertainment industry. Chris has been a freelance writer for both film and television for such notable entities as Sony Pictures, Fox Television, and Columbia Tri-Star Entertainment. As an actor, he has appeared on television shows like *Sabrina the Teenage Witch* and *One On One*.

Investing in the nation's future is a huge priority in Chris's life and he has spent a great deal of time teaching ungrateful children all across the country.

Chris lives in Los Angeles with wife, Nicole, and daughter, Cassidy.

Interesting Tidbit: Chris once appeared with his extended clan on the game-show *Family Feud,* and would have walked away with thousands of dollars in gifts and prizes were it not for the obvious mental shortcomings of his siblings. When asked, "What country are most Americans afraid to go to?" his sister actually answered, "Mexico—because of the water." It's sad really.